GA ARCHITECT

Japanese and English text, Size: 300×307mm
2-5, 9−11, 14号は絶版 Vols. 2-5, 9-11 and 14 are out of print.

現代建築界で活躍している建築家の全貌を，気鋭の批評家書き下ろしの作家論，現地取材の写真，建築事務所の全面的な協力を得た詳細な図面，簡明な作品解説により立体的に編集した大型サイズの作品集。巻末には作品リスト，文献リストを収録。

変貌を続ける現代建築家の肖像を現時点で正確に把握，記録することを試み，現代建築家全集の最新決定版を意図しました。各巻は建築家それぞれの個性を最大限に表現できるよう多彩な構成をとっています。

This is a series c￼
tect and is a con￼
GA ARCHIT￼
tographs most o￼
articles and are ￼
foremost archite￼
tect's own accou￼

an archi-￼
. to date.
ing pho-
ating the
texts by
he archi-

GW00600838

18 KAZUYO SEJIMA RYUE NISHIZAWA 1987-2006

「PLATFORM I」から最新プロジェクトの「ルーブル＝ランス」まで，豊富な写真／図面とテキストで構成される「妹島和世＋西沢立衛全作品集」。
序文は西沢立衛執筆。巻末に全作品リストを収録。

序文「原則をつくる―構造，平面，関係性，風景」：西沢立衛
作品解説：妹島和世，西沢立衛
作品：PLATFORM I，II／再春館製薬女子寮／パチンコパーラー I，II，III／森の別荘／国際情報科学芸術アカデミー マルチメディア工房／ウィークエンドハウス／スタッドシアター／小さな家／金沢21世紀美術館／梅林の家／ディオール表参道／トレド美術館ガラスセンター／森山邸／鬼石多目的ホール／ツォルフェライン スクール／ニューミュージアム／野外芸術文化ゾーン（仮称）アートセンター／EPFLラーニングセンター／ルーブル＝ランス／他，多数掲載

Text: "Creating Principles—Structure, Plan, Relationship, Landscape" by Ryue Nishizawa
Works: Platform I, II; Saishunkan Seiyaku Women's Dormitory, Kumamoto; Pachinko Parlor I, II, III; Villa in the Forest; Multimedia Workshop; 21st Century Museum of Contemporary Art, Kanazawa; Extension of the IVAM; Moriyama House; Onishi Hall; Zollverein School of Management and Design; Naoshima Ferry Terminal; Towada Art Center; Learning Center, EPFL; Louvre-Lens; and others

216 total pages, 114 in color   ¥ 5,667

19 KENGO KUMA

「亀老山展望台」から2005年最新作まで，書き下ろしのテキストと豊富な写真／図面で構成される「隈研吾全作品集」。
論文は隈研吾執筆。巻末に全作品リストを収録。

論文「弱い建築」・作品解説：隈 研吾
作品：亀老山展望台／水／ガラス／ガラス／影／森舞台／川／フィルター／森／スラット／馬頭町広重美術館／高柳町陽の楽家／石の美術館／海／フィルター／銀山温泉共同浴場「しろがね湯」／PLASTIC HOUSE／森／床／奥社の茶屋／古々比の瀧／梅窓院／JR渋谷改修計画／ONE表参道／分とく山／東雲キャナルコートCODAN 3街区／村井正誠記念美術館／LVMH大阪／COCON KARASUMA／ロータス・ハウス／サントリー美術館／朝日放送新社屋／Y-Hütte／コンペティション参加案／他，多数掲載

Text: "Weak Architecture" by Kengo Kuma
Works: Kiro-san Observatory; Water / Glass; Glass / Shadow; Noh Stage in the Forest; Takayanagi Community Center; Stone Museum; Sea / Filter; Ginzan Onsen Hot Spring Bath House; Plastic House; Forest / Floor; Soba Restaurant of Togakushi Shrine; Kogohi Bath House; Baiso-in Temple; One Omotesando; Waketokuyama Restaurant; LVMH Osaka; Lotus House; Suntory Museum; works for competitions; and others

228 total pages, 114 in color   ¥ 6,500

論文・作品解説：磯崎新
作品：チーム・ディズニー・ビルディング／豊の国情報ライブラリー／京都コンサートホール／奈義町現代美術館・図書館／なら100年会館／ラ・コルーニャ人間科学館／静岡県コンベンション・アーツセンター＜グランシップ＞／静岡県舞台芸術センター／オハイオ21世紀科学工業センター／秋吉台国際芸術村／他

Text: Arata Isozaki
Works: Team Disney Building; Toyo-nokuni Libraries for Cultural Resources; Kyoto Concert Hall; Nara Centennial Hall; DOMUS Interactive Museum about Humans; Buss Museum of Art; Shizuoka Convention & Arts Center "Granship"; Shizuoka Performing Arts Center; Akiyoshi International Art Village; and others

15 磯崎新 ARATA ISOZAKI 3 1991-2000

264 total pages, 96 in color
並製：¥ 6,648／上製：¥ 9,333

論文：W・J・R・カーティス 作品解説：安藤忠雄
作品：兵庫県立看護大学／大阪府立近つ飛鳥博物館／兵庫県立木の殿堂／サントリーミュージアム／大山崎山荘美術館／アイキャナー／リー邸／六甲の集合住宅III／FABRICA（ベネトン・アートスクール）／淡路夢舞台／直島コンテンポラリーアートミュージアム・アネックス／ユネスコ瞑想空間／TOTOセミナーハウス／国際子ども図書館／南岳山光明寺／他

Text: William J. R. Curtis/ Tadao Ando
Works: College of Nursing, Chikatsu-Asuka Historical Museum+Plaza; Garden/Lee House; Rokko Hausing III; FABRICA (Benetton Communication Research Center); Awaji-Yumebutai; Naoshima Contemporary Art Museum, Annex; Komyo-ji Temple; and others

16 安藤忠雄 TADAO ANDO 3 1994-2000

276 total pages, 48 in color
¥ 6,648

論文：原広司 作品解説：伊東豊雄
作品：アルミの家／中野本町の家／PMTビル―名古屋／シルバーハット／東京遊牧少女の包／横浜風の塔／中目黒Tビル／八代市立博物館／未来の森ミュージアム／養護老人ホーム八代市立保寿寮／八代市広域消防署／長岡リリックホール／大館樹海ドームパーク／大社文化プレイス／桜上水K邸／せんだいメディアテーク／他

Text: Hiroshi Hara/ Toyo Ito
Works: Aluminium House; White U; PMT Building; Silver Hut; Exhibition Project for Pao, a Dwelling for Tokyo Nomad Women; Tower of Winds; T Building in Nakameguro; Yatsushiro Municipal Museum; Yatsu-shiro Fire Station; T Hall in Taisha; Sendai Mediatheque; and others

17 伊東豊雄 TOYO ITO 1970-2001

217 total pages, 90 in color
¥ 5,700

TADAO ANDO DETAILS
安藤忠雄ディテール集

平面や断面，パースが重ね合わされ，スケールの異なるディテールが挿入された三次元性を持つ独自の図法。その図面には，あらゆる事象を捉えながら結晶化させた建築理念が投影され，建築を創造することの意志が凝縮されています。住吉の長屋から現在まで，主要作品を網羅するこのディテール集の中に，時代に流されず，建築の本質を求めて止まないもう一つの安藤空間が展開します。

Overlayered plans, sections and perspectives, with various details in different scales, Ando's drawing has unique three dimensional character. The drawings represent not only the literal information of details, but also his philosophy of architecture. From "Row house in Sumiyoshi" to recent projects, these two volumes contain Ando's architectural details of major projects and embody the spirits of Ando, who is the evangelist of the essence of architecture.

Japanese and English text
Size: 300×307mm

1 EDITED BY YUKIO FUTAGAWA CRITICISM BY PETER EISENMAN
企画・編集：二川幸夫
論文：ピーター・アイゼンマン

List of Works
Row House in Sumiyoshi (Azuma House)/Wall House (Matsumoto House)/Glass Block House (Ishihara House)/Rokko Housing I/Koshino House/Festival/BIGI Atelier/Town house in Kujo (Izutsu House)/Iwasa House/TIME'S I II/Church on the Water/and others

168 total pages
¥ 4,806

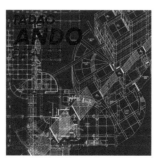

2 EDITED BY YUKIO FUTAGAWA CRITICISM BY FRANCESCO DAL CO
企画・編集：二川幸夫
論文：フランチェスコ・ダル・コ

List of Works
Tea House in Oyodo/Karaza Theater/Rokko Housing II/Galleria[akka]/Collezione/Naoshima Contemporary Art Museum and Annex/Museum of Literature, Himeji and Annex/Otemae Art Center/Matsutani House Addition/and others

148 total pages
¥ 4,714

3 EDITED BY YUKIO FUTAGAWA TEXT BY TADAO ANDO
企画・編集：二川幸夫
文：安藤忠雄

List of works
Pulitzer Foundation for the Arts/Sayamaike Historical Museum, Osaka/The International Library of Children's Literature/Modern Art Museum of Fort Worth/Church of the Light, Sunday School/Komyo-ji Temple/Shiba Ryotaro Memorial Museum/4 × 4 House/and others

148 total pages
¥ 4,714

表記価格には消費税は含まれておりません。

GA DOCUMENT
Global Architecture

GA DOCUMENT presents the finest in international design, focusing on architecture that expresses our times and striving to record the history of contemporary architecture. Striking black-and-white and vibrant color photographs presented in a generous format make for a dynamic re-presentation of spaces, materials and textures. International scholars and critics provide insightful texts to further inform the reader of the most up-to-date ideas and events in the profession.

Vols. 1-16, 18, 20, 23, 25, 28, 36, 47, 51, 54, 68, 70, 73 are out of print.

多様に広がり、変化を見せる世界の現代建築の動向をデザインの問題を中心に取り上げ、現代建築の完全な記録をめざしつつ、時代の流れに柔軟に対応した独自の視点から作品をセレクションし、新鮮な情報を世界に向けて発信する唯一のグローバルな建築専門誌。掲載する作品をすべて現地取材、撮影することで大型誌面にダイナミックに表現し、その空間、ディテールやテクスチャーを的確に再現する。

Size: 300 × 297 mm

1-16, 18, 20, 23, 25, 28, 36, 47, 51, 54, 68, 70, 73号は絶版。(17, 19, 21, 22, 24, 26, 27, 29-35, 37-46, 48-50, 61, 65, 79号は在庫僅少)

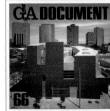

表記価格には消費税は含まれておりません。

表記価格には消費税は含まれておりません。

GA JAPAN
Global Architecture

ENVIRONMENTAL DESIGN

日本の新しい優れた現代建築のエッセンスを主に国内に向けて発信する隔月刊の建築デザイン専門誌。建築思想，技術思想を照射しつつ，建築のデザインに迫る本格的建築総合誌です。

Japanese Text Only／Size: 300 × 228mm

GA JAPAN ENVIRONMENTAL DESIGN 9-10/2007

88

作品：バルセロナ見本市・グランビア会場（エントランスホール，パヴィリオン1）／伊東豊雄，坂の上の雲ミュージアム，直島ベネッセハウス パーク／ビーチ棟／安藤忠雄，川口クリニック（川口皮フ科）／米田明，スタッドシアター・アルメラ／SANAA

記事：図式と空間化のあいだ／妹島和世＋西沢立衛

プロジェクト：Besancon City of Arts and Culture／隈研吾，Budapest Urban Design Project／Janesch Peter＋隈研吾，and Team

PLOT：「Competition for "Les Halles"」編　phase 0：コンペティション案に見る新しいフェーズ／伊東豊雄，「C project」編　phase 1：教育施設の新しいシステムを構築する／山本理顕，「EPFLラーニング・センター」編　phase 1：自由な曲面を合理的につくるために／佐々木睦朗

連載：「GA日記」／二川幸夫

GA広場：「世界の現場」二川由夫・斎藤日登美，「超高層の可能性とは」OMA，「Y字型プランがもたらす建築的効用」宇野享／CAn，「新素材を用いて建築的にアッセンブルするには」隈研吾建築都市設計事務所，「芝居小屋らしい形とつくり方とは」山梨知彦＋羽鳥達也，「スケールレスに実現するザハの形」ザハ・ハディド，「思いがつながり生まれる風景」安藤忠雄

160 pages, 88 in color　¥2,333

GA JAPAN ENVIRONMENTAL DESIGN 3-4/2007

85

座談会：［総括と展望・続編］建築2006／2007　藤森照信・二川幸夫
特集：［Contemporary Skin］［記事］亀井忠夫・隈研吾
［事例］伊東豊雄／SANAA／OMA／モーフォシス／大江匡　他
NEWS：*4 projects in Saadiyat Island of Abu Dhabi*／T. Ando, F. O. Gehry, J. Nouvel, Z. Hadid
PLOT：「杉並区立杉並芸術会館」編　phase 1／伊東豊雄＋S.S.，「多摩美術大学新図書館」編　phase 1／中山英之・庵原義隆，phase 2／編集部，phase 3／藤江和子，「豊田市生涯学習センター逢妻交流館」編　phase 1／宇野享，「（仮称）城下町ホール」編　phase 1／山本理顕
作品：大江匡／ソニーシティ　戸尾任宏／三重県立熊野古道センター　高橋統一＋清水建設／清水建設技術研究所安全安震館
記事：熊野古道センターの等断面集積木材構造，現場レポート「IRONY SPACE 2」／梅沢良三
GA広場：世界の現場，「〈構え〉と〈居場所〉をつくるデザイン」高宮眞介，「中と外を同時に考えた集合住宅」妹島和世，「強さと暖昧さを両立させるには」柳澤潤，他

168 pages, 88 in color　¥2,333

GA JAPAN ENVIRONMENTAL DESIGN 5-6/2007

86

座談会：「21_21 DESIGN SIGHT」安藤忠雄・鈴木博之・二川幸夫
「サントリー美術館」隈研吾・鈴木了二・二川幸夫
作品：21_21 DESIGN SIGHT／安藤忠雄＋日建設計　サントリー美術館／隈研吾＋日建設計　千葉市美浜文化ホール・保健福祉センター／小泉雅生　ふじようちえん／手塚貴晴＋手塚由比，池田昌弘　東京ガス ガスの科学館／日建設計
記事：構造の特徴と設計上のポイント／吉田一彦，施行計画と現場の観点から／津山皓司，市民利用に最適なホール規模の模索／本杉省三，アメンボみたいな建築／池田昌弘
プロジェクト：13号線東急東横線渋谷駅，東急大井町線上野毛駅／安藤忠雄
PLOT：「十和田市現代美術館」編　phase 3／西沢立衛，「豊田市生涯学習センター逢妻交流館」編　phase 2／妹島和世
GA広場：世界の現場，「隙間を薄い曲面壁でつくる」山本理顕・佐藤淳，「雑木林のような広場のような図書館」藤本壮介，「長さ16メートルのキャンティレヴァー」米田明，「断熱性能と剛性を追求したミニマムな木製サッシュ」隈研吾，「初期イメージを現実化する試み」石上純也・佐藤淳，「ハドソン河を見渡すランドマーク」ジャン・ヌヴェル，他

168 pages, 88 in color　¥2,333

GA JAPAN ENVIRONMENTAL DESIGN 7-8/2007

87

座談会：「多摩美術大学附属図書館・横須賀美術館」伊東豊雄・山本理顕・二川幸夫
作品：多摩美術大学附属図書館／伊東豊雄　横須賀美術館／山本理顕　KEYFOREST871228／北川原温　ねむの木こども美術館／藤森照信＋内田祥士　島根県立古代出雲歴史博物館／槇文彦　セントルイス ワシントン大学サム フォックス視覚芸術学部／槇文彦＋Shah Kawasaki Architects　オムロン京都センタービル啓真館／竹中工務店
記事：最新技術を使って一気に原初まで遡る／佐々木睦朗，不均質な皮膜を綺麗な二枚の面に見せる／金田勝徳，場所・時間を読み解いて，新たな空間をつくる／槇文彦
PLOT：「東京大学情報学環・福武ホール」編　phase 1／安藤忠雄，「湯町地区観光交流センター（仮称）」編　phase 1／隈研吾，「多摩美術大学附属図書館」編　phase 4／伊東豊雄
連載：GA日記／二川幸夫
GA広場：世界の現場，「均質な空間が纏うものとは」SANAA，「最先端のマテリアルがもたらすバランス」鈴木康広，「床と家具の境界を溶かす」藤江和子，「ミラノ・サローネで向けられた期待感」斎藤日登美

168 pages, 100 in color　¥2,333

Japanese Text Only
Size: 300 × 228 mm

安藤忠雄／建築手法

今や国民的建築家と言える，安藤忠雄の建築の秘密を解き明かす。
最初期から試みられてきた数多くのコンセプトについてのロング・インタヴューとともに，事務所開設以前からの思考の軌跡を書き下ろした原稿と数多くのスケッチ，図版で収録。

論文：
1970年まで（出自から，事務所開設まで）
70年代，都市ゲリラの時代
都市ゲリラ住居※
抽象と具象の重ね合わせ※
考え続ける苦痛—持続する困難※
理想の風景
※は再録

インタヴュー：
壁と柱のこと
ガラス・ブロックのこと——壁に穴を開けたくない
無我夢中で走り続けること
小篠邸のこと，「まる」の問題
六甲Ⅰ，現場のリアリティと強い気持ち
光のこと
水のこと
スケールが大きくなってきた
木造の精神
建築と時間
建築のクライアント
敷地を考えると，意識が広がっていく
アーティストのこと
これはアートか建築か？——地中美術館のこと
住宅を巡る状況
表参道のこと——都心の風景

320 total pages, 64 in color　¥2,800

隈研吾 読本 Ⅱ —2004

1999年出版の読本から5年。数多くのプロジェクトを手がけ，建築界のメインストリームを躍進していく隈研吾。その建築哲学の成熟とアクティビティの多様化をインタヴューにより解き明かす。

収録作品・プロジェクト：
石の美術館／馬頭町広重美術館／銀山温泉共同浴場「しろがね湯」／PLASTIC HOUSE／GREAT（BAMBOO）WALL／梅窓院／ONE表参道／安養寺木造阿弥陀如来坐像収蔵施設／長崎県立美術館／水／ブロック／サントリー美術館／他

256 total pages, 104 in color　¥2,333

妹島和世＋西沢立衛読本 —2005

妹島和世と西沢立衛のユニット，SANAAの世界中に散りばめられたプロジェクトを収録。1998年から，現在までの妹島＋西沢の展開する建築の真髄を長時間にわたるインタヴューにより紹介。

収録作品・プロジェクト：
飯田市小笠原資料館／岐阜県営住宅ハイタウン北方集合住宅・hhstyle.com／小さな家／梅林の家／市川アパートメント／ディオール表参道／金沢21世紀美術館／トレド美術館／ガラスパビリオン／ニューミュージアム現代美術館／ツォルフェライン スクール／他

320 total pages, 112 in color　¥2,800

妹島和世 読本 —1998

生い立ち，学校，就職，独立……。
建築家＝妹島和世の歩んできたバックグラウンドと初期の作品から現在進行中のプロジェクトまでを収めた，インタヴュー形式による「読む妹島和世」。

収録作品・プロジェクト：
PLATFORM Ⅰ，Ⅱ，Ⅲ／再春館製薬女子寮／パチンコパーラーⅠ，Ⅱ，Ⅲ／森の別荘／Y-HOUSE／調布駅北口交番／岐阜県営北方住宅／S-HOUSE／M-HOUSE／マルチメディア工房／熊野古道なかへち美術館／K本社屋／牛久新駅駅前利便施設／他

336 total pages, 80 in color　¥2,800

表記価格に消費税は含まれておりません。

GA 素材空間

20世紀の建築は、様々な素材の登場により、新しい建築様式が生まれました。21世紀を迎えるにあたって、建築デザインを素材面から考えてみようと、この雑誌では、ほかの産業で開発されている材料も含めて、建築に応用できる素材の発見と、現在、一般的に使用されている建築材料についても、研究・改良されていく様子をレポートしていきます。

Japanese Text Only, Size: 300×228 mm

03 木の21世紀

ノスタルジー素材から未来素材へ

木──創造の最前線から：8人の建築家、構造家の話─石井和紘・岡村仁・北川原温・高松伸・内藤廣・難波和彦・宮本佳明・六角鬼丈
対談：木の素養─藤森照信×二川幸夫／木の現代性とは─隈研吾×二川由夫／今日の木の世界─中村義明×二川幸夫
論文：森を見てつくる木構法 網野禎昭／パルテノン神殿から五重塔へ─花里利一
インタヴュー：木造建築への疑問と実践 納賀雄嗣／現代における木質空間のエッセンス 齋藤裕／民家再生から見えてきたこと 降幡廣信／伝統工法の21世紀 稲山正弘／木の暗黒時代は終わったのか？ 林知行
巻頭インタヴュー：地球と素材 石田秀輝／燃えて燃えない素材 菅原進一
技術最前線：インセクト・テクノロジー 長島孝行
新素材の現在：「DUCTAL」とは何か？ 松岡康訓
連載：記憶に残る素材とディテール 第3回 松村秀一／素材探訪 第2回 杉本賢司

144 total pages, 40 in color ￥2,476

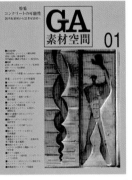

01 コンクリートの可能性
──20世紀素材から21世紀素材へ

対談：原広司×二川幸夫
コンクリート建築1900-2000：20世紀を代表する104作品
論文・インタヴュー：柳田博明／岡部憲明／渡辺邦夫／高橋靗一／菊竹清訓／安藤忠雄／樫野紀元／山本理顕／黒沢亮平／梅沢良三／松岡康訓／金森康史／五十嵐純／坂牛卓／二川由夫／アラン・バーデン
連載：石山修武／松村秀一

160 total pages, 16 in color ￥2,476

02 GLASS
──ガラスの可能性

ガラス建築選集：19～20世紀を代表する72作品
ガラスの空間：最近作10題
論文・インタヴュー：谷川晃一／鈴木了二／桑久庵節郎／伊藤節郎／大西博＋杉崎健一／仁藤喜徳＋岡村仁／アラン・バーデン／林昌二／コリン・ヤーカー／鈴木博之／横内暢生／葉祥栄／岡部憲明／赤坂喜顕／池内清治／近藤靖史
連載：松村秀一／杉本賢司

160 total pages, 16 in color ￥2,476

PLOT
Global Architecture

従来の、建築家から発信されるフォーマルなプレゼンテーションを集めただけの作品集から脱却した、わかる建築書＝PLOT（プロット）。
建築の設計は、完成するまで紆余曲折のスタディが成されています。一人の建築家の背景と、プロセスの発展を追い、何故この建築が完成したのかを、完成作品と現在進行中のプロジェクトと共に、詳細に編集しました。

Japanese Text Only, Size: 300×228mm

01 山本理顕

作品
岡山の住宅、岩出山町立岩出山中学校、埼玉県立大学、広島市西消防署、公立はこだて未来大学、横浜市営住宅「三ツ境ハイツ」他

プロジェクト
東雲集合住宅A街区、北京建外SOHO、岡山の住宅2、和歌山市立大学（仮称）設計競技案、公園レストハウス

184 total pages, 56 in color ￥2,333

02 小嶋一浩

作品
ビッグハート出雲、スペースブロック上新庄、吉備高原小学校、宮城県迫桜高校

プロジェクト
ハノイモデル、東京大学先端科学技術研究センター（IV-1）、北京建外SOHO/SOHO別荘、カタールエデュケーションシティ／ブリッジ・アーツ＆サイエンス・カレッジ、氷室ハウス 他

絶版

200 total pages, 64 in color ￥2,333

03 伊東豊雄

掲載作品
横浜市営地下鉄M駅インテリア・デザイン、桜上水K邸、ブルージュ・パヴィリオン、フローニンゲン・アルミニウム・ハウジング、コニャック・ジェイ病院、マーラー4 ブロックス、松本市市民会館（仮称）、北京CCTVプロジェクト、リラクゼーションパーク イントレヴィエハ、オスロ・ウエストバーネン・プロジェクト、トッズ表参道ビル 他

絶版

184 total pages, 64 in color ￥2,333

GA JAPAN 別冊①

GA JAPAN 1999 別冊
20世紀の現代建築を検証する
○と×

磯崎 新
鈴木博之

20世紀の現代建築を検証する ○と×

鉄・ガラス・コンクリートの出現から、ミース・コルビュジエ・ライトの巨匠時代を経て、現代日本建築にいたるまで。建築家・磯崎新と建築史家・鈴木博之による20世紀の横断。

第1章：新古典主義からモダニズムの誕生へ
第2章：技術とその意味
第3章：一つで歴史に残る家
第4章：前衛か、体制か
第5章：大戦前後
第6章：南北米・欧、それぞれの展開
第7章：最後の巨匠、そして日本

Japanese Text Only, Size: 300×228 mm

198 total pages, 72 in color ￥2,800

小住宅の構造
Integrated Identity
Masahiro Ikeda

小住宅の構造　池田昌弘

構造家として建築デザインをバックアップするだけでなく、建築家のコラボレーターとして、構造、意匠といったセクションの枠組みを外し、それらの境界を自由に横断することで、そこにあるすべての才能を統合する「インテグリスト」＝池田昌弘。建築家と共同で進めた小住宅の設計プロセスとその思想を、インタヴューと、写真／ドローイング／模型／CGなどの豊富なヴィジュアルで紹介します。

掲載作品：Ta house／Y house／O house／s house／S/N／八王子の家／腰越のメガホンハウス／屋根の家／ambi-flux／Beaver House／Conoid／BLOC／町屋project、C House、Théa-ory House、nkm／RECO-house／ペンギンハウス／Lucky Drops／ナチュラルイルミナンス／ナチュラルスラット／ナチュラルエリップス／ナチュラルウェッジ／ナチュラルストラータ／Y House

208 total pages ￥2,200

絶版
Japanese Text Only, Size: 210×148mm

日本の現代建築を考える II
○と×

日本の現代建築を考える II ○と×

磯崎 新：静岡県コンベンションアーツセンター・グランシップ、なら100年会館、秋吉台国際芸術村 槇 文彦：ヒルサイドテラス 山本理顕：埼玉県立大学 伊東豊雄：大社文化プレイス、せんだいメディアテーク 小嶋一浩：ビッグハート出雲 黒川紀章：大阪府立国際会議場 磯崎 新：建築とアメリカの運命 地方都市と共同都市 工業生産と文化の危機 栄久庵憲司 伊藤節郎＋杉崎健一 仁藤喜徳＋岡村仁 青木淳：せんだいメディアテーク 妹島和世＋西沢立衛 工藤国雄 原 広司：札幌ドーム 石山修武：世田谷村 高橋靗一：群馬県立館林美術館

312 total pages ￥1,900

近代建築の黎明
MA
1851-1919
TEXT BY KENNETH FRAMPTON
EDITED AND PHOTOGRAPHED BY YUKIO FUTAGAWA

MA MODERN ARCHITECTURE 1851-1919

第1章：ガラス、鉄、鋼、そしてコンクリート 1775-1915 第2章：シカゴ派の建築─都市と郊外 1830-1915 第3章：アール・ヌーヴォーの構造と象徴主義 1851-1914 第4章：オットー・ワグナーとワグナー派 1894-1912 第5章：工業生産と文化の危機 1851-1910

224 total pages, 48 in colors ￥2,300

近代建築の開花
MA
1920-1945
TEXT BY KENNETH FRAMPTON
EDITED AND PHOTOGRAPHED BY YUKIO FUTAGAWA

MA MODERN ARCHITECTURE 1920-1945

第6章：北ヨーロッパの風土建築としての煉瓦造近代建築 1914-1935 第7章：古典主義の伝統とヨーロッパのアヴァンギャルド 1912-1937 第8章：ヨーロッパの芸術と建築における千年王国的な衝撃 1913-1922 第9章：地方都市と共同都市 建築とアメリカの運命 1913-1945 第10章：インターナショナル・モダニズムと国民的自覚 1919-1939

288 total pages, 48 in colors ￥2,300

反回想 I
磯崎 新

反回想 I 磯崎 新

GA JAPANで好評を博した同名タイトルの連載をもとに、新たな原稿を加えて単行本化しました。1960年代から80年代初頭までの氏の作品を振り返り、その背景と時代を浮彫りにします。作品集「GA ARCHITECT ARATA ISOZAKI」の裏読本的内容。

320 total pages ￥2,380

超大数集合都市へ
篠原一男

超大数集合都市へ 篠原一男

アフリカ・ヨーロッパ・南北アメリカ・日本という地域軸と、古代から現代までの2000年を超える時間軸を、縦横に織り上げることによって論じられる「都市」。

160 total pages ￥1,900

建築のエッセンス
齋藤 裕

建築のエッセンス 齋藤 裕

木や漆喰、コンクリートなどの材料から空間の構成法まで、時代や風土を越えてエッセンスを抽出し、再解釈することで現代の建築家が忘れかけている建築の本質にせまります。

320 total pages ￥2,476

表記価格に消費税は含まれておりません。

A.D.A. EDITA Tokyo

GA DOCUMENT 99
Publisher: *Yukio Futagawa*
Editor: *Yoshio Futagawa*

Published in September 2007
© A.D.A. EDITA Tokyo Co., Ltd.
3-12-14 Sendagaya, Shibuya-ku,
Tokyo, 151-0051 Japan
Tel. 03-3403-1581
Fax.03-3497-0649
e-mail: info@ga-ada.co.jp
www.ga-ada.co.jp

Logotype Design: *Gan Hosoya*

Printed in Japan by
Dai Nippon Printing Co., Ltd.

All rights reserved.

Copyright of Photographs:
© *GA photographers*
*All images are provided by Zaha
Hadid Architects except as noted.*

GA DOCUMENT 99
発行：二川幸夫
編集：二川由夫

2007年9月25日発行
エーディーエー・エディタ・トーキョー
東京都渋谷区千駄ヶ谷3-12-14
電話(03)3403-1581(代)
ファクス(03)3497-0649
e-mail: info@ga-ada.co.jp
www.ga-ada.co.jp

ロゴタイプ・デザイン：細谷巌

印刷・製本：大日本印刷株式会社

禁無断転載

ISBN978-4-87140-199-9 C1352

取次店
トーハン・日販・大阪屋
栗田出版販売・誠光堂
西村書店・中央社・太洋社

*Cover page: Abu Dhabi Performing Arts Center
Abu Dhabi, United Arab Emirates*

Copyediting: Takashi Yanai (pp.9-15)
和訳：谷理佐 (pp.9-15)，菊池泰子 (pp.16-169)，
佐藤圭 (pp.179-201)

Contents

Global Architecture

GA DOC

99

SPECIAL ISSUE

CUMENT

Interview with Zaha Hadid

ザハ・ハディド・インタヴュー

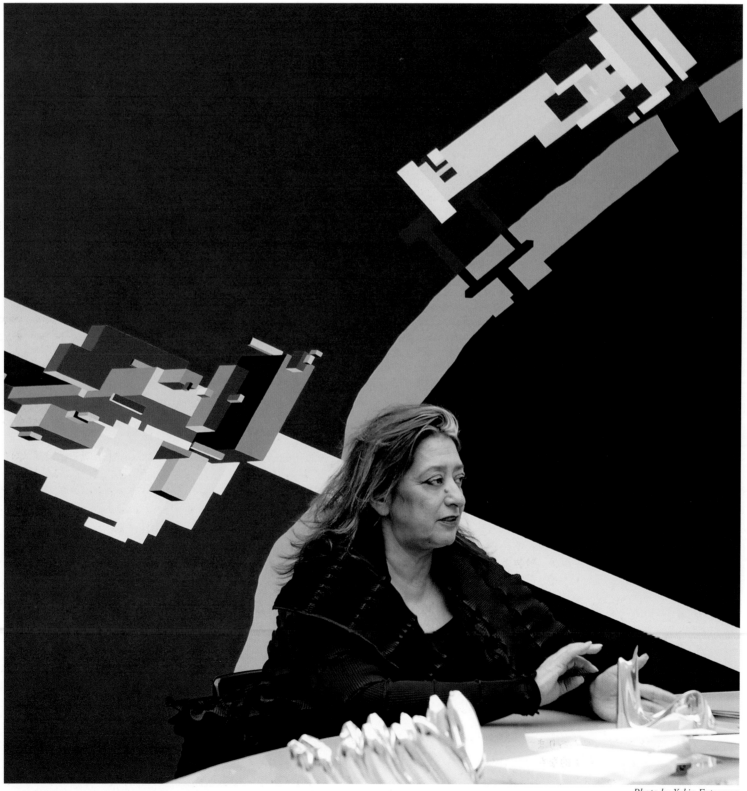

Photo by Yukio Futagawa

GA: I'd like to talk about how your practice has evolved since 1994. The projects have become much larger and more complex. You now have an office of more that 200 people here. How do you handle this change in scale?

Zaha Hadid: Every time the office grows it's a difficult transition. The first time we went from twenty to fifty it was very difficult. The next time we went from fifty to a hundred it was very difficult. But now it has settled down. I have very good senior people who are partners now and there are about twenty to twenty-five people here that are very good and capable who direct the others who are still very young and need guidance.

GA: When did you move into your new apartment?

ZH: About a year and a half ago. I still have the other place. I wanted to renovate it but then I would have to move out and rent. So instead I decided to move here and see if I liked it. It's a nice location and very convenient. I can walk here.

GA: What have you done with your old place?

ZH: Nothing yet. I will either renovate it or sell it. One or the other.

GA: And how has the design process changed for you now that the work is much more complex? How do you start a design? Years ago the work manifested itself in your beautiful drawings, but now you are doing these concrete buildings and the image of your work has changed a lot. Before you did a lot of sketches, how do you generate early ideas now?

ZH: I still do sketches. I have a lot of new beautiful sketches. They're next to my desk. A lot of them are about abstract ideas that I would like to try generally and

that may be applied to a specific project. When a project is being developed by my staff on the computer I will get print outs and sketch over them again.

GA: How about working in model?

ZH: We do some models. Now of course the drawings and the models are the same. Before there were always discrepancies that arose out of the translation between drawing and model and vice versa. Now the models can practically be printed. So there is no interpretation. It is more direct, and faster. I think the new technologies available are quite exciting.

It vastly speeds up the design and production process. For example, we're doing a complex structure for the Serpentine Gallery ("Lilas, 2007") in under two months. It's phenomenal. Are you coming to the Venice Biennale? You should see our installation.

GA: Who introduces this new technology to your office?

ZH: Computer programs have become incredible and the young people are amazing with them. For example, we have someone who used to work at Arup who is used to working with complex geometry. As you know, I love to work with engineers. The programs are all parametric now.

GA: I can see how this would work with furniture. But what about buildings? Do you start with the interior spaces? Or the exterior form?

ZH: Well it's not really an issue with the computer because we are not generating exterior form only. We always consider the design the way we always have which is to design it all at the same time.

GA：1994年以降の展開についてお伺いします。より大規模で複雑なプロジェクトへとシフトされていますね。今や，この事務所で働くスタッフは200名以上。これほどの規模拡大にはどう対応されているのでしょうか。

ザハ・ハディド（ZH）：事務所が拡大するたび苦労をしますね。最初20人から50人に増えたときも大変でしたし，その次に50人から100人に増えたときも大変でした。でも今は落ち着いています。パートナーとして参画してくれる優秀な年長者の人材もありますし，指導が必要な若いスタッフ達をとりまとめる有能なスタッフが20〜25人いますので。

GA：新しいアパートに移られたのはいつですか？

ZH：1年半ほど前です。前のアパートも手放してはいません。改装するつもりだったのですが，そのためには中を空にしてどこかを間借りしないとならないので，かわりにここに引っ越して様子を見る事にしたのです。なかなか便利で良い場所ですよ。歩いて通えますし。

GA：前のアパートは今どうなっているのですか？

ZH：まだ何もしていません。改装するか売却するか。どちらかでしょうね。

GA：より複雑な仕事を手がけるようになり，デザインのプロセスにはどのような変化が生じましたか？ 仕事の取りかかり方は？ 以前はあの素晴らしいドローイングから全てが始まっていたと思うのですが。現在ではコンクリートの建物も多く，かなり作品イメージが変わってきています。以前はたくさんスケッチを描かれていましたが，現在，最初のアイディアはどのように生まれてくるのでしょうか。

ZH：今でもスケッチはしますよ。新しい佳作がたくさんあります。ほら，デスクの横に。だいたいは，思い浮かんだアイディアをスケッチした抽象的なもので，特定のプロジェクトのためのものではありません。ほかのスタッフがパソコン上で作業をするようなプロジェクト

の場合，プリントアウトをしてもらい，自分でスケッチをし直します。

GA：模型はどうですか？

ZH：時々，つくります。もちろん，今ではドローイングと模型は同じですよね。以前はドローイングから模型をおこす際，あるいはその逆方向でも，解釈のギャップがつきものでしたが，今は模型はほぼ完璧にプリントアウトできるものですから，解釈自体が不要になり，もっと手早く，ダイレクトになりました。今のテクノロジーはなかなか素晴らしいもので，デザイン・制作プロセスにかかる時間が大幅に短縮されました。例えば，今進行中の曲がりくねった複雑な構造ですが，作業期間は2ヶ月弱です。驚きますよね。ヴェニスのビエンナーレには行きますか？ ぜひ私たちのインスタレーションを見てみて下さい。

GA：事務所では，どなたがそういった新しいテクノロジーを導入するのですか？

ZH：パソコンのプログラムの進化には目を見張るものがあります。若い人には親和性があるようですね。オヴ・アラップ出身で，複雑な構造を扱うのに慣れたスタッフもいます。ご存知の通り，わたしはエンジニアと一緒に仕事をするのが好きです。今のプログラムはすべてがパラメトリックですね。

GA：家具のデザインにぴったりだというのは分かります。では建築ではどうでしょう？ 内部空間から着手されますか？ それとも外観から？

ZH：そうですね，パソコンを使うかどうかはあまり関係がないです。外形だけをつくるわけではありませんから。デザインについては，以前と変わらず，すべてを同時に考えるというやり方をとっています。また，長年この仕事をやっていると，自然と自分なりのレパートリーが出来上がってくるものです。それを壊そうとしたり，新たに増やそうとしたりする。パソコンで作業をする時でもチャレンジ精神は同じです。そういった意味で仕事のプロセスに

Also after a long time, you learn from your own work and develop a repertoire. Sometimes you break this repertoire or add to it. You challenge it. Working with computers hasn't changed this aspect of the practice. The process has not changed in this sense, but the computer does allow you to make these leaps. It is easier to resolve complexity. Before you had to build it, analyze it, slice it. So as a tool the computer has added many dimensions, but it doesn't help you create the ideas. Sure, there are those that use computers to generate form. But for me it doesn't help me make ideas. It is however a tool that helps me think seriously about form.

GA: Is there a particular program that you use?

ZH: There are several and they get more and more incredible every year. But you can't just use them on their own. You can't use them without an idea. It's changed the process. For example we used to look at a form by drawing a thousand perspectives. It was time consuming. The computer makes this easier to generate the same number of views. It's made the design process much more elastic.

But in the end you have to make a building stable and stand up. Even a dramatic cantilevered table has to stand up. A building is complex. You have mechanical and electrical and structural engineers. That's what makes architecture very rich. There is a complexity with so many layers. And so it makes creating architecture and thinking about architecture very difficult and very exciting. Not to generalize, but you can always tell when something is not designed by an architect even if a space looks nice, because it will not have a sense of organization.

GA: So your office continues to work at a variety of scales.

△▽Phaeno Science Center, 2000-05

変わりはありませんが，パソコンのおかげでステップの省略が出来ることも事実です。以前なら，複雑な形を扱う際，実際に組み立てて，分析して，切断して，という作業が必要でしたが，パソコンでなら簡単に解析が出来ます。道具としてのパソコンは可能性を広げてくれましたが，アイディアが生まれる場面で使う物ではありません。もちろん，フォルムをつくるのにパソコンを使う人もいるでしょうが，私にとってはクリエイティブな道具ではないのです。フォルムを熟考する際に使うことはありますが。

GA：どんなプログラムを使用されていますか？

ZH：使用するプログラムはいくつかありますが，毎年どんどん進化していきますね。でも，プログラムを使いさえすればいいわけではなくて，はじめにアイディアありき，です。プロセスは変わりましたね。以前は，1つのフォルムに対して膨大な枚数のパースを描くため，非常に時間がかかったものです。パソコンはそういう作業は得意ですから，デザインのプロセスに柔軟性をもたせてくれます。

でも最終的に重要なのは，建物が安定して建ち上がることです。派手なキャンティレバー・スタイルのテーブルでも，ちゃんと自立しないとならない。建物には様々な分野の要素がからみあっていて，機械，電気，構造のエンジニアの助けが必要です。それが建築の豊かさなのです。そして，だからこそ建築をつくったり考えたりすることは非常に難しく，面白味のあるものなのです。偏見ではありませんが，建築家がデザインしていないものは，一目でそうとわかってしまいます。見た目は良くても，まとまりに欠けるんですね。

GA：さまざまな規模の仕事を手がけていらっしゃいますが。

ZH：ええ。同じ人間が大規模なものから小規模なものまでを担当します。アイディアや語法の断絶があってはいけませんから。

ZH: Yes. In fact the same people often work on some of the largest projects and then some of the smallest. The ideas have to relate to each other and be of the same language.

For example when we did Vitra we also needed to design bicycle parking—a shed for the bicycles. We did something like mushrooms or trees.

GA: Furniture design has always been an integral part of the practice.

ZH: Yes. I can show you some very nice furniture pieces we are developing. They're all done in aluminum. They're very stunning. For instance, we're doing a very nice table, all made of one piece of aluminum ("Crater" for David Gill Galleries, 2007). With the computer these are designed and built in months.

I don't know if you remember but many years ago when I was doing my other furniture I did a table, and when I compare them to this, they are almost identical except the first one had more straight lines.

GA: You have a lot of furniture commissions?

ZH: This year we do. We're doing a thing for Established & Sons. (The Seamless Collection, 2006)

GA: How are sales?

ZH: They are doing well. The limited editions are all gone.

GA: Few people can do both architecture and furniture. I think the attitude is similar but really it is totally different. What do you think about that? How do you go about thinking about tables, chairs and sofas.

ZH: I think about it at the same time. It's all floating in my head. For instance, I want

たとえば，ヴィトラのプロジェクトでは，駐輪場もデザインしました。自転車用の車庫ですね。キノコと樹木をいっぺんに手がけたようなものです。

GA：以前から家具デザインも手がけていらっしゃいますね。

ZH：ええ。こちらが現在とりかかっている家具シリーズ。アルミ製です。なかなか良いでしょう。このテーブルはアルミの削りだしです。パソコンを使って，デザインから作製まで数ヶ月で出来上がります。

憶えているかもしれませんが，何年か前に別シリーズの家具を手がけた際，テーブルもつくったのですが，それとこれを比べてみるとほとんど一緒なのです。昔のものの方が直線が多めだったくらいで。

GA：家具デザインの依頼は多いですか？

ZH：今年は多いですね。Established & Sonsからのオーダーなど。

GA：売り上げはいかがですか？

ZH：好調です。限定モデルは完売しました。

GA：建築と家具の両方ができる人は，あまりいません。心構えは似ていても，まったく別のものだと私は思うのですが，ご自分ではどうお考えですか？　テーブルや椅子やソファーなどをどのように考えていらっしゃいますか？

ZH：それらを考えるのは同時に，ですね。すべて私の頭の中に浮かんでいるのです。例えばテーブルを考えながら，その表面がランドスケープになればいい，という具合に。いろいろなイメージが頭の中にあって，そこから運良く形になるものがいくつか出て来るので，そこに意識を集中するのです。

GA：だからこのテーブルはあなたの建築にマッチするものだと。

to do a table where the surface becomes a landscape. So I'm thinking of many things and luckily a few things come out and I'm able to focus on it.

GA: So this table goes with your architecture.

ZH: Yes, but I think it can work in other houses as well.

GA: I see so many iterations of the designs in your studio.

ZH: We vary it until it works just as you would study the geometry of the building.

GA: In sketches?

ZH: I still love hand drawing you know. But young people can't do draw anymore.

GA: There hasn't been much talent after the emergence of your generation.

ZH: I think that will change eventually. It takes a long time to build a career in architecture. It's very competitive. And also there are other social factors. Many things overlap at the same time and produce these generational shifts.

GA: How do you feel at school teaching young people?

ZH: I think teaching is interesting because you train people who can move on to different things. There's a lot going on right now that's really exciting. And also there's the opportunity to have these discussions with others.

GA: The way of teaching has changed a lot since you were in school.

ZH: Well. It wasn't all digital before.

GA: Yes. When we saw the studio we were so surprised by the desks with just a computer. It used to be that you needed drafting tables.

ZH: Well, that's partially because we're renovating. But it's true. Sometimes a com-

△▽BMW Plant Leipzig—Central Building, 2002-05

ZH：ええ，でも他の家にも合うと思いますよ。

GA：最近では，デザインの転用がいろいろな建物で見られるようになってきましたね。

ZH：建物の形状を決める時と同様に，たくさんのバリエーションを考えます。

GA：スケッチでですか？

ZH：いまだに手描きのスケッチが好きなんですよ。でも最近の若い人々はスケッチができなくなりましたね。

GA：あなたの世代以降は，才能のある人があまり出てきていません。

ZH：そんな状況もいずれ変わると思います。建築でキャリアを積むには時間がかかるし，競争も激しい。またそれとは別に，社会的な要因もあります。世代交代というものは，さまざまな条件が重なり合って起きるものですから。

GA：学校で若い人々を教えることについてはどう思われますか？

ZH：人に教えるのは，面白いです。将来さまざまな方向へ進む可能性を持つ生徒を相手にしますから。今はエキサイティングなことが沢山ありますし。それに，学校は他の人々と議論が出来る場でもあります。

GA：ご自分が学生だった頃とは教え方もずいぶん変わってきているのでは。

ZH：そうですね。こんなにデジタル化されてはいませんでした。

GA：ええ。スタジオを拝見した時，デスクがとても小さく，パソコンが置いてあるだけなのに，たいへん驚きました。昔は製図台が必要だったのに。

ZH：今ちょうど改装中だということもありますが。そうなんです，パソコン一台あれば事足りてしまう。彼らはスケッチもできないし，模型もつくれない。こんな状況が変わるには，も

puter is all they need. They can't draw and they can't make models. It will take another moment in history for this to change. You can't teach these skills that take ten years to develop in a month or a year.

GA: So you don't think it's a problem that there's a lack of skill today?

ZH: I think it's a problem but then again there always new skills that emerge. For instance, for my generation there was a critical moment in the early 80s when some people showed others that there was another way to do things. And that was very subversive. And it was met with resistance from the schools, and the architects and the builders and everyone. But look at how many architects have thrived from that period.

GA: Whenever I try to meet architects like you, it's impossible, because everyone is traveling. I would have thought with the internet that communication would be easier, but the opposite has happened for architects. There is more traveling than ever before.

ZH: Yes it's true. The world has opened up a lot. It's really exhausting.

GA: You travel a lot lately but haven't been to Japan in many years.

ZH: I know. I must go back to Japan. I haven't been in fifteen years, since before Fukuoka in the early 1990s. I will try to go back sometime.

Looking back, I must say that my trips to Asia in the 1980s had an incredible impact on me and my work. This impact stays on even today. It's another universe in a positive way. If you look at Japanese fashion, street fashion, photography and makeup, it's quite interesting and inspiring.

GA: How do you keep up with this information?

ZH: Oh, magazines, TV programs. I just think it's incredible. I remember walking

う少し時間がかかりそうですね。本来なら10年かかって習得するスキルを1ヶ月や1年で教える事はできませんから。

GA：では昨今の人材のスキル不足は問題ではないとお考えですか？

ZH：問題だと思ってはいますが，新しく出現するスキル，というものもあるわけです。たとえば，私の世代にとって80年代初頭は重大な節目といえる時期でした。今までとは違う，別のやり方を提示する人々が現れたのです。それは非常に破壊的なパワーを持っていました。学校や建築家や建設業者や，みんなからの抵抗にあいましたが，今まわりを見廻してみると当時の混乱の中から成長した建築家がたくさんいます。

GA：あなたのような建築家と会って話をしようとしても，みなさん出張中で，つかまえられません。インターネットの普及でコミュニケーションが楽にとれるようになると思いきや，建築家に関してはその逆のようです。以前よりも出張が増えていますね。

ZH：その通りです。世界は広がりましたが，その分，体力を消耗します。

GA：近頃は特に出張が多いようですが，日本には数年来いらしていませんね。

ZH：そうなんです。日本にはまた行かないと。もう15年，訪れていません。1990年代初めに福岡に行って以来。いつかまた訪れるつもりです。

振り返ってみると，1980年代にアジア諸国をまわった経験は，自分自身と作品に相当なインパクトを与えています。その影響は今なお残っていると思います。いい意味で，別世界なのです。日本のストリート・ファッションや写真，メークアップなどは，とても興味深く，インスピレーションを与えてくれます。

GA：そういった情報はどのように入手されるのですか？

ZH：雑誌とか，テレビ番組とか。すごいものがあると思います。東京の街を訪れたときに見

around Tokyo looking at all these gadgets. At the time, those kinds of things weren't available in Europe. I think it's a shame there was a recession in the 90s because Japan at the time was very advanced and exciting. I think they were breaking the boundaries and they were hiring architects to do very experimental and interesting work. But then again, when one goes back to these places it's never the same.

GA: Where do you get inspiration from these days?

ZH: Right now when I'm traveling it's too hectic to see things. I don't have time to really see the things around me. I would love to go to India because I've never been. I would love to go to Chandigarh. I would love to go to Dhaka by Louis Kahn. It's just fantasies right now. A visit to Japan would be a little easier because I know people there. I would have to plan an agenda for India. But once I was flying over India and the plane was flying very low, the cities were vast and enormous. It made me very curious about them.

GA: Now you often go to China don't you?

ZH: No not really. Not in the last year. They've changed a lot of laws about working in China. We are doing the Guangzhou Opera House which should be open next year.

GA: How about the Middle East. You have several projects there currently.

ZH: Yes. In Dubai and Abu Dhabi and we've been approached about a project in Beirut which could be very interesting and even about work in Syria and North Africa.

GA: When you work in the Middle East is there a kind of empathy with the culture for you?

ZH: It's the language that ties us together. Of course if I worked in Iraq it would be quite emotional for me since I lived there. But I must say this past year I drove from Beirut to Damascus and I went to see a particular Mosque again and it was very stunning. As a child in Iraq, I went to a nun's school, a Christian school. I used to pass by these things on the bus on the way to, say, a school picnic. These places are, apart from their religious significance, very stunning, and beautiful, with elaborate mysterious interiors. A mosque is very deliberately done and beautiful. It's meant to evoke heaven and it is absolutely stunning. And it's very curious to me the connection between these beautiful worlds and all the geometry and the mathematical roots of the structures. So when I saw them again, I became very curious about it. So I guess these are the kinds of things you get to confirm when you travel.

It is also interesting to see the combinations when you travel. For instance, Moorish Hollywood. When you go to Hollywood there are houses with Moorish influences. Once in Los Angeles, I was visiting a house in Pasadena built for an actor from the 30s. It was this fantastic Hollywood version of Moorish architecture. It was very well done and quite stunning. And now they are doing this hybrid style in Morocco. From Morocco to Los Angeles to Morocco again. They're miles away. The influence comes from the new world back through Spain. It's very interesting how these languages travel in this way. So the process of globalization has been happening for a hundred years.

GA: What's the situation with British architecture?

かけた雑貨やおもちゃ。当時ああいう物はヨーロッパには無かった。90年代の不況は残念なことだったと思います。あの頃の日本は最先端を進んでいて，とてもエキサイティングでしたから。枠にとらわれずに，建築家を雇って実験的で面白い仕事をさせていました。でも，変わらずにいるものなど無いのは，日本だけではありませんからね。

GA：最近はどのようなものからインスピレーションを受けましたか？

ZH：今は旅行ばかりでバタバタしていて，周りを見回す時間がとれません。今まで訪れたことのないインドには興味があります。チャンディガールに行ってみたい。ルイス・カーンのダッカに行ってみたい。現段階ではただの思いつきですが。日本には知人が何人かいるので，行くのはいくぶん簡単なのですが，インドの場合は事前のプランニングが必要です。以前に一度，乗っていた飛行機がインド上空を低空飛行したことがあって，巨大な広がりを持つ市街地を見て，好奇心を大いにかきたてられました。

GA：最近では中国に何度もいらしていますよね？

ZH：いえ，そうでもないです，特に昨年は。中国では法律がだいぶ変わったようで。来年オープン予定の広州オペラ・ハウスを手がけています。

GA：中東はいかがですか。現在進行中のプロジェクトがいくつかありますが。

ZH：ええ。ドバイとアブダビで。ベイルートでのプロジェクトについて，かなり面白そうなオファーがありました。シリアと北アフリカのプロジェクトの話もあります。

GA：中東での仕事をされる際，文化的な共感が得られることは？

ZH：中東諸国と私自身を結ぶ絆は，言語です。もちろん，もしイラクで仕事が出来たなら，それはとても感動的なことだと思います。昔住んでいた場所ですので。昨年，ベイルートからダマスカスまで車で移動した際，とあるモスクを見学しに行ったのですが，これが非常に

素晴らしかった。イラクでの子供時代，私はキリスト教の修道女学校に通っていたのですが，学校の遠足などでは，そういった建造物の前をバスで通ることがありました。モスクは，宗教的な意味合いはさておき，それ自体がとても美しく素晴らしい建物で，内部は精巧につくり込まれ，ミステリアスな雰囲気があります。天国を喚起させるよう，非常に美しく緻密につくられています。そういった美しい世界と，その構造の幾何学・数学的ルーツの関係性は，とても興味深いところです。久しぶりにモスクを見て，好奇心をかきたてられました。こんな風に，旅行をしたおかげで再確認ができることもあるんですね。

もうひとつ，旅行につきものなのは，面白いコンビネーションを見つけることです。例えば，ムーア様式とハリウッド。ハリウッドに行くと，ムーア様式の影響を受けた家々を見かけることができます。ロサンジェルスのパサデナに，とある俳優のために1930年代に建てられた家があります。ムーア様式のハリウッド版といったところの，実に立派な建築でした。そして今度はそんなハイブリッド・スタイルをモロッコに持って行くそうです。モロッコからロサンジェルスへ，そしてまたモロッコへと長い距離を渡ってゆく。文化や言語が新世界からスペインを通って戻ってくる。とても面白いですね。グローバリゼーションは，もう100年ほど前から始まっていたのです。

GA：イギリス建築の現状についてお聞かせ下さい。

ZH：そうですね，経済は上向きです。今日のロンドンは20年前の日本と同じです。アメリカ人がどうしているかはわかりませんが。世界のどこよりも物価が高い。ニューヨークの物価の2倍です。多くの才能ある建築家が，商業的な建築家へと転向しています。若手で突出した人はあまりいませんね。そしてここでは，アメリカやヨーロッパと違い，年が若いうちに

ZH: Well the economy is thriving. London now is like Japan 20 years ago. I don't know Americans manage here. It's double anywhere else. It's double New York prices. A lot of talented architects have become commercial architects. There are not a lot of young architects that stand out. And also unlike America or Europe there are no opportunities to make a name for yourself when you are young. In Europe they might win a competition. In America there is always the opportunity to do a family house.

GA: Same as Japan.

ZH: I think it's a problem. These kids come out of school. They may go off on their own after one or two years. They have no experience and work on art projects. They don't develop their repertoire. They either don't stay long enough at an office or they stay too long. They aren't very practical.

In Europe at least everything is a competition. So there are a lot of young people who win these projects. There's more opportunity. For example there are lot of young architects that have graduated from the AA School that are building interesting work in Eastern Europe.

GA: How about Russia?

ZH: We have a house project in Moscow. But in Russia you have no control over what they might do to it. I love Moscow, but it is crazy. It's an amazing city. The Russians are crazy.

GA: Any comments on your contemporaries? Rem Koolhaas, Frank Gehry, Jean Nouvel?

ZH: We are all competitors but also friends. I support them, they support me.

I saw Frank at an event a few weeks ago. I saw Wolf Prix yesterday. I saw Steven Holl in New York and Jacque Herzog in London recently. I don't see Rem much, But we're all very good friends. Architecture is very tough and so it makes you very competitive. It's really difficult.

GA: You've been competing with them for a long time.

ZH: It's true. It's amazing that the scene has not changed that much in the last thirty years. The work has changed but the people in the game are the same. So it just means that these people have incredible perseverance and agility at the same time.

GA: Do you ever discuss projects with each other?

ZH: No. But for example I'm teaching in Vienna so I was there yesterday with people like Jeff Kipnis and Greg Lynn. And younger people from New York like Jesse Reiser and Ali Rahim. And there's a discussion between us. I give a lecture. So we meet on reviews, but there's no forum really for us to discuss architecture. It's not like when Alvin was here and he would arrange these discussions at the AA School. It does occur sometimes. Like when I was at Yale, Eisenman was on my review. So it happens, but not in any organized way. It's a shame; we're all too busy these days.

June 27, 2007, London
Interview by Yoshio Futagawa,
Copyediting by Takashi Yanai

名声が得られるようなチャンスはほとんどありません。ヨーロッパでならコンペティションで優勝すれば名をあげることができますし，アメリカではいつでも個人宅を手がけるチャンスがあるのですが。

GA：それは日本も同じですね。

ZH：これは問題だと思っています。若い子が学校を卒業して，1〜2年したら独立する。ところが実務経験がなく，アート・プロジェクトに関わったこともない。自分の中にレパートリーの蓄積がない。1つの事務所に腰掛け程度にしか所属しないか，必要以上に長く居続けてしまうかのどちらかです。人材として，あまり実践的とは言えません。ヨーロッパではすべてがコンペティションですから，そのおかげで若い人でもプロジェクトに参加するチャンスに恵まれています。AAスクール出身の若手建築家でも，西ヨーロッパで面白い建築をやっている連中がたくさんいます。

GA：ロシアはどうでしょう？

ZH：モスクワで住宅プロジェクトが進行中です。でもロシアでは，こちらの希望通りにいかないことばかりで。モスクワは大好きなのですが，とんでもない場所です。素晴らしい都市ですが，ロシア人はクレージーですね。

GA：レム・コールハース，フランク・ゲーリー，ジャン・ヌヴェルといった，あなたと同時代の人々についてどう思われますか？

ZH：ライバルでもあり，友人でもあります。互いにサポートし合う関係です。

フランクには数年前，とあるイベントで会いました。昨日はウォルフ・プリックスに会いました。最近ではロンドンでジャック・ヘルツォークに，ニューヨークでスティーヴン・ホールに会っています。レムはあまり見かけませんね。皆よい友達です。建築の世界は厳しい

ので，競争も激しい。なかなか大変です。

GA：彼らとは長い間，共に競争をされてきました。

ZH：そうです。ここ30年ほどシーンがほとんど変わっていないのには驚きますね。仕事自体は変わりましたが，立役者は同じ顔ぶれです。単に，彼らが途方もない根気と機敏さを併せ持っている，というだけのことなのかもしれませんが。

GA：お互いのプロジェクトについて語り合うことはありますか？

ZH：ありません。ただ例えば，今私はウィーンの学校で教えていて，昨日はそこで講演をしてジェフ・キプニスやグレッグ・リン，それからニューヨークの若手ジェシー・ライザーとアリ・ラヒームといった人たちと会って話をした，というようなことはあります。講評の時に顔を合わせることもあります。でも建築について議論をかわすフォーラムのようなものは存在しません。例えば，アルヴィンがやって来るからAAスクールでディスカッションの場を設けよう，というようなことはほとんどありません。時々，例えば私がイェールにいた時にアイゼンマンが講評に現れた，というようなことはありますが。あくまで偶然の産物で，計画的なものではありません。残念なことですが……皆それぞれが忙しすぎるのですね。

2007年6月27日，ロンドンにて
インタビュー：二川由夫
和訳：谷理佐

MAXXI: NATIONAL MUSEUM OF XXI CENTURY ARTS

Rome, Italy
Design: 1997–   Construction: –2008

Architectural Concept and Urban Strategy:
Staging the Field of Possibilities

The Museum for Contemporary Arts addresses the question of its urban context by maintaining an indexicality to the former army barracks. This is in no way an attempt at topological pastiche, but instead continues the low-level urban texture set against the higher level blocks on the surrounding sides of the site. In this way, the Museum is more like an 'urban graft', a second skin to the site. At times, it affiliates with the ground to become new ground, yet also ascends and coalesces to become massivity where needed. The entire building has an urban character: prefiguring upon a directional route connecting the River to Via Guido Reni, the Museum encompasses both movement patterns extant and desired, contained within and outside. This vector defines the primary entry route into the building. By intertwining the circulation with the urban context, the building shares a public dimension with the city, overlapping tendril like paths and open space. In addition to the circulatory relationship, the architectural elements are also geometrically aligned with the urban grids that join at the site. In thus partly deriving its orientation and physiognomy from the context, it further assimilates itself to the specific conditions of the site.

Space VS Object

Our proposal offers a quasi-urban field, a "world" to dive into rather than a building as signature object. The Campus is organised and navigated on the basis of directional drifts and the distribution of densities rather than key points.

This is indicative of the character of the Museum as a whole: porous, immersive, a field space. An inferred mass is subverted by vectors of circulation. The external as well as internal circulation follows the overall drift of the geometry. Vertical and oblique circulation elements are located at areas of confluence, interference and turbulence.

The move from object to field is critical in understanding the relationship the architecture will have to the content of the artwork it will house. Whilst this is further expounded by the contributions of our Gallery and Exhibitions Experts below, it is important here to state that the premise of the architectural design promotes

a disinheriting of the 'object' orientated gallery space. Instead, the notion of a 'drift' takes on an embodied form. The drifting emerges, therefore, as both architectural motif, and also as a way to navigate experientially through the museum. It is an argument that, for art practice is well understood, but in architectural hegemony has remained alien. We take this opportunity, in the adventure of designing such a forward looking institution, to confront the material and conceptual dissonance evoked by art practice since the late 1960's. The path lead away from the 'object' and its correlative sanctifying, towards fields of multiple associations that are anticipative of the necessity to change.

Institutional Catalyst

As such, it is deemed significant that in configuring the possible identity of this newly estab-

Site

lished institution (housing both Art and Architecture), with its aspiration towards the polyvalent density of the 21st century, conceptions of space and indeed temporality are reworked. Modernist Utopian space fuelled the white 'neutrality' of most 20th century museums. Now, this disposition must be challenged, not simply out of wilful negation, but by the necessity for architecture to continue its critical relationship with contemporary social and aesthetic categories. Since absolutism has been indefinitely suspended from current thought on the issue of art presentation, it is towards the idea of the 'maximising exhibition' that we gravitate. In this scenario, the Museum makes primary the manifold possibilities for the divergence in showing art and architecture as well as

catalysing the discourse on its future. Again, the 'signature' aspect of an institution of this calibre is sublimated into a more pliable and porous organism that promotes several forms of identification at once.

Walls/Not-Walls: Towards a Contemporary Spatiality

In architectural terms, this is most virulently executed by the figure of the 'wall'. Against the traditional coding of the 'wall' in the museum as the privileged and immutable vertical armature for the display of paintings, or delineating discrete spaces to construct 'order' and linear 'narrative', we propose a critique of it through its emancipation. The 'wall' becomes the versatile engine for the staging of exhibition effects. In its various guises—solid wall, projection screen, canvas, window to the city—the exhibi-

tion wall is the primary space-making device. By running extensively across the site, cursively and gesturally, the lines traverse inside and out. Urban space is coincidental with gallery space, exchanging pavilion and court in a continuous oscillation under the same operation. And further deviations from the Classical composition of the wall emerge as incidents where the walls become floor, or twist to become ceiling, or are voided to become a large window looking out. By constantly changing dimension and geometry, they adapt themselves to whatever curatorial role is needed. By setting within the gallery spaces a series of potential partitions that hang from the ceiling ribs, a versatile exhibition system is created. Organisational and spatial invention are thus dealt with simultaneously amidst a

rhythm found in the echo of the walls to the structural ribs in the ceiling that also filter the light in varying intensities.

Stage for Thought/Art as Drama

It is in this way that the architecture performs the 'staging' of art, with moveable elements that allow for the drama to change. 'Sets' can be constructed from the notional elements of the gallery spaces. These are attuned to the particularities of the exhibition in question, materialising or dematerialising accordingly.

The drift through the Museum is a trajectory through varied ambiences, filtered spectacles and differentiated luminosity. Whilst offering a new freedom in the curators' palette, this in turn digests and recomposes the experience of art spectatorship as liberated dialogue with artefact and environment.

Architects: Zaha Hadid Architects—
Zaha Hadid with Patrick Schumacher, design;
Gianluca Racana, project architect;
Paolo Matteuzzi, Anja Simons, Mario Mattia, site supervision team; Paolo Matteuzzi, Anja Simons, Fabio Ceci, Mario Mattia, Maurizio Meossi, Paolo Zilli, Luca Peralta, Maria Velceva, Matteo Grimaldi, Ana M.Cajiao, Barbara Pfenningstorff, Dillon Lin, Kenneth Bostock, Raza Zahid, Lars Teichmann, Adriano De Gioannis, Amin Taha, Caroline Voet, Gianluca Ruggeri, Luca Segarelli, design team; Ali Mangera, Oliver Domeisen, Christos Passas, Sonia Villaseca, Jee-Eun Lee, James Lim, Julia Hansel, Sara Klomps, Shumon Basar, Bergendy Cooke, Jorge Ortega, Stephane Hof, Marcus Dochantschi, Woody Yao, Graham Modlen, Jim Heverin, Barbara Kuit, Ana Sotrel, Hemendra Kothari, Zahira El Nazel, Florian Migsch, Kathy Wright, Jin Wananabe, Helmut Kinzer, Thomas Knuvener, Sara Kamalvand, competition team
Local architect: ABT srl
Client: Italian Ministry of Culture
Consultants: Anthony Hunt Associates, OK Design Group, structural; Max Fordham and Partners, OK Design Group, mechanical & electrical; Equation Lighting, lighting; Paul Gilleron Acoustic, acoustic
Total floor area: 30,000 m²

Site: under construction

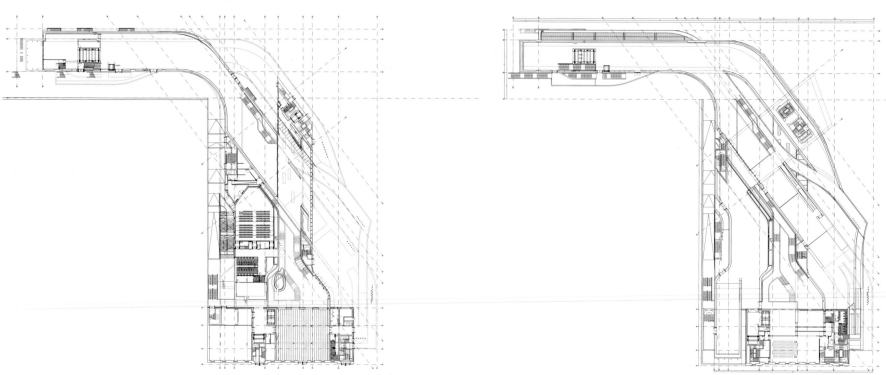

Level 1

Level 2

〈建築的コンセプトと都市的ストラテジー：可能性のフィールドを演出する〉

現代美術館は，以前ここにあった兵舎を連想させるような性格を維持することで，その都市文脈に対する問題提示を行う。これは，地形の寄せ集めをしようというのではなく，敷地を囲む高層の建物が並ぶ街区側に対抗させて，低層の都市構造を連続させるのである。この方法においては，美術館は“街の接ぎ木”，敷地の第2の皮膚のようなものである。時々，それは地とつながって新たな地を形成するが，必要な箇所では，立ち上がり合体してマッシブなものとなる。建物全体は都市的な性格をもつ。川とグゥイド・レーニ通りをつなぐ方向への道筋を想定しつつ，美術館は，既に存在するもの，望まれるもの，両方の通路パターンを，内，外に包含する。このベクトルは建物へ入る主要な道筋を規定する。通路を都市文脈と撚り合わせることで，巻きひげのような通路やオープン・スペースが重層しながら，建物は都市の公共的な尺度を共有する。循環的な関係に加えて，建築的要素はまた，敷地に合流する都市グリッドと幾何学的に整列する。こうして，部分的にはコンテクストが備える方位や外形から生まれた建物は，敷地固有の状況にさらに深く同化する。

〈空間対物体〉

提示案は署名入りのオブジェクトとしての建物ではなく，都市に似たフィールド，飛び込んでいく“世界”を表現する。このキャンパスは漂流する方向性であり，主要地点の点的な分布ではなく密度の配分に基づいて組織され，航行していく。

全体の性格を暗示するのは，多孔性，沈潜性，フィールド・スペースである。埋葬されたマッスは通路のベクトルによって転覆される。内部同様，外部の通路も幾何学の全体的な漂流に従う。垂直方向や斜めに進む通路は，合流，衝突，乱流地点に位置する。

オブジェクトからフィールドへの移行は，この建築が中に収めることになる芸術作品の内容との関係を理解する上で重要である。これは，ギャラリー／展覧会専門家の尽力によりさらに詳述されることになるが，この建築デザインの前提が，“オブジェクト”指向のギャラリー空間という遺産からの撤退を促進させるものであるとここで述べておくことは重要である。それに代わって“漂流”という概念が具体化された形のなかに取り入れられる。従って，漂流は，建築的な主題にも，館内を経験しながら航行していく道筋にも出現する。それは，芸術作品ではよく理解されているが，建築世界の中では，依然として異質な主張である。この機会をとらえて，こうした先進的な建物をデザインするという冒険のなかに，1960年代後半以来，芸術活動によって喚起されてきた材料やコンセプトの不協和音的構成と向き合うことにしたのである。通路は“オブジェクト”とその相互依存関係にある神聖化から離れ，変化の必要が予測される多様な連関のフィールドへと導く。

〈インスティテューショナルな触媒〉

こうして，この新たに設立されるインスティテューション（芸術と建築を共に収める）に可能な独自性を設計することが重要であると考えた。21世紀の多様な複雑さに対する願望と共に，空間構想とテンポ

ラリティそのものが再生される。モダニストの夢想的な空間は20世紀の美術館の大半を白い“ニュートラリティ”で覆い尽くした。今，これは異議を申し立てられるに違いない。単に意志的な否定からではなく，建築はコンテンポラリーな社会とその美的規範との関係を持ち続ける必要が重要であるゆえにである。芸術作品の展示法に対する絶対主義的な考え方は，現在，不確定的な留保状態にあるので，われわれが強く惹かれている“展示を最大限に活用する”アイディアへ向かうことができる。このシナリオのなかで，美術館はまず第一に，未来を見据えた論考のための触媒となると同時に，芸術を見せることと建築との分岐に対する多様な可能性をつくりだす。さらにまた，この重要なインスティテューションの“署名的”側面は，独自性を備えたいくつもの形態を同時に進展させる，よりしなやかで多孔性の有機体へと昇華される。

〈壁／非壁：今日的な空間性へ向けて〉

建築的な点からは，これは“壁”という表象によって，最も悪意的につくられている。絵画の展示のための，“秩序”や線形の“物語”を構築するための，分離した空間の輪郭を描くための，特権的で，不変の垂直の骨格としての，美術館内の伝統的な符号である“壁”に対決して，壁を束縛から解放することで，その批評を提起する。“壁”は展示効果の演出のための万能のエンジンとなる。多彩な外貌を持つ展示壁は──ソリッドな壁，映写スクリーン，キャンバス，都市を望む窓──主要な空間構成の装置である。敷地を横断し，隅々まで巡らされ，流れるように，身振りをつけながら，壁を構成する線は内部と外部を進んでいく。都市空間は，同じ操作のもとで，連続する変動のなかでパヴィリオンとコートを交換しながら，ギャラリー空間と同時存在する。そして壁の古典的構成からのさらなる逸脱は，壁が床になり，あるいはねじれて天井になり，あるいは取り除かれて外を見る大きな窓になるところで，偶発的事件として発生する。不断にディメンションと幾何学を変えることで，壁はどのようなキュレーター的役割が必要となろうと自身を適応させる。ギャラリー空間内に，天井のリブから吊り下げられた一連の有効な間仕切りを設置することで，多様な展示空間がつくられる。こうして，構成的，空間的な工夫は同時に，天井のリブへの壁の共鳴のなかに見つかるリズムそのものと関わることになる。天井はまた様々な明るさの光を濾過する。

〈ドラマとしての思考／芸術のための舞台〉

ドラマを変えることのできる可動要素，建築が芸術の“演出”を行うのはこの方法によってである。“舞台装置”はギャラリーの概念的な要素から構築できるだろう。これらは物質化するか非物質化するかに応じて，その時々の展示の独自性に適合される。

美術館全体の緩やかな流動性は，多様な環境，フィルターをかけられた光景や様々な光の中を貫く軌道である。キュレーターの手に新たな自由を付与する一方で，逆に，これは芸術品とそれが置かれる環境の解放された対話として，芸術鑑賞者の経験を要約し再構成する。

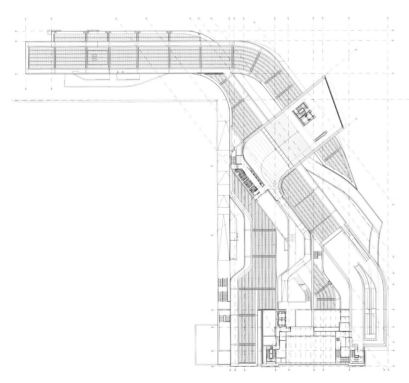

Level 3

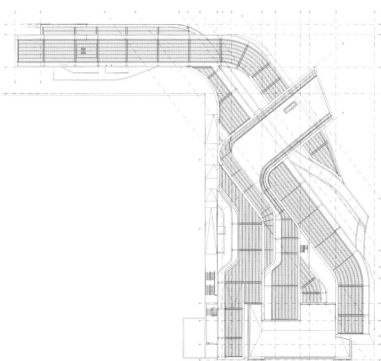

Level 4

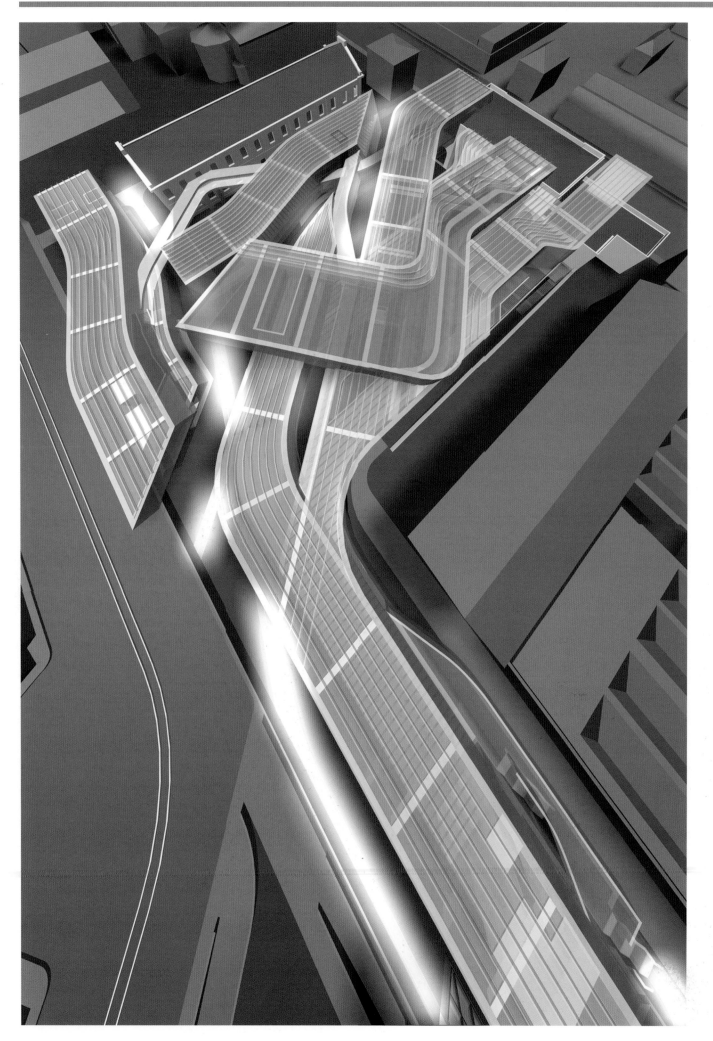

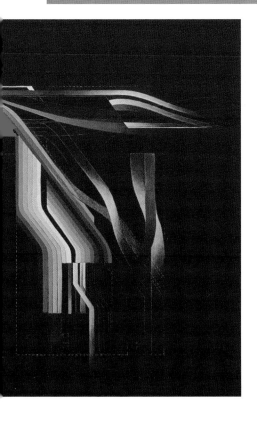

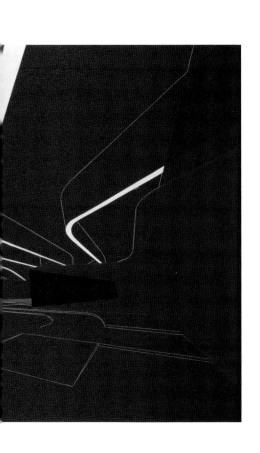

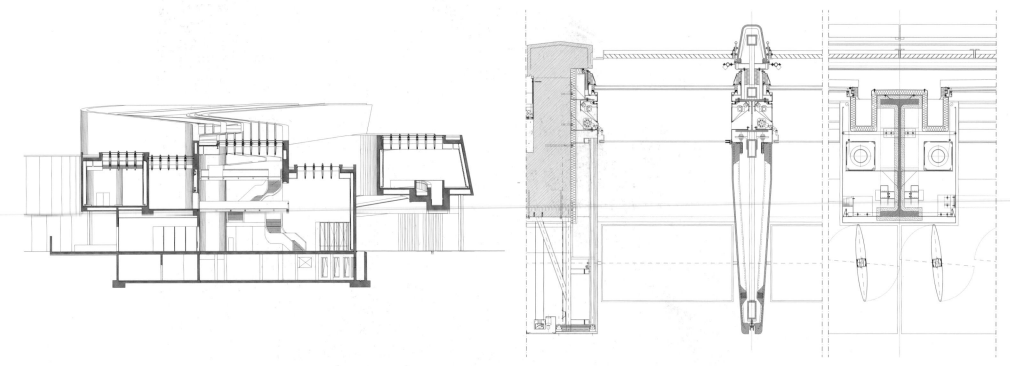

Cross section

Detail: ceiling

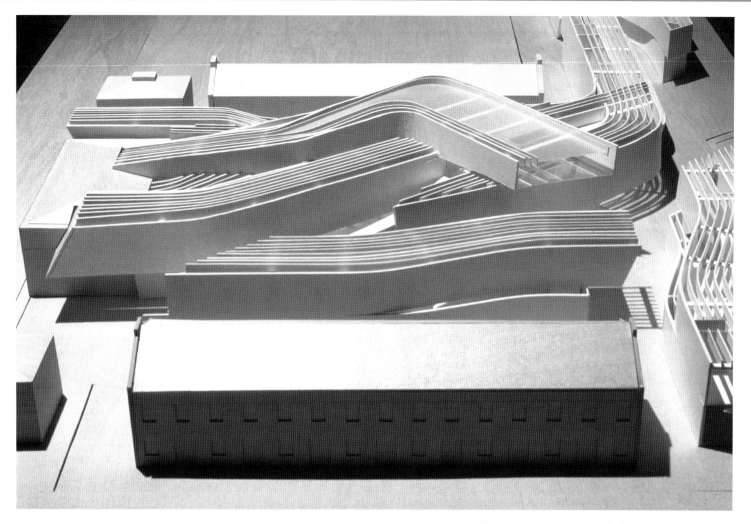

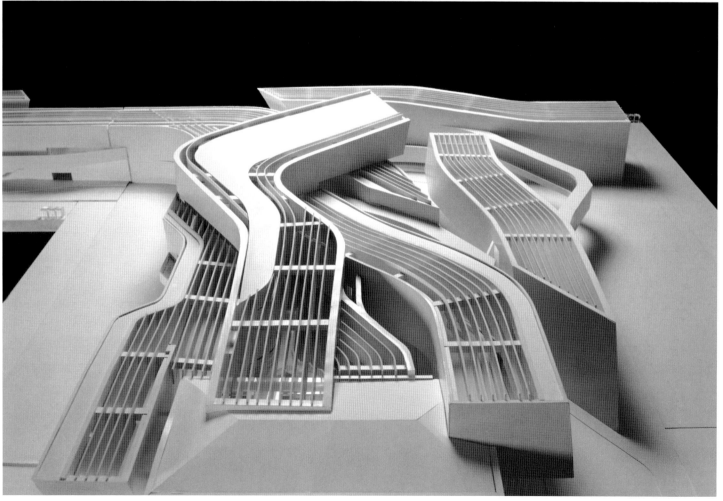

Construction site

Construction site△▽

◁△*Photos: ©Hélène Binet*

SHEIKH ZAYED BRIDGE

Abu Dhabi, United Arab Emirates
Design: 1997–   Construction: –2009

The UAE has a highly mobile society that requires a new route around the Gulf South shore, connecting Abu Dhabi city and the highways to other emirates, notably Dubai and the Northern Emirates. In 1967 a steel arch bridge was built to connect the fledgling city of Abu Dhabi Island, to the mainland followed by a second bridge built in the seventies, connecting downstream at the south side of Abu Dhabi Island. The location of the new (third) Sheikh Zayed Bridge, close to the first bridge, is critical in the development and completion of the highway system. Conceived in an open setting, the bridge has the prospect of becoming a destination in itself and a potential catalyst in the future urban growth at the mainland tip of Abu Dhabi Island. The need for a third crossing to Abu Dhabi Island was first realised 10 years ago at a time when the two other bridges—the four-lane Maqta Bridge and the six-lane Mussafa Bridge—provided access to the capital.

In 1994 engineers were first invited to submit tenders for the new crossing, and after re-tenders and re-submissions and a design competition High-Point Rendel's tender was selected as the most favourable. Supplementary data and various alternatives were considered by 1997 the Client—the Works Department of Abu Dhabi—decided that the Sheikh Zayed Bridge would be a 'Landmark Structure' and invited architect Zaha Hadid to submit proposals. Zaha Hadid's special architectural design for the bridge makes for a challenging assignment. A collection, or strands of structures, gathered on the shore, are lifted and 'propelled' over the length of the channel. A sinusoidal waveform provides the structural silhouette shape across the channel. The mainland is the "launch pad" for the bridge structure emerging from the ground. The road decks are cantilevered on each side of the rising and falling spine structure. Steel arches rise and spring from concrete piers laid asymmetrically, in length, between the road decks. The main bridge arch structure rises to a height of 60 m above water level with the road crowning at 20 m above mean water level.

The geometry of the steel arches and the concrete piers made it necessary to develop a highly detailed computer model of the bridge in order to determine its behaviour. Structural engineers COWI, hired by the Client to independently check if the bridge fulfils the design requirements, have used the Integrated Bridge Design and Analysis System (IBDAS) programme developed by them. IBDAS is a unique programme that allows 3D analysis models to be developed based on detailed geometric models of the bridge—including arches and girders. In addition, the programme features a wide range of analysis procedures for verification of the effects of e.g. earthquakes, strong winds, ship collisions and heavy traffic crossing the bridge. The bridge is about 61 m in width and 842 m in length, with a central steel arch span of 234 m, with their cross-sections measuring up to 6 m x 8 m. The central pier alone contains enough concrete to cover a football pitch to a height of five metres. The first phase involved the 3.8 km approach to the bridge from the Dubai road on the Mainland and included a 350 m seven-span viaduct as well as a 200 m two-lane link viaduct. The second phase, scheduled to end this year, provides the 2.8 km link to the bridge from the Eastern Ring Road on Abu Dhabi Island, and includes a 280 m five-span and a further 300 m five-span link viaduct. The 1.4 km section of the three-part scheme, costing US$ 175 m, involves the crossings of the Maqta channel and includes the Sheikh Zayed Bridge with an overall length of 845 m. The new crossing which will provide a four-lane dual carriageway with two hard shoulders and pedestrian walkways has been designed to the recently published AASHTO LRFD standard.

UAE は高度な車社会で，ペルシャ湾の南岸沿いに，アブダビ市と他の首長国，特にドバイと北部の首長国を高速道路で結ぶ新しいルートを必要としている。1967年，アブダビ島のまだ発展途上にあった都市を本土に結ぶために鋼鉄製のアーチ型ブリッジが建設され，続いて70年代にアブダビ島南側の下流域を結んで2つ目の橋が建設された。新しい（3番目の）シェイク・ザイード・ブリッジは，最初の橋に近く，高速道路システムの発展と完成にとって重要な位置を占めている。見通しのよい環境を考えると，橋そのものが目的地になること，アブダビ島の本土先端にあって，将来，都市が成長して行くための潜在的な触媒となることが予想された。アブダビ島への3番目の橋の必要性は，10年前，他の2つの橋，4車線のマクタ・ブリッジと6車線のムッサーファ・ブリッジが首都へのアクセスを提供した時に，既に理解されていた。

1994年，技術者たちは新しい橋の請負見積書の提出を最初に要請され，再見積，再提出，設計競技の後，ハイポイントレンデル社の見積が最も望ましいものとして選ばれた。補足的なデータや様々な代替案が提示され，1997年，クライアントのアブダビ当局は，シェイク・ザイード・ブリッジは"ランドマーク・ストラクチュア"とすべきことを決定し，ザハ・ハディドに設計を依頼した。ザハ・ハディドの個性的なデザインは，刺激的な課題を提起することになった。海岸に集められた集積物，つまり橋を構成するストランドは海峡の全長に渡って引き上げられ，駆り立てられるように前進する。正弦曲線を描くその波形は，海峡を横断して構造のシルエットを浮かび上がらせる。本土側は地表から現れるブリッジの構造体の"発射台"となる。床版は立ち上がり，下降する背骨を構成する構造体の両側にキャンチレバーで支えられる。鋼鉄のアーチは床版の間に，全長に渡って非対称に並べられたコンクリートの橋脚から立ち上がり，飛び跳ねる。ブリッジのメイン・アーチは水面から60mの高さまで立ち上がり，床版は平均水位の上20mに架け渡される。

鋼鉄のアーチとコンクリートの橋脚の幾何学形態は，その挙動を測定するために，橋の高精度のコンピュータ・モデルを開発することを必要とした。橋がデザインの要求を満たしているか独自にチェックするために雇用された構造エンジニアのCOWIは，彼らが開発した橋梁総合分析システム（IBDAS）プログラムを使用した。IBDASはアーチやガーダーを含め，橋梁を詳細な幾何学モデルに基づいて開発するための三次元解析ができる優れたプログラムである。加えて，プログラムには，地震，強風，船の衝突，橋を渡る激しい交通量などの影響の検証のための広範な分析方法が組み込まれている。ブリッジは幅約61m，長さ842m，中央の鋼鉄アーチはスパン234m，その横断面は6 m×8 mに達する。中央の橋脚だけでも，5 mの高さのサッカー・フィールドを包むに足るコンクリート量である。第一期では，本土側のドバイ・ロードからブリッジへの3.8kmの進入路がつくられ，7スパン，350mの高架橋と，200m，4車線の連絡高架橋が含まれる。今年終了予定の第二期では，アブダビ島の東環状道路からブリッジへの2.8kmの連絡高架橋がつくられ，5スパン，280mと5スパン，300mの連絡高架橋が含まれる。三部構成の計画中1.4km分で1億7千500万ドル掛かり，これにはマクタ海峡を横断する部分と全長845mのシェイク・ザイード・ブリッジが含まれる。この新しい横断橋は，4車線の往復分離道路と2本の待避線と歩道で構成され，最近公布されたAASHTO LRFD（アメリカの荷重係数抵抗設計法）基準によって設計されている。

Architects: Zaha Hadid Architects—Zaha Hadid, design; Graham Modlen, project architect; Garin O'Aivazian, Zahira Nazer, Christos Passes, Sara Klomps, Steve Power, design team
Client: Sheikh Sultan Bin Zayed Al Nahyan, Chairman Public Works Department
Consultants: High-Point Rendell, civil and structural; Mike King, project engineer; Hollands, lighting
Contractors: Archirodon
Program: highway bridge to Abu Dhabi Island
Size: 800 m long, 64 m high, 61 m wide

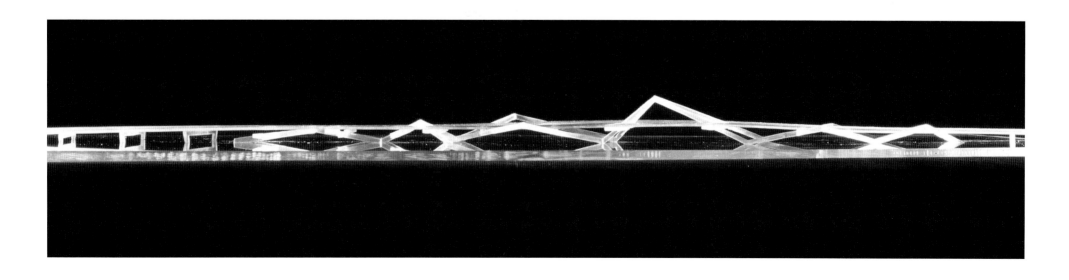

Construction site

MARITIME TERMINAL SALERNO

Salerno, Italy
Design: 1999–   Construction: –2008

View from west

View from south

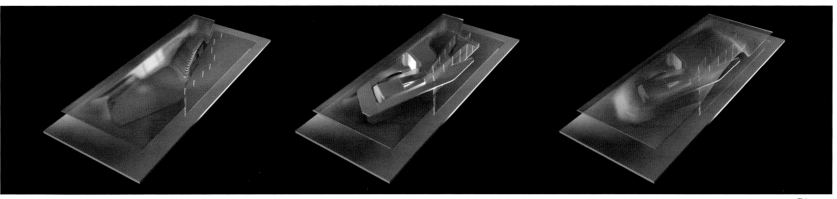

Diagram

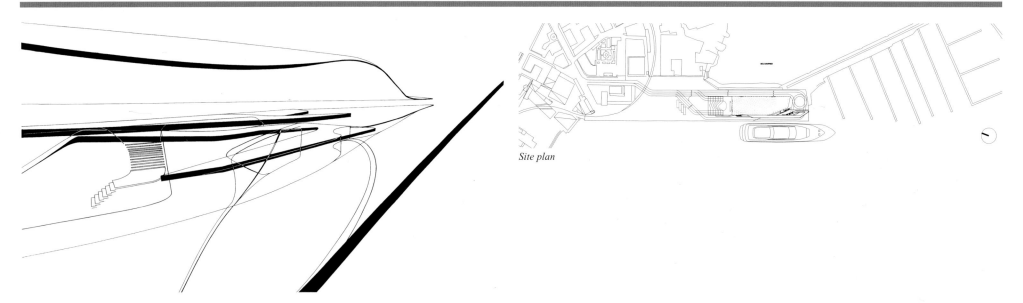

Site plan

The New Salerno Ferry Terminal will forge an innovative, intimate relationship between the city and the waterfront. Like an oyster, the building has a hard shell that encloses soft, fluid elements within. A 'nerved' roof acts as an extended protection against the intense Mediterranean sun.

When passengers arrive at the terminal, their drifting begins in dynamic spaces organized around focal points such as the restaurant and the waiting room. The aquatic topography offers insistently differentiated spaces, and experience, whilst providing clear orientation.

The ground is sculpted as a smooth hill upon which the sloped path begins. This whole area is indicatively lit to guide passengers through the length of the building. The idea of the lighting operates at another level too: from the outside, the glow of the terminal will act like a lighthouse to the port, a symbolic mark on the complex set of traces belonging to its former Norman and Saracen past.

Functionally speaking, the terminal is composed by three main interlocking elements: the offices for the administrative section; the terminal for the ferries and the terminal for the cruise ships. The daily ferry passengers' movements are fast and intense, and the organization of the plan enhances the speed and efficiency of the visit. Passengers arrive on the ground level, buy their ticket, coffee and newspaper. They then ascend via ramps, to the upper level and reach the vessel entrance.

As a whole, the new terminal operates, both visually and functionally, as an intensified, smooth transition between the land and the sea; an artificial landform that is constantly mediating, as if melting, from the solid into the liquid.

サレルノ・フェリー新ターミナルは、街と海岸との間に革新的で、親しみのある関係をつくりだすだろう。牡蛎のように、建物はその内側に柔らかく流れるようなエレメントを包む、堅い殻を持っている。"大胆な"屋根は、地中海の強烈な陽射しを防ぐ、拡張した日除けとなる。

乗客がターミナルに着くと、レストランや待合室のような焦点のまわりに組み立てられたダイナミックな空間の中での漂流が始まる。"水の地形"は、際立って差異化された空間とその体験を与えてくれ、同時に明快な方位を指し示す。

1階はスロープとなった通路の起点でなめらかな丘のように形作られる。このエリア全体が、建物全長に渡って乗客を誘導するために、進行方向を示唆するように照明される。この照明のアイディアはもう一つの階でも同じように機能する。外からは、ターミナルの輝きは港を照らす灯台、かつてこの街を支配したノルマン人やサラセン人の歴史に属する、錯綜する一群の痕跡を象徴する標識のように見えるだろう。

機能的には、ターミナルは互いに組み合わされた3つの主要素、つまり管理部門のオフィス、フェリーのターミナル、クルーズ船のターミナルで構成される。毎日やってくるフェリーの乗客の動きは素早く集中的で、平面構成は客の迅速で無駄のない動きを一層強める。乗客は1階に到着し、切符を買い、コーヒーや新聞を買う。次に、スロープを上階へ上り、乗船口へ出る。

全体として、新ターミナルは、視覚的にも機能的にも、陸と海の間の強く滑らかな移動を操作する。あたかも、固体から液体へと溶けて行くかのように、常に介在する人工の地形。

Architects: Zaha Hadid Architects—Zaha Hadid, design; Paola Cattarin, project architect;
Andrea Parenti, Giovanna Sylos Labini, Cedric Libert, Filippo Innocenti, Paolo Zilli, Eric Tong, design team;
Paola Cattarin, Sonia Villaseca, Chris Dopheide, competition team
Local architect: Interplan Seconda—Alessandro Gubitosi, Piero Speranza, Stefano de Clemente, Giovannella Pezzullo, Alessandro Claudi
Client: Comune di Salerno
Consultants: Ingeco—Francesco Sylos Labini, Paolo Antonini, structural; Ove Arup and Partners—Sophie Le Bourva, structural (preliminary design); Macchiaroli and Partners—Roberto Macchiaroli, Itaca srl—Felice Marotta, mechanical & electrical; Ove Arup and Partners, mechanical & electrical (preliminary design); Ove Arup and Partners—Greg Haigh, maritime/transport engineer; Equation Lighting Design—Mark Hensmann, Paolo Giovine, lighting; Building Consulting—Pasquale Miele, costing
Program: ferry and cruise-line terminal, cafe, shops
Total floor area: 4,500 m²

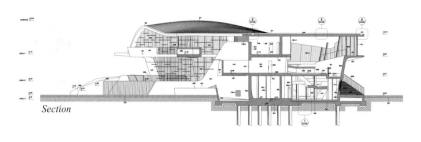

Section

Northwest elevation

Southeast elevation S=1:650

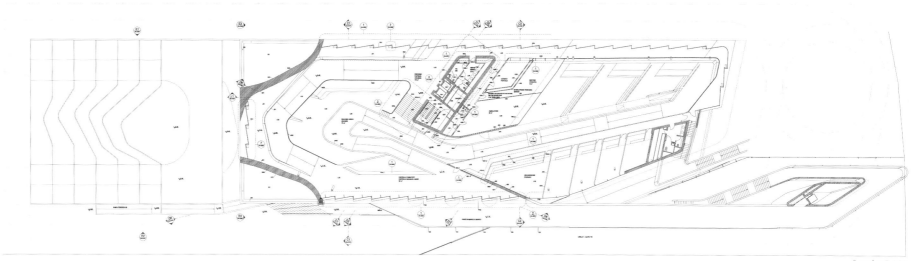

Level +7,150

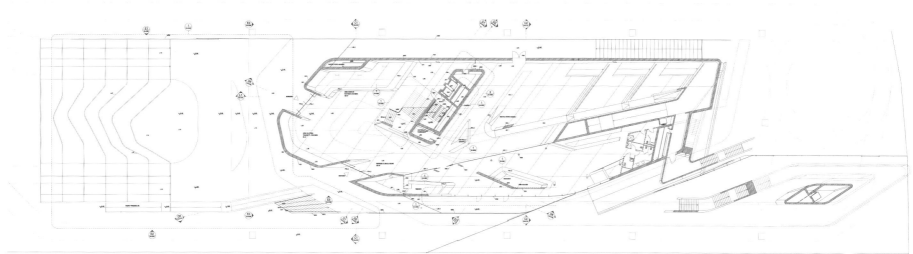

Level +2,450 S=1:650

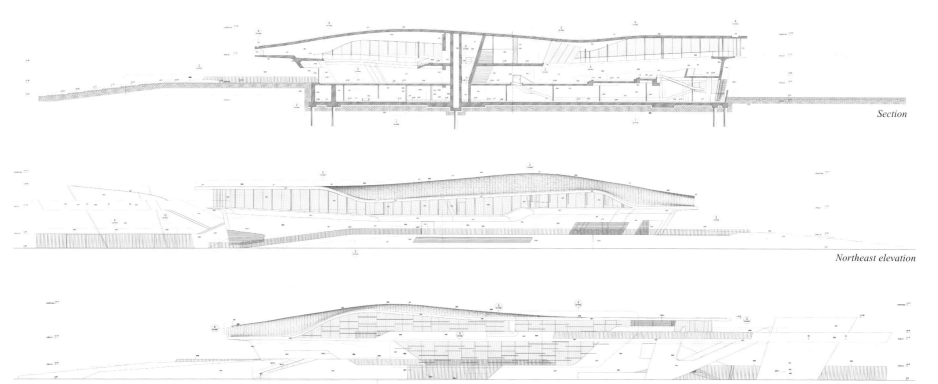

Section

Northeast elevation

Southwest elevation

SINGAPORE SCIENCE PARK – ONE NORTH

Singapore
Design: 2002–   Construction: –2021

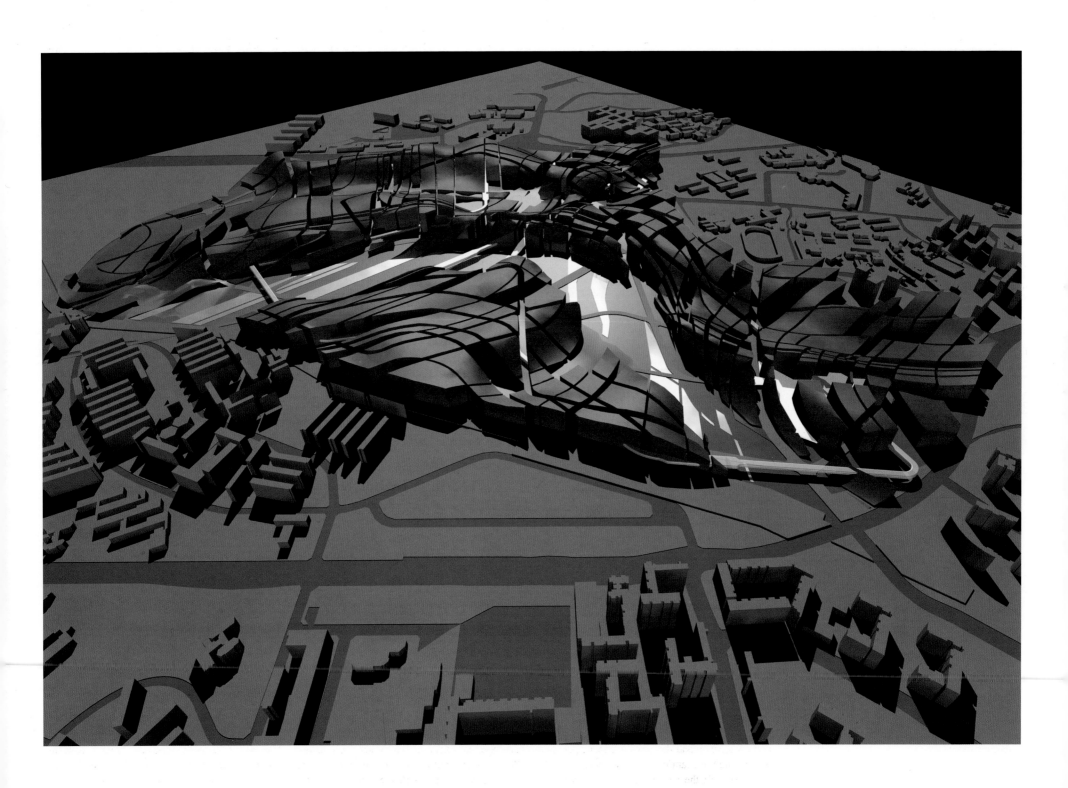

The proposal for the Vista master plan applies the concept of artificial landscape formation to the articulation of the whole urban quarter. The advantages of such a bold move are striking:

Strong sense of identity—the scheme offers an original urban skyline and identifiable panorama visible from without as well as from the park in the heart of the new urban quarter. The rich diversity of squares and alleys engenders a unique sense of place within the various micro environments.

Unity in difference—the concept of the gently undulating, dune-like urban mega-form gives a sense of spatial coherence that has become rare in the modern metropolis. The regulation of the building heights is normal planning procedure

and easily instituted. The powerful aesthetic potential that lies dormant in this ordinary planning tool has never been exploited before. An unusual degree of aesthetic cohesion and unity is achieved by allowing the roof surfaces to join in the creation of softly modulated surface. At the same time a huge variety of built volumes—tall, low, wide, small—is brought under the spell of a unifying force.

Integrating heterogeneity—the softly swaying pattern of lines that defines the streets, paths as well as the built fabric allows the mediation and integration of the various heterogeneous urban grids of the adjacent areas. The curvilinear pattern is able to absorb and harmonize all the divergent contextual orientations.

Flexibility without chaos—the proposed morphological system allows for infinite variation within the bounds of a strong formal coherence and lawfulness. This is a great advantage of working with a "natural" geometry rather than with a strict Platonic geometry. The form is "free" and therefore malleable at any stage of its development while traditional interpretations of Platonic figures (squares, circles, strict axes etc.) are too exacting and therefore vulnerable to corruption and degradation by later adaptations. The proposed natural morphology is no less lawful and cohesive than the Platonic system; but it is much more pliant and resilient, always able to absorb adaptations into its system of natural beauty. The idea of an artificial landscape

formation occurs not only on the level of the overall urban form.

Not only the mega-form but also some of the micro-environments could benefit from the landscape analogy. In particular in hub areas where one of the possibilities of developing could be to introduce a raised plaza level about 5 meter above the street level. Since these areas would need to be well serviced by street access, parking and deliveries, while at the same time aspiring to a lively pedestrian scene, it seems opportune to double the ground surface in these areas. This would allow to bring the elevated APMS system onto the same level with the plane of pedestrian communication.

These raised plazas would not be vast, flat

and vacant fields but would be articulated through terraces and gentle slopes. These raised grounds will be connected to the ground proper through the interiors of the buildings as well as by means of broad staircases and shallow ramps on the exterior.

Within Zaha Hadid's oeuvre there is a long series of urban schemes, which explore various artificial landscapes as a means to sculpt public space and to impregnate it with public programme. These schemes manipulate and multiply the ground surface by means of sloping, warping, peeling or terracing the ground.

Three important advantages may be achieved by such manipulation: the visual orientation within the public realm is enhanced by means of tilting the plane into view and allowing for vistas overlooking the scene from above. By means of a gentle differentiation of slopes, ridges, terraces etc. the ground plane can be used to choreograph and channel movements across the plane in an unobtrusive and suggestive manner.

The landscaped surface is rich with latent places. Articulations like shallow valleys or hills might give a foothold to gatherings and become receptacles for outdoor events without otherwise predetermining or obstructing the field.

Vista Xchange contains one of the three epicentres initiating the urban technopole at one-north, defined by the broad range of producer services associated with the new economy industries. Thus, Vista Xchange's identity will not stem from a single-industry synergy; the plan for Vista Xchange highlights the balanced interweaving of contrasts between local heritage and new economy to articulate an alternative, strong identity.

ヴィスタ・マスタープランでは，街区全体を分節するために，人工的なランドスケープ構成の考え方を適用している。こうした大胆な方法の利点は際立っている。

アイデンティティへの強い意識——計画案は都市の新しい地区の中心に，公園からも外側からもよく見える，独創的なスカイラインと識別可能なパノラマを提供する。広場や小路の豊かな多様性は，様々なミクロの環境のなかに場所に対する独特な感覚を生み出す。

差異の統合——ゆるやかに起伏する，砂丘に似た都市のメガ・フォームというコンセプトは，現代の大都市では稀になった統一感のある空間イメージを与えてくれる。建物の高さに対する規制は一時的な計画手法であり，制定も容易である。この平凡な計画立案のための道具のなかに眠っている強力な美的可能性は，これまで開発されることは決してなかった。この並外れたレベルの美的凝集力と統合は，屋根面を柔らかに調整されたサーフェスとしてつくり上げることで達成されている。同時に，高い，低い，幅が広い，小さいなど，建物のヴォリュームがつくりだす様々な差異は，統合力という呪文の下に抑制される。

融合される異質性——道路，小道，建物の境界を定める線の緩やかに揺れるパターンは，隣接するエリアの，様々に異質なものが混ざり合う都市グリッドを調停し，統合する。曲線でかたちづくられたパターンは逸脱するすべての文脈上の方位を吸収し調和させることができる。

混沌のない柔軟性——提案した形態学的なシステムは，形態の強い統一と合法性による強い拘束の範囲内で無限の変奏を容認する。これは，厳格なプラトン幾何学よりも"自然"幾何学と作業することの大きな利点である。形態は"自由"で，従って，その展開のどの段階でも融通性がある。一方，プラトン図形（四角，円，厳格な軸線，etc.）の伝統的解釈は，あまりに正確で，従って，後からの適合による改悪や劣化に負けやすい。提案した自然な形態構造はプラトンのシステムに劣らないほど合法的で，結合力があるが，はるかに柔軟で，回復力があり，常に，自然の美しさというそのシステムのなかに適合を吸収してしまう。人工的なランドスケープ構成というアイディアは都市形態全体のレベルのみに発生するわけではない。

メガ・フォームだけではなく，ミクロの環境も多少，ランドスケープの類似性から恩恵を受けるはずだ。とりわけ，展開の可能性の一つであるハブ・エリアには，道路レベルから約5m高く持ち上げられた広場を導入できるだろう。これらのエリアは，アクセス道路，駐車場，配送網によって十分にサービスされることが必要であり，一方同時に，活気のある歩行者の姿も望まれるので，ここでは地表を二重に構成することが適切であるように思われる。これによって，歩行者が行き交う面と同じ高さに持ち上げられたAPMS（動く歩道）システムを導入することができるだろう。

高く持ち上げられた広場は，広大で，平坦で，空っぽのフィールドにするのではなく，テラスや緩やかなスロープで分節されるだろう。持ち上げられた"地表"は，建物の内部を抜けて，また，屋外の幅の広い階段や浅いスロープによって本物の地表と連結される。

ザハ・ハディドの仕事には，長期にわたる一連の都市計画があり，そのなかで，公共空間をかたちづくり，それを公共のプログラムで満たす方法としてさまざまな人工のランドスケープを開発している。これらのスキームは，"地表"に勾配を付け，ねじれを与え，はぎとり，テラス状に構成するなどの方法でその表面を巧みに操作し，多面的なものにしている。

こうした操作によって，3つの重要な利点が生まれるだろう。公共領域内の視覚による方位の把握が，面を眺めに向けて傾ける方法で強化され，上から風景を見晴らす，見通しの利く眺望が与えられる。スロープ，細長い隆起，テラスなどの適度な差異化によって，"地表"は，控えめで，暗示的な作法で面全体を振り付け，人々の動きを特定の方向に向けるだろう。

ランドスケープ構成された"地表"は潜在する場所により豊かなものとなる。浅い谷や丘のような分節は，集いのための足がかりとなり，他の状況では必要とされる，フィールドをあらかじめ方向付けたり，遮ることなく，戸外イベントのための器となる。

ヴィスタ・エクスチェンジは，ワン・ノース地区に，ニューエコノミー産業と関わる広範な生産者サービスによって特徴づけられた，都市のテクノポールを創始する3つの中心の一つを内包する。従って，ヴィスタ・エクスチェンジのアイデンティティは，単独の産業の共同作用からは生まれないだろう。ヴィスタ・エクスチェンジは，既存のものに代わる強い独自性を明確に表現するために，地元の遺産とニューエコノミーの調和のとれたコントラストを浮き上がらせる。

Architects: Zaha Hadid Architects—
Zaha Hadid with Patrik Schumacher, design;
David Gerber, Dillon Lin, Silvia Forlati, project leaders (masterplan phase);
David Mah, Gunther Koppelhuber, Rodrigo O'Malley, Kim Thornton, Markus Dochantschi, project team (masterplan phase);
Gunther Koppelhuber, project leaders (Rochester detail planning phase);
Kim Thornton, Hon Kong Chee, Yael Brosilovski, Fernando Perez, project team (Rochester detail planning phase); David Gerber, Edgar Gonzalez, Chris Dopheide, David Salazar, Tiago Correia, Ken Bostock, Patrik Schumacher, Paola Cattarin, Dillon Lin, Barbara Kuit, Woody K.T. Yao, competition team
Consultants: Lawrence Barth, Architectural Association, urban strategy; Ove Arup and Partners, infrastructural engineers; JTC Consultants Private Limited, infrastructural audits; MVA, transport engineers; Cicada Private Limited, landscape architects; Lighting Planner Associates Incorporated, lighting planners; B consultants, planning tool consultants

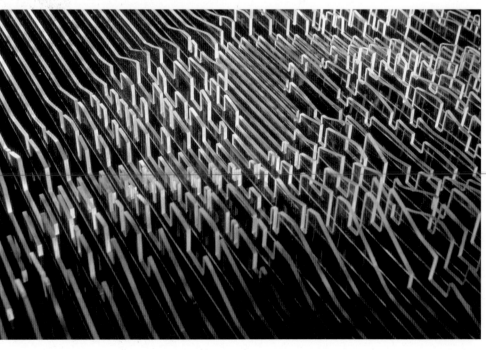

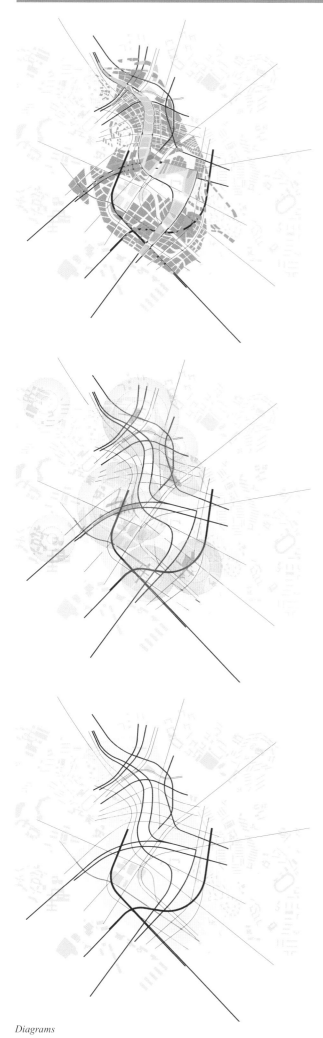

Diagrams

Painting

Night view

PRICE TOWER ARTS CENTER

Bartlesville, Oklahoma, U.S.A.
Design: 2002–

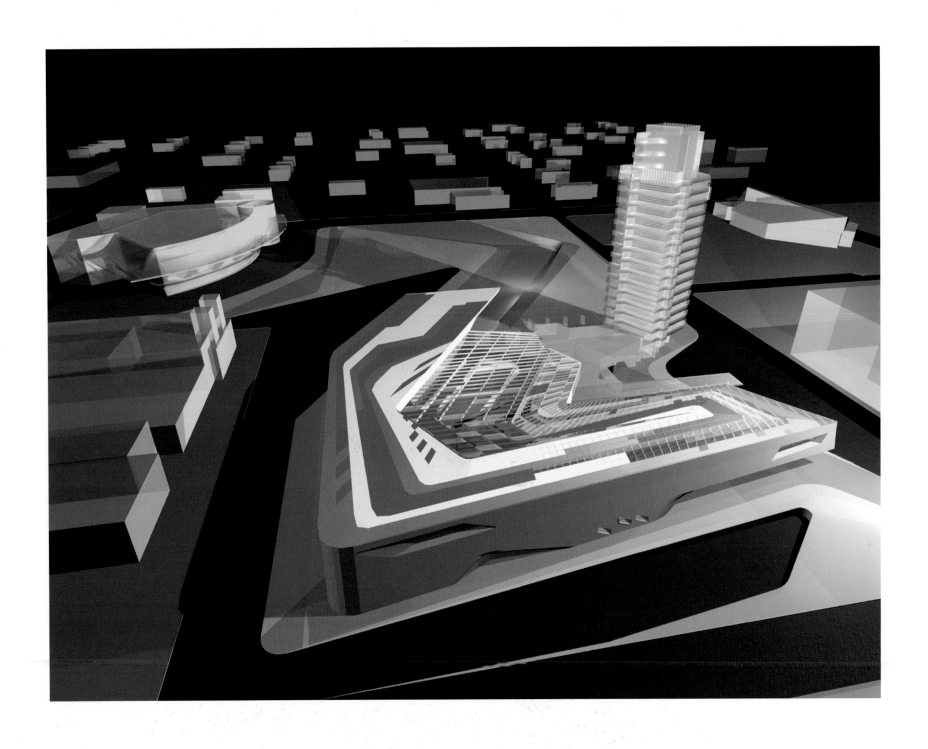

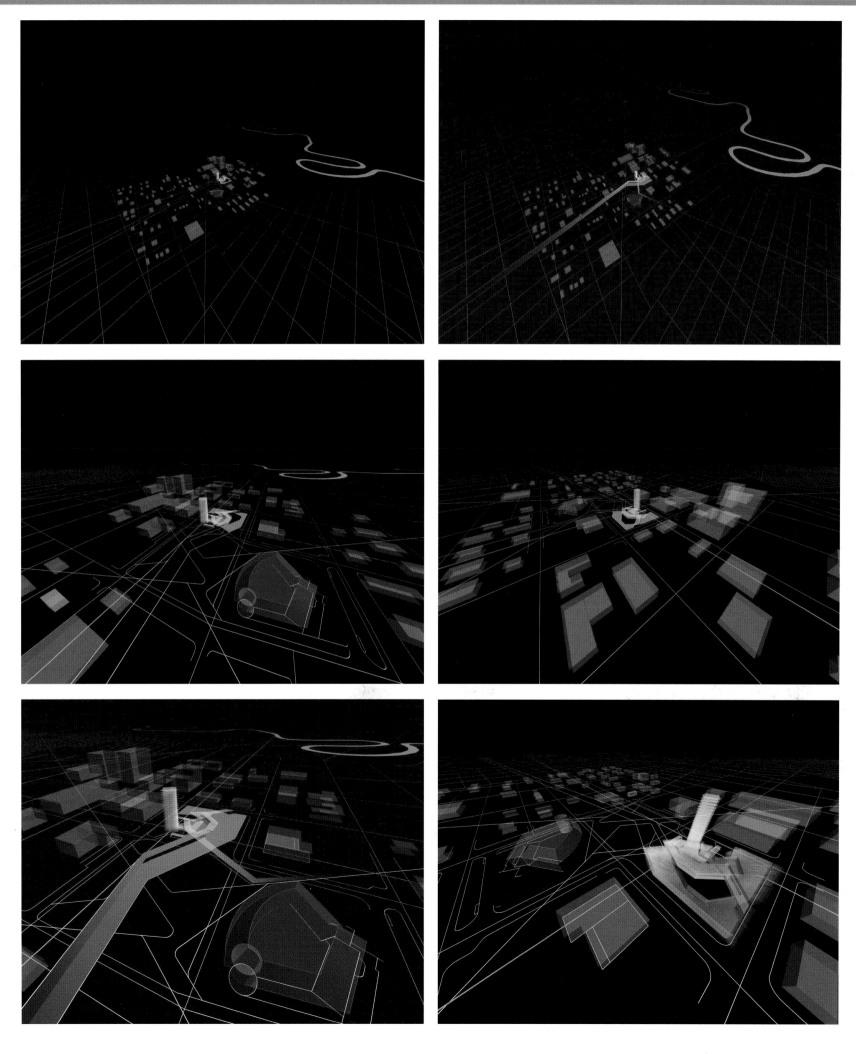

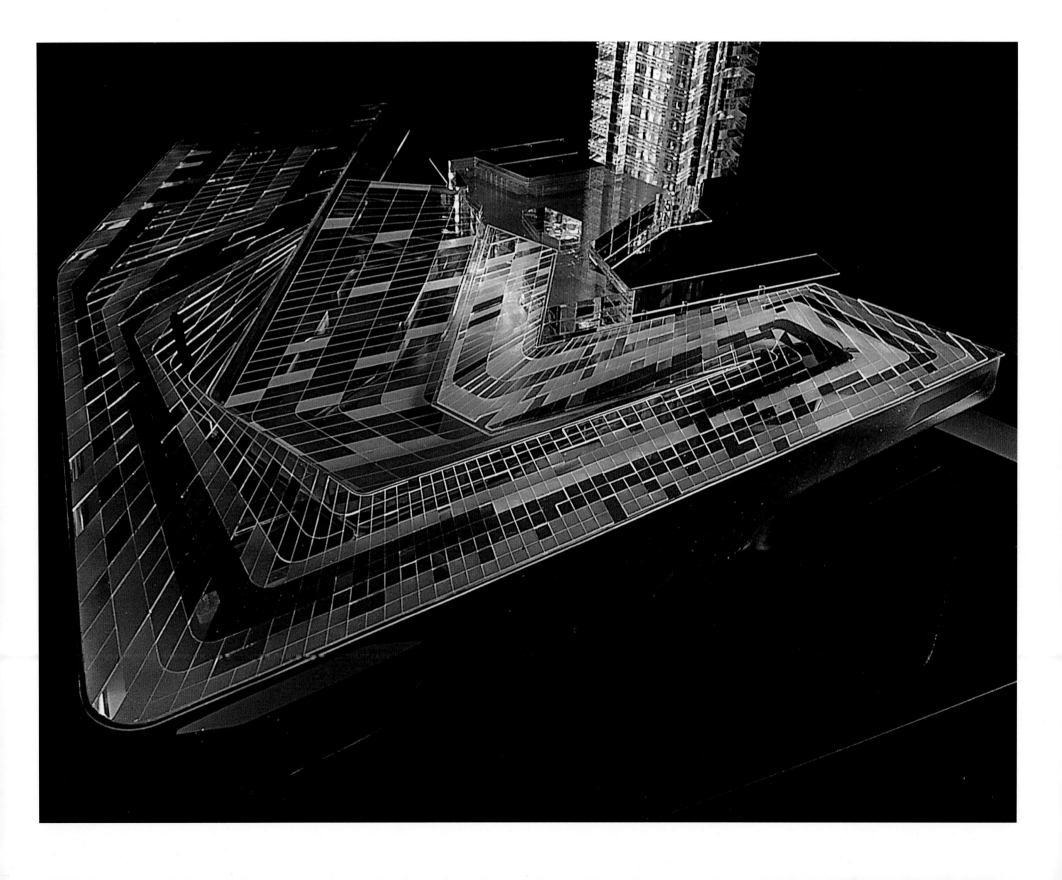

Architects: Zaha Hadid Architects—
Zaha Hadid with Patrik Schumacher; design
Markus Dochantschi, project architect;
Matias Musacchio, Ana Cajiao, Jorge Seperizza,
Mirko Becker, Tamar Jacobs, Viggo Haremst,
Christian Ludwig, Ed Gaskin, project team
Client: The Price Tower Arts Center, Bartlesville
Program: study center with adjoining storage to
house growing collection of works on paper

The Price Tower is the only fully realized skyscraper by Frank Lloyd Wright: a 19-story landmark completed in 1956 in Bartlesville, Oklahoma. Wright's innovative and honest use of materials plus his daring geometry and his dynamic sense of space. These were the inspiration and the challenges of the new Price Tower Arts Center. (PTAC)

The new building wraps around the original building, bringing the project's sense of energy to the very limit of the site.

Extending and transforming the geometry of the Price Tower, the new facility creates a continuum of fluent and dynamic space, were the oppositions between exterior and interior, old and new, geometry and nature are synthesized. The lines of energy that converge within the building also radiate outwards—redefining the quality of the surrounding urban space; guiding the movement through this emerging urban field; suggesting new uses for the surrounding areas and creating an engaging campus that gives a new spatial relationship to the PTAC and the nearby performing arts center. (designed by William Wesley Peters of Taliesin Architects) and the city library.

The galleries of the PTAC are arranged to form a dynamic spiraling loop. The project conceives three large, open spaces: 5,000 square feet for the permanent collection, 5,000 square feet for temporary exhibitions and 2,000 square feet for a "swing gallery", which can be used for either the collection or exhibitions.

These galleries are located on the second floor—offering for the potential of daylight from above, while the first floor contains the main entrance lobby as well as all the back-of-house functions. The lobby mediates interior and exterior, old and new, as well as first and second floor. It is a bright space which offers a generous reception and orients visitors upwards to the galleries via an open cascade of intermediate levels. This space is fully glazed while the gallery spaces are differentiated by the way the sky-lights are modulated—from potentially bright to more closed areas. However, all spaces have the capacity to control light, including being totally blacked-out.

A walkway, which passes dramatically over the lobby, houses the Architecture Study Center.

プライス・タワーはフランク・ロイド・ライトが設計した高層建築のなかで実際に建てられた唯一の作品である。19階建てのランドマークは，オクラホマ州バートルズヴィルに1956年に竣工した。ライトによる材料の革新的で正当な使い方に，彼の大胆な幾何学形と空間に対するダイナミックな感覚を加えることが，新しいプライス・タワー・アーツ・センター（PTAC）設計の発想源となり挑戦となった。

　新しい建物は，オリジナルの建物の周りを包み，プロジェクトのエネルギー感を敷地境界ぎりぎりまで運ぶ。

　プライス・タワーの幾何学形を広げ，変形させながら，新しい施設は，よどみのない，ダイナミックな空間の連続体をつくりだし，内と外，新と旧，幾何学と自然の対立を統合する。建物内に収斂するエネルギーのラインは外部に向かっても放射状に広がり，周囲の都市空間の性格を再定義し，この新たに生まれた都市域全体の動きを導き，周辺領域の新しい使い方を示唆し，PTACとすぐそばにある舞台劇術センター（タリアセン・アーキテクツのウィリアム・ウェスリー・ピータース設計）及び市立図書館との新たな空間関係を確立させて，お互いに連繋するキャンパスをつくりだす。

　PTACのギャラリーはダイナミックな螺旋状のループを形成するように配置される。プロジェクトでは3つの，広いオープン・スペースを想定している。パーマネント・コレクションに5,000平方フィート，企画展示のために5,000平方フィート，どちらにも転換できる“スウィング・ギャラリー”のために2,000平方フィート。

　これらのギャラリーは，上から日中の光が射し込むように2階に配置され，1階には正面玄関ロビーとすべてのサポート施設が置かれる。ロビーは，内部と外部，新と旧，1階と2階を仲介する役割を果たす。ここは明るい空間で，広いレセプションを提供し，2つの階の間に階段状に広がるオープン・カスケードを経て来館者を上階に向かわせる。ロビー空間が全面ガラス張りであるのに対し，ギャラリー空間はスカイライトを調節することで，明るい空間からより閉ざされた空間まで変化をつけられる。その一方で，すべてのスペースで，全面的な暗転を含め，光の調節が可能である。

　ロビー上方に，ドラマティックに架け渡された通路にはアーキテクチュア・スタディ・センターが置かれる。

PIERRES VIVES

Montpellier, France
Design: 2002–   Construction: –2009

Elevation

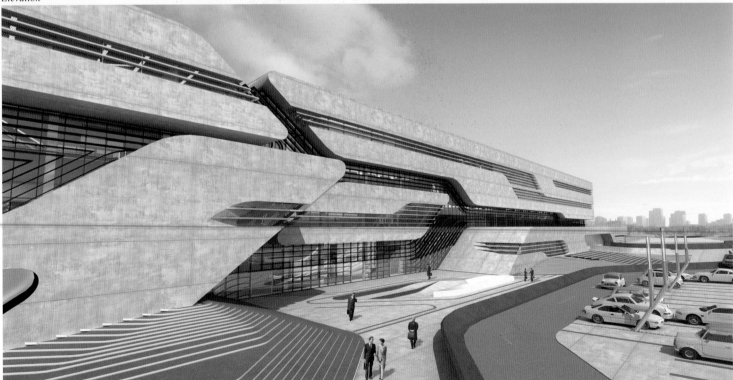

View toward entrance

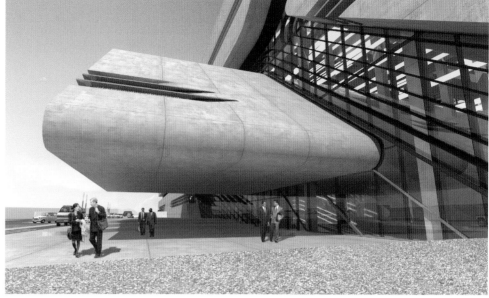

Interior view

Architectural Concept

Our design is based on a series of key qualities that characterise the new building for the Department of Herault:

1. The building should be a new landmark on the edge of Montpellier, a visible icon of progressive regional government.

2. This large complex of institutions requires an efficient and clear organisation, both for the benefit of easy public access/orientation and for the sake of a productive and pleasant working atmosphere.

The three institutions—the archive, the library and the sports department—are unified within a single, envelope. The three parts of this "cite administrative" combine into a strong figure visible far into the landscape. As one moves closer, the division into three parts becomes apparent. The building has been developed on the basis of a rigorous pursuit of functional and economic logic combined with the organisational diagram of a 'tree of knowledge'. The resultant figure is reminiscent of a large tree-trunk with the archives located at the solid base of the trunk, followed by the slightly more porous library with the sports department and its well-lit offices on top where the trunk bifurcates and becomes much lighter. The branches projecting off the main trunk articulate the points of access and the entrances into the various institutions. All the public entrances are located on the western side of the building; whilst the service entrances for staff and loading bays are on the eastern side. In this way, the tree-trunk analogy is exploited to organise and articulate the complexity of the overall "cite administrative".

Spatial Organisation

The main vehicular access road for visitors as well as for staff and service vehicles is from Rue Marius Petipa, and provides access to either side of the building. There is a generous visitor car park in front of the main entrance lobby. The service access is stretched along the opposite side of the building. This longitudinal division of serviced and servicing spaces is maintained within the ground floor along the full length of the building. The front side contains all the public functions of each institution, linked by a linear lobby and central exhibition space. To the rear of the building, all the service, storage and garage areas are located. Above the ground level, the three institutions remain strictly separated. Each institution has its own internal vertical circulation and is laid out following its specific functional logic.

Upon arrival at the main entrance, visitors are directed from the lobby to the educational spaces of the archives on ground level; or via lifts and escalators to the main public artery on level 1. This artery runs the entire length of the building and is articulated all along the facades as a recessed glass strip. Here, reading rooms of both the archives and library are immediately accessible. Central to this artery and therefore located at the heart of the building, are the main public facilities shared between the three institutions: the auditorium and meeting rooms. These shared public facilities also create the central volume that cantilevers from the trunk, providing a grand canopy for arriving visitors.

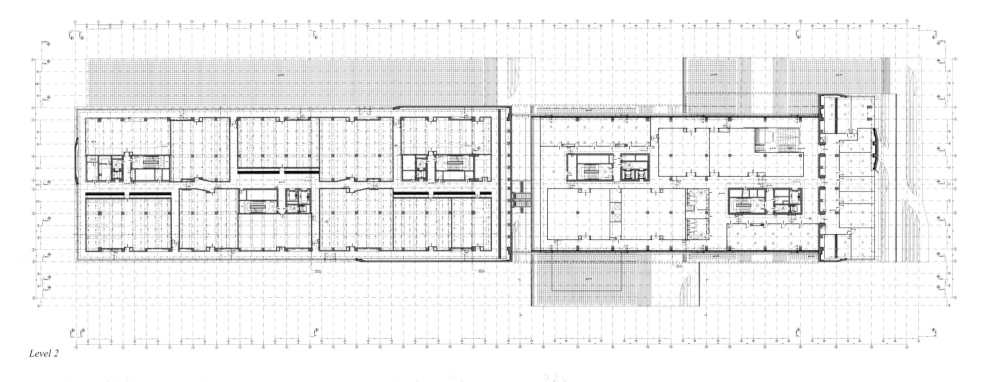

Level 2

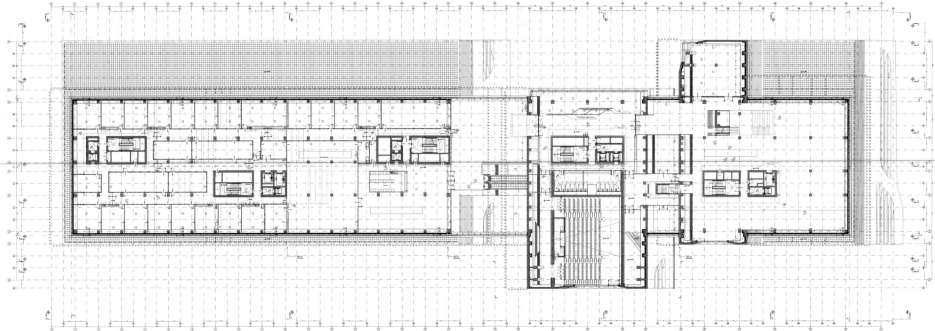

Level 1 S=1:850

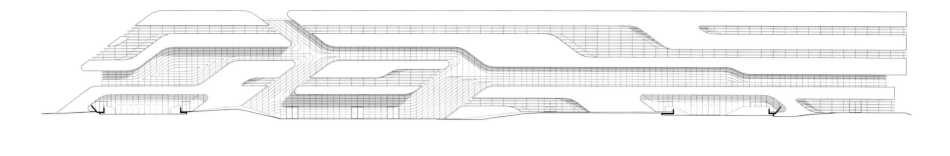

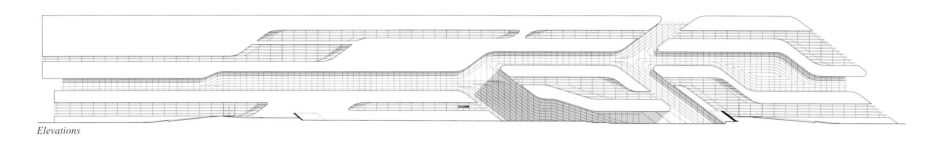

Elevations

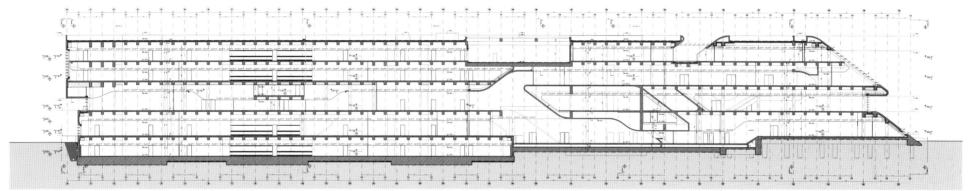

Section

〈コンセプト〉

私たちのデザインは、エロー県庁の3機関を納める新しい建物を特徴づける、いくつかの重要な特質に基づいている。

1）建物はモンペリエの周縁部に位置する新しいランドマーク、革新的な地方行政府の目に見えるイコンとなるものであること。

2）この政府機関の大規模な複合体には、利用者が簡単にアクセスでき、どこに何があるか分かるように、また、生産的で快適な仕事場の雰囲気をつくるために効率的で明快な構成が求められる。

アーカイブ、ライブラリー、体育局から成る3つの機関は単一の被膜のなかに統合されている。この"官庁街"を構成する3機関は結合して強く印象的な姿を風景のなかに現し、遥か先からも見える。近づくにつれて3つの区分が明快となる。建物は、"知恵の木"の系統的なダイアグラムと組み合わされた、機能・経済論理の厳格な追求を基盤にして展開されている。この結果生まれた形態は、大きな木の幹を連想させる。幹の堅い根元にあるアーカイブ、続いてわずかに多孔性の強いライブラリーと体育

局、そして、幹が分岐し、さらに明るくなる最上部の陽射しがよく入るオフィス。中心的な幹から張り出した枝は、アクセス・ポイントと様々な部門への入り口を明快に示す。一般の入り口はすべて建物の西側に位置している。一方、職員用の入り口と荷積み用区画は東側にある。こうした方法で、木の幹に似たシステムは"官庁街"全体の複雑さを組織立て、明快にするために活用されている。

〈空間構成〉

職員、サービス車両と同様、訪問者の車での主要アクセス路はマリウス・プティパ通りからで、建物の両側へアクセス路が通じている。メインエントランス・ロビーの前には広い訪問者用の駐車場がある。サービス路は建物の向かい側に沿って伸びる。こうしたサービスされる空間、サービスする空間の長手方向での分割は、1階では建物全長に沿って継続されている。正面側には各機関のすべての公的機能が配置され、リニアなロビーと中央展示空間がこれらを連結する。建物背面側には、すべてのサービス機能、倉庫、ガレージが位置している。1階より上のレベルでは3つの機関の厳格な分離は残されてい

る。各部局にはそれぞれ専用の内部垂直動線があり、それぞれの機能に従って配置されている。

メインエントランスに着くと、訪問者はロビーから1階アーカイブの教育関連スペースに向かう。あるいはエレベータかエスカレータでレベル1の一般用主要通路へ進む。この通路は建物全長を貫き、後退したガラスの帯としてファサード全面に沿って明快に表現されている。ここから、アーカイブとライブラリーの閲覧室へすぐに入ることができる。この幹線通路の中心、従って建物の中心には3つの機関で共有される主要公共施設であるオーディトリアムと集会室がある。これらの公共施設はまた、建物の中央に幹から片持ちで張り出し、訪れる人に大きなキャノピーを差し掛ける。

Architects: Zaha Hadid Architects—Zaha Hadid, design; Stephane Hof, project architect;

Joris Pauwels, Philipp Vogt, Rafael Portillo, Melissa Fukumoto, Jens Borstelman, Jaime Serra, Kane Yanegawa, Loreto Flores, Edgar Payan, Lisamarie Villegas Ambia, Stella Nikolakaki, Karouko Ogawa, Hon Kong Chee, Caroline Andersen, Judith Reitz, Olivier Ottevaere, Achim Gergen, Daniel Baerlecken, Yosuke Hayano, Martin Henn, Rafael Schmidt, Daniel Gospodinov, Kia Larsdotter, Jasmina Malanovic, Ahmad Sukkar, Ghita Skalli, Elena Perez, Andrea B. Caste, Lisa Cholmondeley, Douglas Chew, Larissa Henke, Steven Hatzellis, Jesse Chima, Adriano De Gioannis, Simon Kim, Stephane Carnuccini, Samer Chamoun, Ram Ahronov, Ross Langdon, project team;

Thomas Vietzke, Achim Gergen, Martin Henn, Christina Beaumont, Yael Brosilovski, Lorenzo Grifantini, Carlos Fernando Perez, Helmut Kinzler, Viggo Haremst, Christian Ludwig, Selim Mimita, Flavio La Gioia, Nina Safainia, competition team

Client: Departement of Herault

Consultants: Ove Arup & Partners—Paul Nuttall, Sophie Le Bourva, Mits Kanada, David Rutter, structural; Ove Arup & Partners—Emmanuelle Danisi, Michael Stych, services (concept design); GEC Ingenierie—Francis Petit, Philippe Vivier, Rene Andrian, Gregory Makarawiez, services; GEC Ingenierie—Jean Paul Sulima, infrastructure; Rouch Acoustique—Nicolas Albaric, acoustics; Gec LR—Ivica Knenovic, cost

Program: archives, library, office

Site area: 35,000 m²

Total floor area: 28,500 m²

SMARGON VITERBI RESIDENCE

La Jolla, California, U.S.A.
Design: 2003–

The brief called for a single family house located at the top of a residential area overlooking the Pacific Ocean. A contained synthetic new topography is imposed over the existing site in order to shelter the structure from the adjacent houses. A perimeter fence contains the dynamic roof span where private and family spaces are clustered emphasizing the ocean view. The structural geometry responds to this internal dynamic by a polar distortion in plan and section. This enables the incorporation of all structural elements into one seamless skin with unimpeded ocean views and clear access to the forecourt and the interior landscape.

Mainly following a parallel axis from the distant shoreline, the main areas of the house are distributed linearly along a porous gallery. Vertical ramps and connections spill into this linear space opening multiple interior readings and most importantly, they allow for a relative flexibility in regards to programmed activities. The domestic in this case, is married to an open loft interior where traditional notions of family life are injected with a new dynamism that responds to the particularity of the site and emphasizes a light materiality in regards to the structure.

This same dynamic character is applied to the main facades where structure is treated as tissue, expanding and contracting depending on use and environmental criteria. The materials are wrapped unto the roof, opening a habitable depression that serves as a second elevated terrace. A double landscape datum sandwiches the architectural object that restricts the overall geometry to limited variation in height. This single volume contracts with the neighbouring structures, critical of typological notions common in most American suburbs.

Architects: Zaha Hadid Architects—
Zaha Hadid with Patrik Schumacher, design;
Kenneth Bostock, project architect;
Christos Passas, associate director;
Barbara Pfenningstorff, Daniel Fiser, design team
Client: Dan Smargon Audrey Viterbi
Consultants: Buro Happold UK US, structural; CS inc.
California, mechanical & environmental; Isometrix,
lighting

プロジェクトは太平洋を見晴らす丘の頂上に建てられる。ドラマチックな眺めと自然の主だった特徴を際立たせるために，構造的な要素が人工の地形を構成して敷地を広げる。

　家の最高点は，最も低い地点へとなめらかにならされ，屋根に向かう主階段をつくりだす。この操作から，敷地を横断して対角方向に鏡像のように転写され，逆方向を向いた"双子の一方の"エレメントである広々とした居間が生まれる。双子の空間は，海の向こうまでシームレスな，遮るもののない眺めへの道筋を開く。一つは内側に，一つは外側に。

　構造は，建物全体のパターンのなかで非還元的な部分としてデザインされる。

　それは内部空間をオープンロフトとして活用させ，その様々な機能エリアは，構造的に独立した要素の挿入によって区画される。これらの挿入された"石"は自由にプログラムでき，将来の内部構成の変更を容易にし，変更を促す。

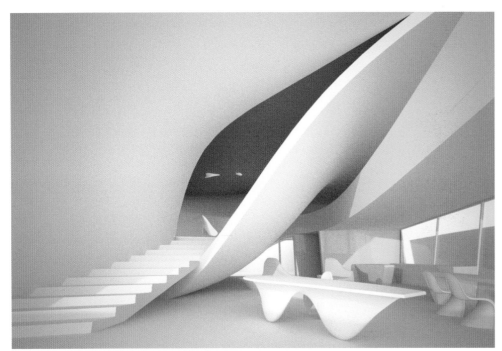

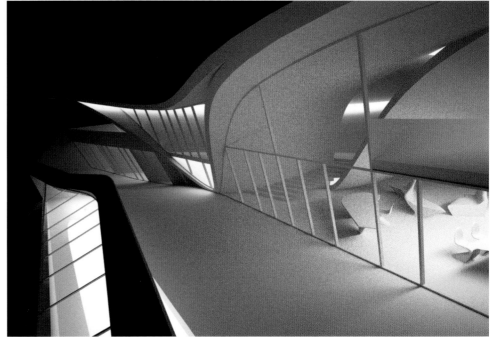

GUANGZHOU OPERA HOUSE

Guangzhou, China
Design: 2003–   Construction: –2008

Conceptual Interpretation
Overlooking the Pearl River the Guangzhou Opera House is at the heart of Guangzhou's cultural sites development. Adopting state of the art technology in its design and construction it will be a lasting monument to the New Millennium, confirming Guangzhou as one of Asia's cultural centres. Its unique twin boulder design will enhance urban function by opening access to the riverside and dock areas and creating a new dialogue with the emerging new town.

Urban Strategy/Landscape
The structure rises and falls at the foot of Zhujiang Boulevard, bringing together the two adjacent sites for the proposed Museum and Metropolitan Activities. As an adjunct to the Haixinsha Tourist Park Island, the Opera House presents a contoured profile to provide a large riverside focus to visitors.

When viewed from the park at the centre of the Zhujiang Boulevard, the Opera House creates a visual prelude to the Tourist Park Island beyond. When viewed from the river, the towers of Zhujiang New Town provide a dramatic backdrop to the Opera House and give a unified vision of civic and cultural buildings on a riverside setting.

An internal street, an approach promenade, is cut into the landscape, beginning at the proposed Museum site at the opposite side of the central boulevard, leading to the Opera House. Cafe, bar, restaurant and retail facilities which are embedded shell-like into these landforms are located to one side of the approach promenade.

Visitors arriving by car or bus are deposited at a "drop-off" on the north side of the site on Huajiu Road. Service vehicles access the Opera House and Theatre Buildings at either end of the Huajiu Road. VIP access to the Opera House is from the western boundary facing Huaxia Road.

〈コンセプト〉
珠江を見渡す広州オペラハウスは，広州の文化開発地区の中心に位置する。芸術的な技術がデザインと建設に適用され，この建物は新しい千年紀の永続的なモニュメントとなり，広州はアジアの文化中心地の一つとして認められることになるだろう。一対の丸い巨岩を想わせる独特のデザインは，川岸と埠頭エリアへ開かれたアクセスを提供し，都市機能を強化すると同時に，新興のニュータウンと新たな対話を生み出す。

〈都市のストラテジー／ランドスケープ〉
構造体は珠江大道の足下に上昇し，また下降しながら広がり，隣り合って並ぶ美術館予定地とメトロポリタン・アクティビティのための敷地の二つを結びつける。海心沙ツーリストパーク・アイランドの付属施設として，オペラハウスは訪れる人たちにとって川岸の大きな核を形成する。

珠江大道の中央に位置する公園から見ると，オペラハウスはその先に広がるツーリストパークへの視覚的な前奏となる。川から眺めると，珠江ニュータウンのタワーがオペラハウスに劇的な背景を提供し，都市施設や文化施設を収めた河岸の建築群が一体となって見える。

敷地内の通路や遊歩道はランドスケープを切り進み，オペラハウスに続く中央大通りの反対側に計画されている美術館の敷地の端へ至る。これらの地形に貝殻のようにはめ込まれたカフェ，バー，レストラン，店舗がオペラハウスへ至る遊歩道の片側に並ぶ。

車かバスで到着した観客は，华就路に面した敷地の北側にある"降車地点"で降りる。サービス車両のオペラハウスと劇場建物への進入路は华就路の両端にある。VIPは华夏路に面した西側境界から入る。

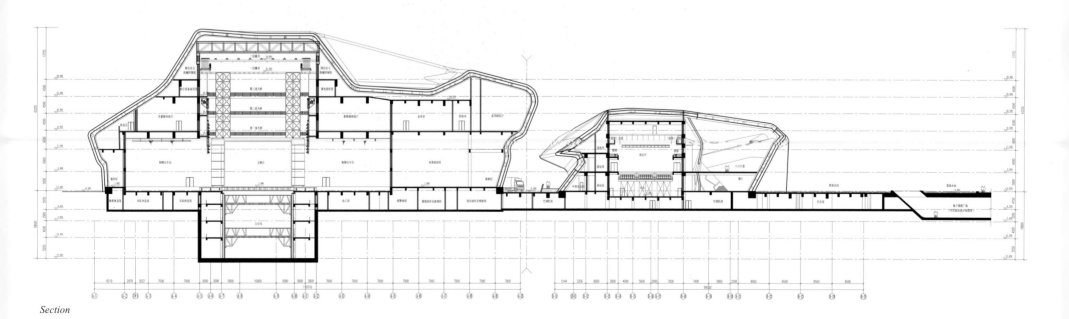

Section

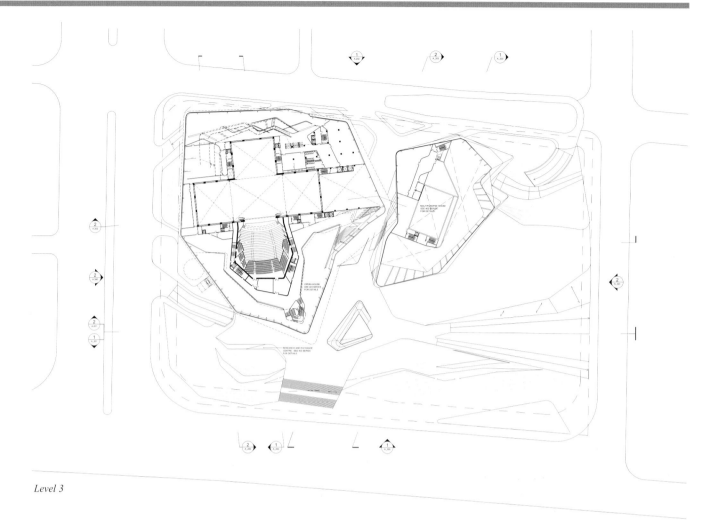

Level 3

Architects: Zaha Hadid Architects—Zaha Hadid, design;
Woody K.T.Yao, Patrik Schumacher, project director;
Simon Yu, project architect; Jason Guo, Yang Jingwen,
Long Jiang, Ta-Kang Hsu, Yi-Ching Liu, Zhi Wang,
Christine Chow, Cyril Shing, Filippo Innocenti,
Lourdes Sanchez, Hinki Kwong, project team;
Filippo Innocenti, Matias Musacchio, Jenny Huang,
Hon Kong Chee, Markus Planteu, Paola Cattarin,
Tamar Jacobs, Yael Brosilovski, Viggo Haremst,
Christian Ludwig, Christina Beaumont,
Lorenzo Grifantini, Flavio La Gioia, Nina Safainia,
Fernando Vera, Martin Henn, Achim Gergen,
Graham Modlen, Imran Mahmood, competition team
(1st stage); Cyril Shing, YanSong Ma, Yosuke Hayano,
Adriano De Gioannis, Barbara Pfenningstorff, compe-
tition team (2nd stage)
Client: Guangzhou Municipal Government
Consultants: Ove Arup & Partners (London & Hong
Kong), structural, services & acoustics (competition
stage); Guangzhou Pearl River Foreign Investment
Architectural Designing Institute, local design insti-
tute; SHTK, Guangzhou Pearl River Foreign Invest-
ment Architectural Designing Institute, structural;
KGE Engineering; facade engineering; Marshall Day
Acoustics, acoustic; ENFI, theatre consultant; Beijing
Light & View, lighting
Principal contractor: China construction third engi-
neering bureau co. ltd.
Total floor area: 70,000 m²
Program: 1,800 seats grand theatre, entrance lobby
& lounge, multifunction hall, other auxiliary facilities
& support premises

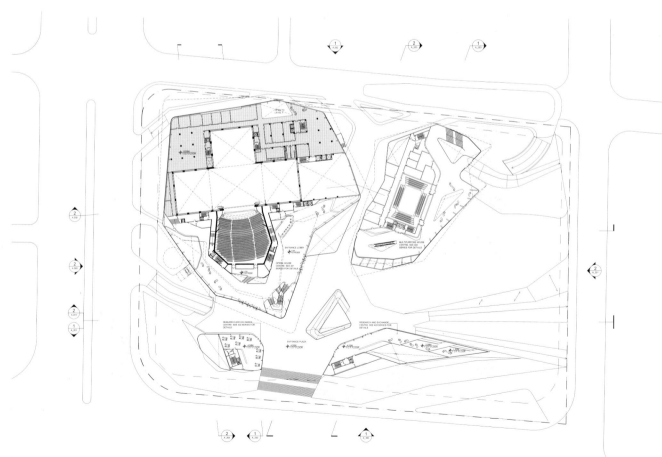

Level 1

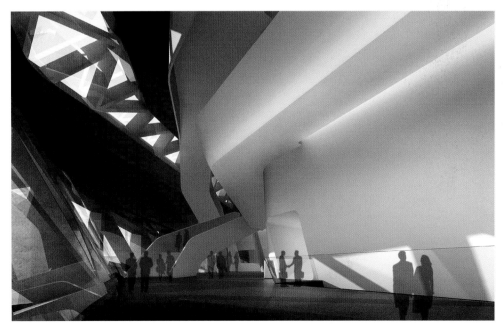

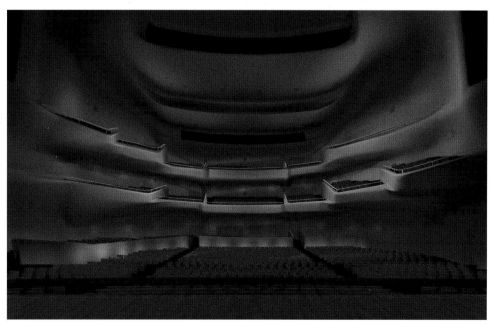

ZORROZAURRE MASTER PLAN, BILBAO

Bilbao, Spain
Design: 2003–   Construction: –2009

Zaha Hadid has completed the conceptual masterplan for Zorrozaurre in Bilbao, a 60 hectare area cradled in a long curve of the Nervion River just across from the city's centre. This former port and industrial area will become home to nearly 15,000 new residents and will provide workshops, labs, studios, and offices for nearly 6,000 working people. Zorrozaurre has been nearly separated from its neighbouring communities by a canal opened to enlarge the port during its heyday, and this canal is destined to be extended for flood-control purposes in future years. This will make Zorrozaurre an island occupying a strategically key position in the future expansion of the city and integration of the region.

The plan permits the dramatic character of Zorrozaurre's surrounding topography and the broad curve of the Nervion to subtly influence Bilbao's well-defined urban grid. The resulting building alignment generates a finely textured ground sweeping the length of the site, contracting to conform to the small scale of existing fabric and expanding in response to more open spaces. In this way the plan accommodates both historic buildings and major new investment, while linking both to a generous public waterfront. Zorrozaurre's future skyline presents a jagged profile with fine gaps, reminiscent of densely built waterfronts around the world. Zorrozaurre will be well integrated with its neighbours on both banks of the Nervion by an exciting sequence of bridges. These will allow the river itself to become a meaningful part of the daily life of local communities along the banks. Equally important to the transport system, Bilbao's existing tram system will be extended the length of Zorrozaurre and beyond, establishing a central spine of activity running through the island and linking the region's downstream communities to the city's centre. The plan aims to set the trend for a regionally integrated city, defining new patterns of living and working within the context of a distinctively strong local identity.

At the heart of the plan for Zorrozaurre, an elegant system of building blocks enables the achievement of both skyline and collective ground. These building blocks are like a set of "tiles", each over 1,000 m², and they allow the ground formation to respond to the curving

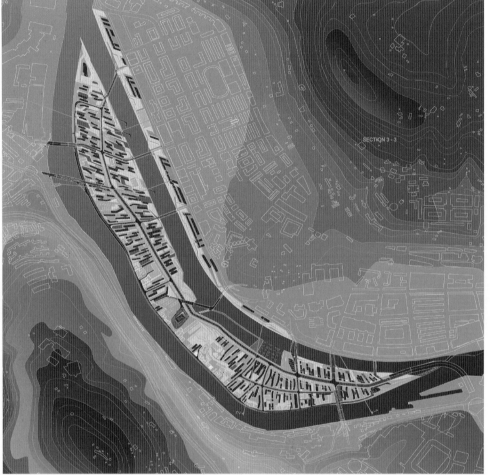

Urban form

spine of the river, the street grid, and the shifting orientation of buildings from upstream to downstream. In this way, the tiles give the plan an overall unity while allowing the differentiation of districts and clusters. The platform level of the tiles establishes the critical level of defense against floods while also creating space for underground parking. By linking this critical level to the development of building clusters, the waterside promenade can dip closer to the normal level of the river, allowing the people of Bilbao a closer engagement with the water's edge. Meanwhile, above the platforms, the buildings are turned perpendicular to the long axes of the river, opening the building fabric so that pathways and views may be enjoyed by all. The rich pattern of public and private spaces we see in the plan can be achieved through the subtle differentiation of levels, promoting an easy balance between the needs of privacy and the pleasures of community life. The overall structure organizing the tiles permits a densely built environment to accompany the fabric's strong feel of porosity, with future residents and workers all enjoying a rich tapestry of outdoor places. Waterside promenades, parks, the tree-lined central avenue, small squares, and public gardens—all link together to create a textured setting for urban social life.

Architects: Zaha Hadid Architects—
Zaha Hadid with Patrik Schumacher, design;
Gunther Koppelhuber, project architect,
Kim Thornton, project manager (competition and phase A); Manuela Gatto, project architect;
Steve Hatzellis, project manager (phases B/C/D);
C. Fernando Perez, project liaison;
Juan I. Aranguren, Daniel Baerlecken, Yael Brosilovski, Helen Floate, Marc Fornes, James Gayed, Fabian Hecker, Alvin Huang, Yang Jingwen, Graham Modlen, Judith Reitz, Brigitta Lenz (model), Jonathan Smith (model), project team
Local architect: Arkitektura Eta Hirigintza Bulegoa S.A.
Client: Management Committee for the urban development of the peninsula of Zorrozaurre Bilbao
Consultants: Ove Arup & Partners, engineer;
Gross Max, landscape; Larry Barth, urban strategy
Program: refurbishment and construction of housing, new industries, tertiary uses, urban and recreational spaces and new connections linking the peninsula, city and surrounding areas
Site area: 60 hectare

ビルバオの中心から真向かいに広がる，ネルビオン川の長い湾曲部に抱かれた60ヘクタールに及ぶソロサウーレ地区のコンセプチュアルな全体計画である。この，以前は港湾と産業で栄えた地域は，15,000人近くの新しい住民の家となり，6,000人近く人々が働くワークショップ，研究所，スタジオ，オフィスを提供するだろう。ソロサウーレは，その全盛期に港を拡張するために開かれた運河で近隣のコミュニティからほぼ切り離されている。この運河は数年先には，洪水調整のために拡張される運命にある。これは，ソロサウーレを，街の将来の拡大と地域の統合にとって戦略的に重要な位置を占める島とすることだろう。

　計画案は，ソロサウーレ周辺の地形とネルビオン川のゆったりした湾曲がつくりだす劇的な性格が，ビルバオの明解に区画された都市グリッドに微妙に影響を及ぼすことを容認している。その結果生まれた建物の整列は，敷地の全長に広がる精密なテクスチャーを持つ"地"をつくりだし，既存の都市構成の小さなスケールに合わせて収縮し，より広々としたスペースに呼応して拡大する。この方法によって，歴史的な建物と，大半を占める新しく資本投下される部分の両方に対応しながら，両者を公共空間である広いウォーターフロントへつなげる。ソロサウーレの将来のスカイラインは，建物が密集する世界中のウォーターフロントを連想させる，細い切れ目の入った，鋸の歯のような輪郭を見せることになる。ソロサウーレは，想像力をかき立てられる一連の橋によってネルビオン川両岸の近隣地区としっかりと結びつけられる。これらの橋は，川そのものを，岸に沿った地元コミュニティの日常生活にとって意味のある一部とするだろう。同様に，交通システムにとって重要なのは，ビルバオを走る路面電車網がソロサウーレ全長を越えてその先まで延長され，島全体を貫いて，人々の動きを支える背骨をつくりあげ，この地域の下流域のコミュニティを市の中心に結ぶことである。全体計画の目的は，地域を統合する都市への大勢を整え，地元の強いアイデンティティを持った文脈のなかに，生活と仕事の新しいパターンを明快に定めることである。

　ソロサウーレ全体計画の中心では，"積み木"の優美なシステムが，スカイラインと集積された地表，その両方をつくりあげる。これらの"積み木"は，それぞれが1,000平米を越える大きさで，一組の"タイル"のように，川の湾曲する"背骨"，道路のグリッド，上流から下流へと変わる建物の方位に呼応して地表を構成する。この方法で，"タイル"は，地区と建築群の分化を容認しながらプランに全体的な統一を与える。"タイル"の基盤レベルは洪水を防ぐぎりぎりのレベルを設定する一方でまた，地下駐車場のためのスペースをつくりだす。このレベルを建築群の展開部と連結することで，水辺側の遊歩道は川の通常水位近くまで下げることができ，ビルバオの人々は，水辺とより身近に結ばれる。同時に，基盤の上で，建物は川の長手軸線に対して垂直に向きを変え，通路や眺めがすべての人に楽しめるように，建物と建物の間を開く。計画案に見られる公私のスペースの豊富なパターンは，階高の微妙な差異によってつくられ，プライバシーの必要とコミュニティーライフの楽しさを簡単に均衡させてくれる。"タイル"を組み立てた全体構造は，将来の住人や

ここで働く人のすべてが，戸外空間がつくる豊かなタペストリーを楽しめるような，有孔性が強く感じられるファブリックが構成する，密度の高い建築環境を可能にする。水辺側の遊歩道，公園，並木のある中央大通り，小広場，公共庭園がすべて一つにつながって，都市の社会生活のために，織り上げられた舞台をつくりだす。

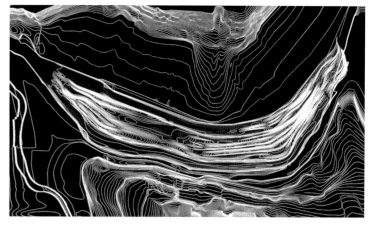

Aerial view

NEW STATION NAPOLI AFRAGOLA

Naples, Italy
Design: 2003–   Construction: –2008

The New High Speed Station Napoli Afragola is a bridge above the tracks. The key challenge of the architectural scheme is to create a well organized transport interchange that can simultaneously serve as a new landmark to announce the approach to Naples—thus a new gateway to the city. The concept of the bridge emerges from the idea of enlarging the overhead concourse, required to access the various platforms, to such a degree that it can become the main passenger concourse itself.

Providing an urbanized public link across the tracks, the task is to give expression to the im-position of a new through-station that can also act as the nucleus of a new proposed business park linking the various surrounding towns. The bridge concept further allows two strips of extended park-land to move openly through the site alongside the tracks opening and connecting the site to the surrounding landscape and business park.

The architectural language proposed, geared towards the articulation of movement, is pursued further within the interior of the building, where the trajectory of the travelers determines the geometry of the space.

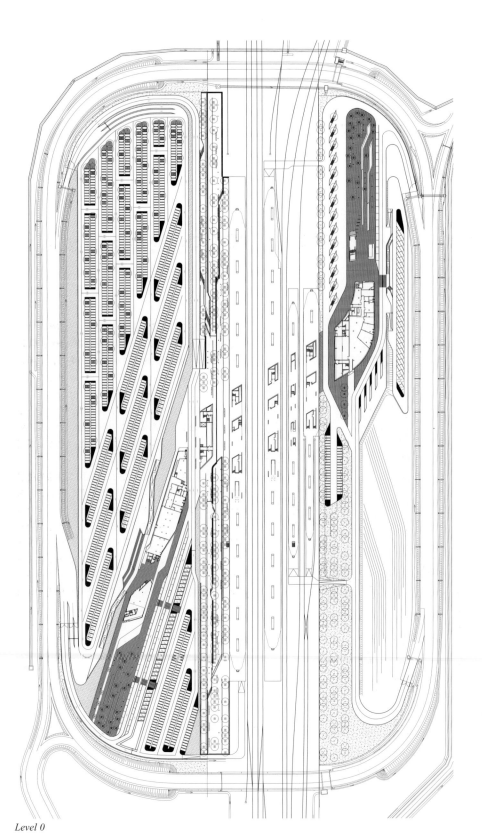

Level 0

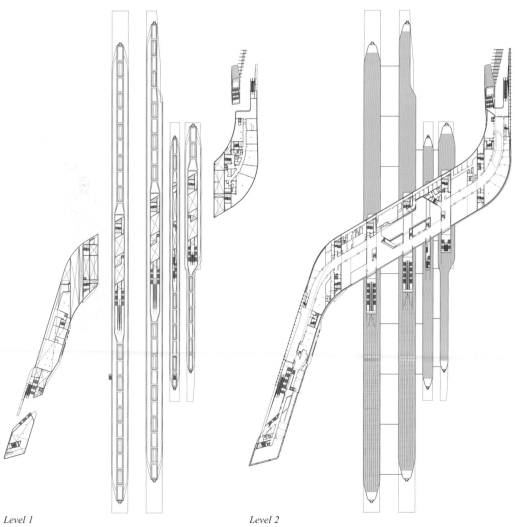

Level 1   *Level 2*

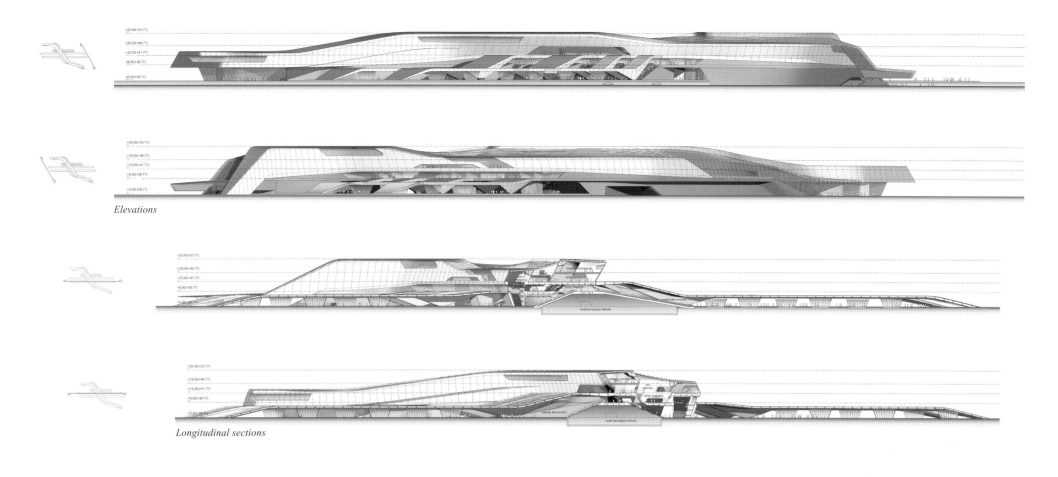

Elevations

Longitudinal sections

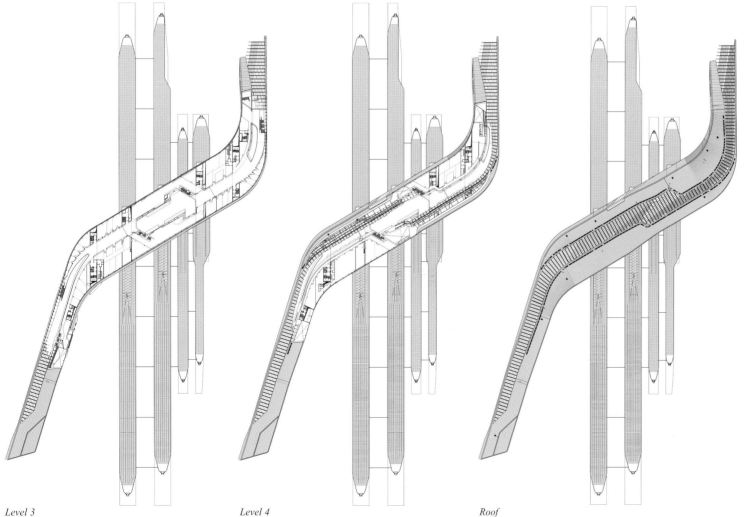

Level 3　　　　　　　　　　　*Level 4*　　　　　　　　　　　*Roof*

ナポリ・アフラゴラ新高速鉄道駅は，軌道の上方に架け渡されたブリッジである。建築計画の目標は，巧みに組織された交通機関の乗換駅であり，同時にナポリへの接近を知らせるランドマークとしての役割も果たす街の新しい玄関をつくることである。ブリッジ・コンセプトは，要求された様々なプラットフォームへ通じる高架のコンコースを，それ自体が乗客のメイン・コンコースになるほど大きく広げて構成するアイディアから生まれている。

軌道を横断する，都市化された公共連絡路を提供しながら，周囲の様々な町を結ぶ，新しいビジネスパーク構想の核としての役割も果たせる新しいスルー・ステーション（駅の通り抜け）という難しい課題に表現を与えることがその任務である。ブリッジ・コンセプトはさらに，パークランドから延びる2本の通りが，敷地を周囲の風景やビジネスパークに開放し，結びつけながら軌道に沿って敷地内を自由に通り抜けて行くにまかせる。

ここで提案されている，動きを関連づけるよう意図された建築言語は，建物内部でもさらに追求され，そこでは旅客の軌跡が空間のジオメトリーを決定する。

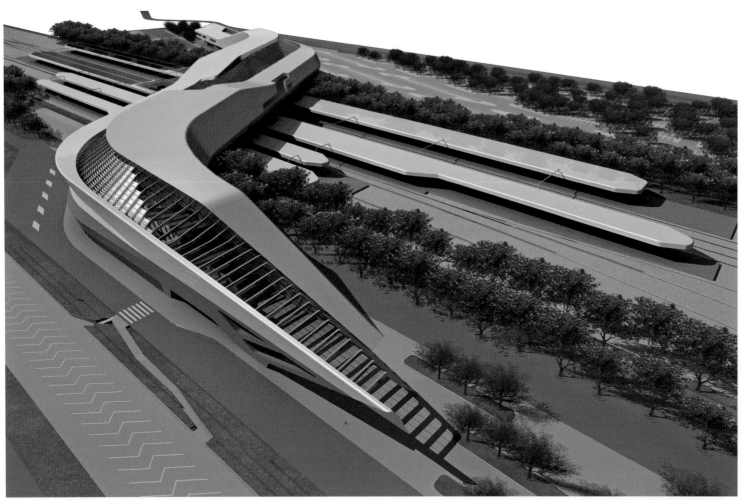

Architects: Zaha Hadid Architects—
Zaha Hadid with Patrik Schumacher, design;
Filippo Innocenti, project architect;
Paola Cattarin, project manager; Fernando Perez Vera,
Ergian Alberg, Hon Kong Chee, Cesare Griffa,
Karim Muallem, Steven Hatzellis, Thomas Vietzke,
Jens Borstelmann, Robert Neumayr, Elena Perez,
Adriano De Gioannis, Simon Kim, Selim Mimita, com-
petition team; Cesare Griffa, Federico Bistolfi,
Mario Mattia, Paolo Zilli, Tobias Hegemann,
Michele Salvi, Chiara Baccarini, Alessandra Bellia,
Serena Pietrantonj, Roberto Cavallaro, Karim Muallem,
design team
Clients: TAV s.p.a.
Consultants: AKT—Hanif Kara, Paul Scott, Interprogetti—
Giampiero Martuscelli, structural and geotechnics; Max
Fordham—Henry Luker, Neil Smith, Studio Reale—
Francesco Reale, Vittorio Criscuolo Gaito, environmen-
tal, mechanical & electrical; Interplan 2 Srl—
Alessandro Gubitosi, building regulation, co-ordination
local team; Gross Max—Eelco Hooftmanc, landscape;
JMP—Max Matteis, transport engineering;
Paul Guilleron Acoustics—Paul Guilleron, acoustic
Program: train station for high speed and regional
services; facilities for bus, taxi and car parking; retail
and civic; rail administration, police and fire services
Total floor area: 20,000 m²

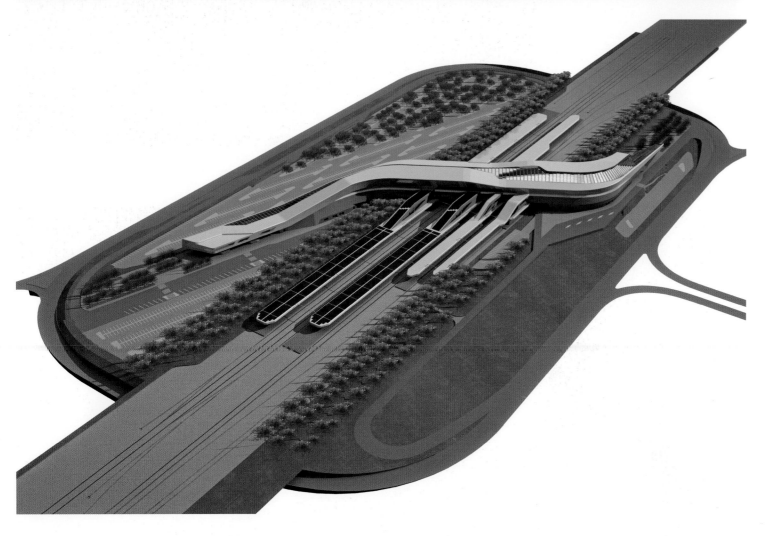

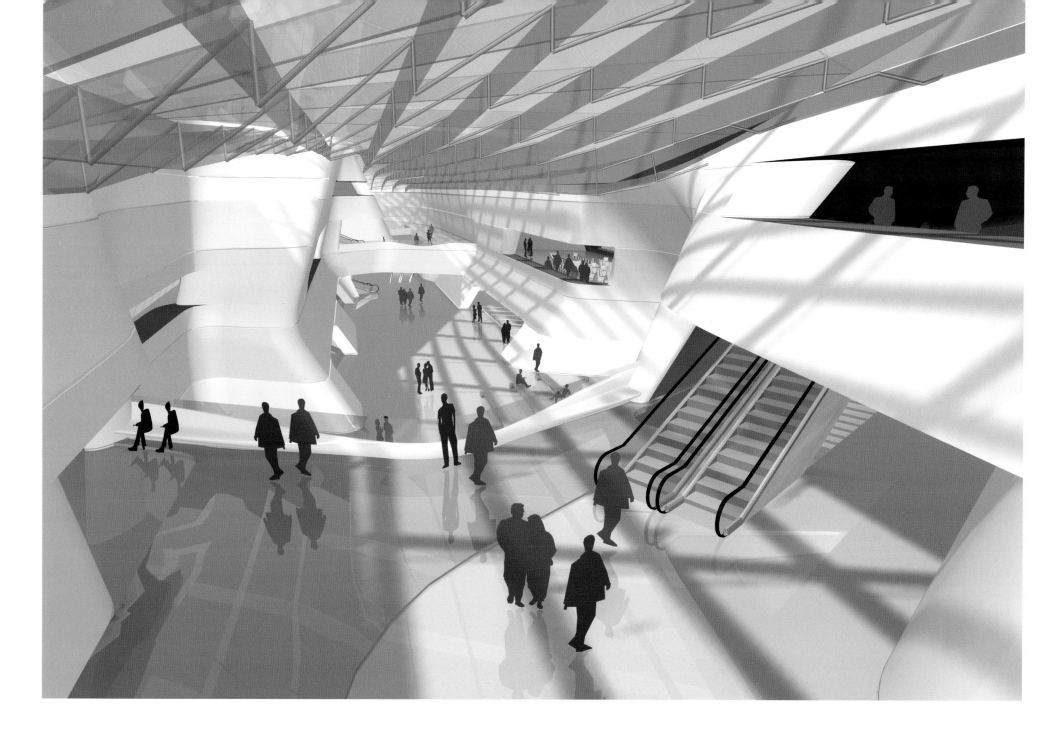

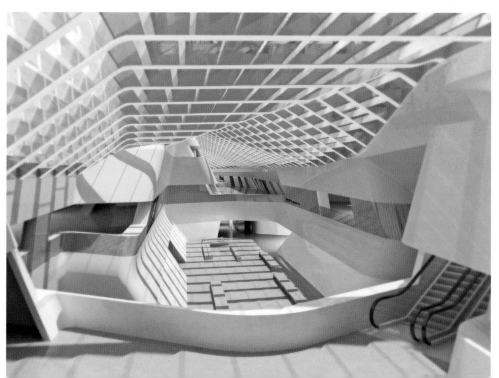

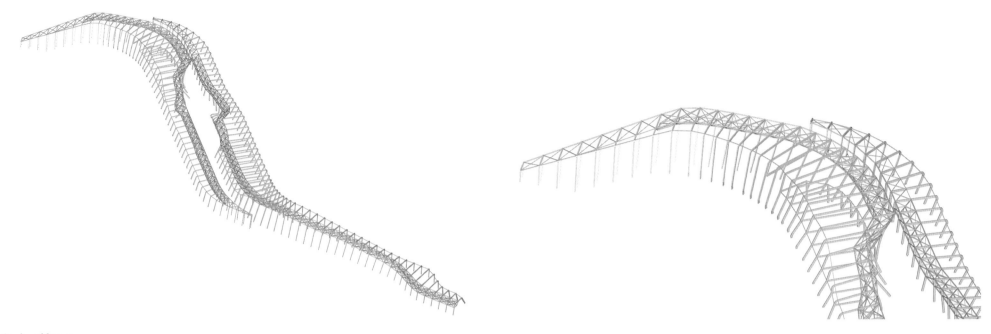

Steel roof frames

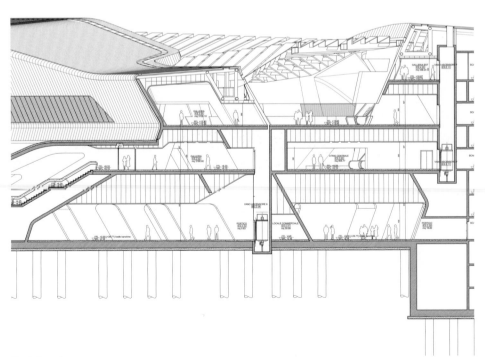

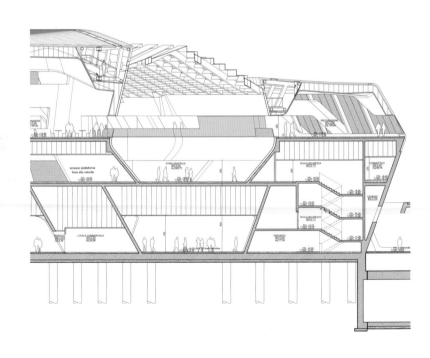

Partial sections

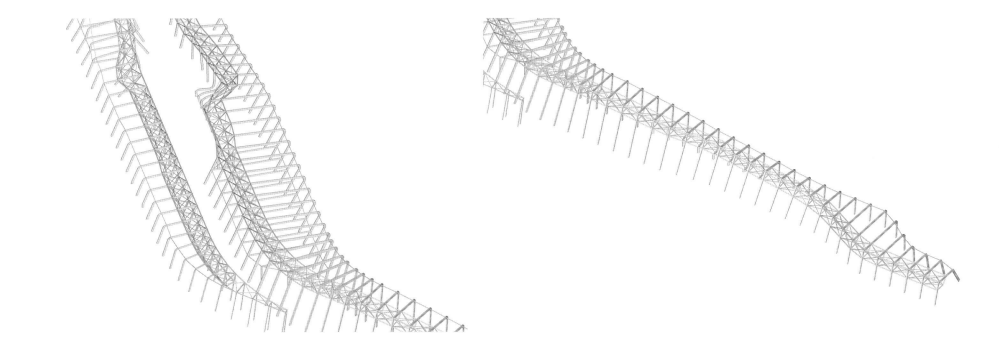

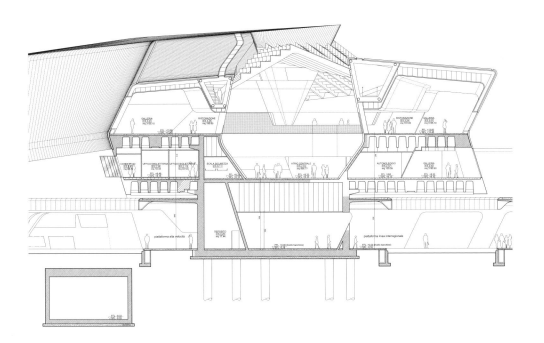

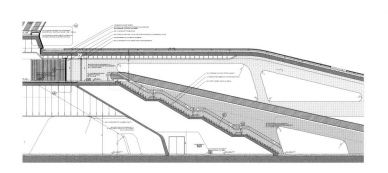

NEW EUSKO TREN CENTRAL HEADQUARTERS AND URBAN PLANNING

Durango, Spain
Design: 2004–

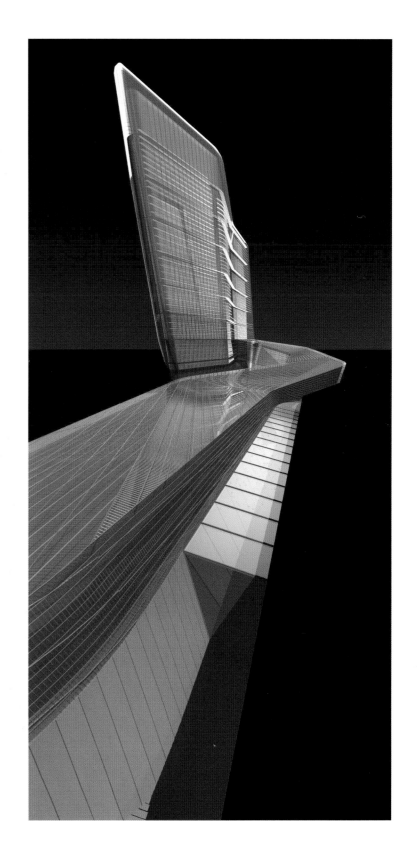

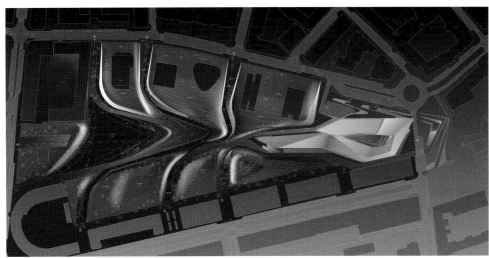

Site plan

Concept

The challenge of the Eusko Tren was integrating a new underground station, the corporate HQ and commercial space to create a new civic landmark for Durango, Spain. The new building provides more than the company's physical needs; it articulates Eusko Tren's new identity and image, symbolising its economic growth and expansion across the region and Europe. The new building is thus a new symbol not only for the company but the citizens of Durango too. It is anticipated the structure will be a catalyst and focus for the transformation of the town centre.

Urban Strategy

The overall concept is one of a conjoined design of buildings emerging at the head of the site from the reformed land. Existing rail tracks at ground level are to be removed and replaced with a new network of underground tracks across Durango allowing the land to return to public use. Foot paths are to be re-established across the site forming a connective urban tissue with a network of open public spaces each graded by topography and enclosure. The paths connect the park directly to the station and commercial space. The subterranean car park is to provide permanent parking for nearby residents and visitors with access and egress to the building provided at key points along its length. Vertical access routes are then generated where higher levels of pedestrian and car circulation flow across the car park's premises.

Important to the planning of the site was how public and private spaces were first anticipated and then realised. Our architectural proposal accentuates these areas with a frequency of circulation strips including the public areas with their converging circulation and the private domains adjacent to the planned residential areas. Topographic differentiations and ground level changes are then employed to create self-separation and allow programmatic connections across the site to both the car park, buildings and adjacent streets.

〈コンセプト〉

エウスコ・トレン（バスク鉄道）プロジェクトの課題は，地下駅・本社屋・商業スペースを統合し，スペイン北部にあるデュランゴ市に新しいランドマークをつくることであった。新しい建物は，エウスコ・トレンが物理的に必要とする以上のものを提供する。社の新しい個性とイメージを明確に表現し，その経済成長，そして地域とヨーロッパへの拡張を象徴する。つまり新しい建物は会社のみならず，デュランゴ市民にとってもまた新しいシンボルとなる。建物には，街の中心を変える触媒となり焦点となることが期待されている。

〈都市戦略〉

全体コンセプトは，再構成された土地の先端から立ち上がる，複数の建物が連接するデザインである。それまで地上を走っていた軌道は撤去されてデュランゴ市を横断する新しい地下の軌道網が取って代わり，地上は公共用途に返還される。歩道が敷地を横断して再構成され，地形や囲みによってそれぞれ徐々に移り変わるオープンな公共空間のネットワークによって接続性の高い市街が形成されるだろう。歩道は公園，駅，商業スペースと直接結ばれる。地下駐車場が近隣住民とこの場所を訪れる人のために常設のパーキングを提供する。その全長に沿って要所要所に建物への進入口と出口が設置される。次に，垂直方向のアクセス・ルートが，駐車場構内全体を横断する歩行者や車の流れの上層につくられる。

敷地計画で重要だったのは，どのように，公私のスペースをまず予測し，次に具体化するかであった。プロポーザルでは，これらのエリアを，動線の集中する公共空間，計画されている住宅地域に隣接する私的領域を含めて，動線の通過する頻度によって強調している。次に，地形的な差異と土地の高さの変化によって自動的に区分けし，プログラムに基づいて，敷地全体を駐車場，建築群，隣接する街路のすべてに連結させる。

Architects: Zaha Hadid Architects—
Zaha Hadid with Patrik Schumacher, design;
Juan Ignacio Aranguren, project architect;
Jimena Araiza, Andrés Arias, Muriel Boselli,
Daniel Dendra, Alejandro Díaz, Elena García,
John D. Goater, Daewha Kang, Kia Larsdotter,
Sophie le Bienvenu, Murat Mutlu, Mónica Noguero,
Markus Nonn, Benjamin Pohlers, Aurora Santana,
project team; Alvin Huang, Yang Jingwen,
Simon Kim, Graham Modlen, Sujit Nair,
Annabelle Perdomo, Makakrai Suthadarat,
Philipp Vogt, competition team
Project manager: MECSA
Local architect: Idom UK
Client: Public Company Eusko Tren,
Department of Transport and Public Works of the
Basque Government
Consultants: Adams Kara Taylor, Idom Bilbao, structural; Idom Bilbao, mechanical and electrical; Idom UK, cost planning; Emmer Pfenninger Partners AG, facade; Arup Acoustics, acoustics; Architectural Lighting Solutions (ALS), lighting; Gross Max, landscape
Program: new central headquarters, railway station, commercial and leisure centre and urban, park development
Total floor area: 26,403.20 m² (7,291.35 m², central headquarters Eusko Tren; 9,575.95 m², commercial & leisure centre; 9,536.00 m², railway station)
Total public park area: 25,192.05 m²

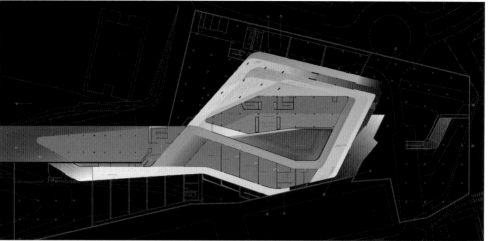

Commercial space level

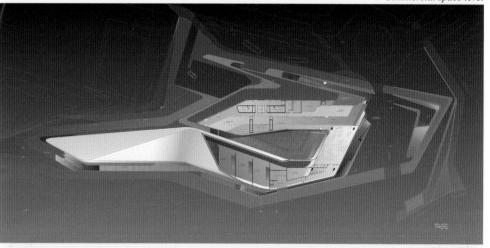

Ground floor

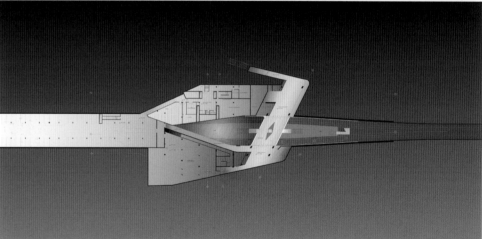

Railway station level

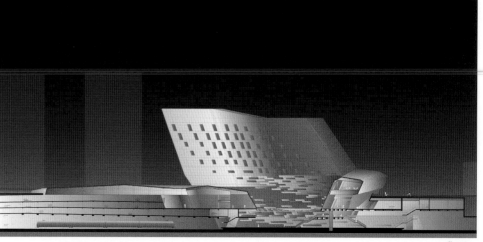

Section

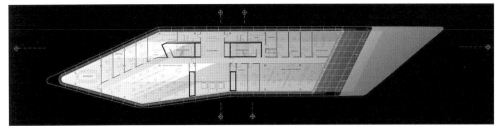

Fourth level

ZHIVOPISNAYA TOWER

Moscow, Russia
Design: 2004–

The new Zhivopisnaya residential tower is located on the Zhivopisnaya riverfront park in Moscow.

The proposed architectural design is a development of the modernist theme of the "tower in the park", dissolving the podium into the towers' body and creating one single entity, embedding the base and roof with civic program, and opening the building into the surrounding parkscape.

The tower's mass is carved by sinuous lines in a choreographed movement, creating four blocks that are joined by a system of three cores. The tower is generated through an elastic extrusion, incorporating diversity in its primary volume and enabling the creation of different apartment typologies within one overall modular frame.

The cores' transparency breaks down the building mass into slender volumes and contains all common circulation and infrastructure. The panoramic lifts capitalize on the breathtaking views over the Moscow River.

The buildings reflective envelope and transparent cores contribute to an interesting play of reflections and intersections with the river and the sky.

The subdivision of the tower into different blocks allows for a differentiation in the access to the reception and concierge services, as well as to the apartments, underlining the exclusive profile of the development.

The apartment types range from studios to four bedroom duplex and work as families, where different spatial modules are combined and organized to create the different dwellings.

The tower base accommodates a retail boulevard as well as other amenities like health club, gym, spa, solarium, nursery and restaurant. The roof garden offers a bar esplanade and winter garden with spectacular views over the city.

ジヴォピスナヤ・タワーはモスクワ川を前にしたジヴォピスナヤ公園に建てられる集合住宅である。

計画案は、"公園のなかの高層建築"というモダニズムのテーマを発展させたもので、ポディウムをタワーの本体に溶解して一体化させ、基部と屋上には都会的なプログラムをはめこみ、建物を周囲の公園風景のなかに開放する。

タワーのマッスは、踊っているかのような動きを持ち、しなやかに連続する線で4つのブロックに切り分けられ、3本のコアがそれを結ぶ。タワーは伸張性のある押し出し成形から生まれたような形をして、その基本的なヴォリュームに多様性を組み入れ、全体を覆うモジュラー・フレームの範囲内で、様々な住戸タイプを創出できる。

コアのガラス壁の透明性は建物の量塊を細身のヴォリュームへ解体する。コアにはすべての共有動線とインフラ設備が収まっている。エレベータからはモスクワ川を望む素晴らしい眺めが見える。建物を包む反射する外被とコアの透明な壁に、川や空が反射交錯して戯れ、目を引きつけるだろう。

4つのブロックへの細分によって、レセプションとコンシェルジュ、住戸への個別のアクセスが確保され、タワーの特権的な側面が強化される。

住戸タイプはスタジオ・タイプから4寝室デュプレックス、さらには異なる空間モデュールを組み合わせて独自の住居をつくれる家族向きのものまで多岐にわたる。

タワーの基部は、商店街や、ヘルスクラブ、ジム、サウナ、ソラリウム、保育所、レストランなどのようなアメニティに利用できる。屋上庭園にはモスクワ市外を見晴らす、バーのある散歩道やウィンターガーデンが設置される。

Living room

Living room

Kitchen

Living room

Lobby

Pool

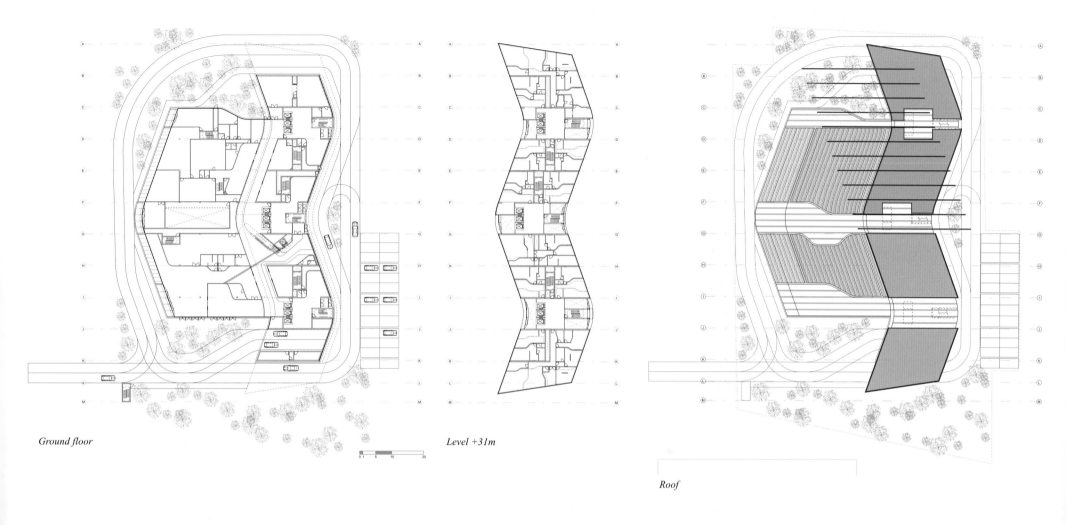

Ground floor

Level +31m

Roof

West elevation

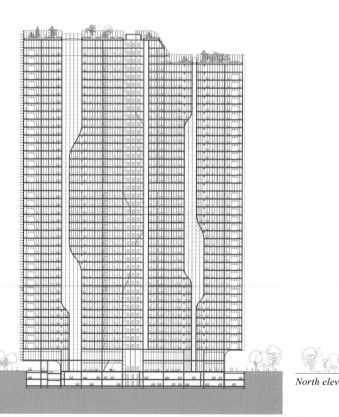

Longitudinal section

North elevation

Architects: Zaha Hadid Architects—
Zaha Hadid with Patrik Schumacher, design;
Tiago Correia, project architect;
Christina Beaumont, Achim Gergen, Nils Fischer,
Feng Chen, Larissa Henke, Sujit Nair, Agnes Koltay,
Makakrai Suthadarat, Atrey Chhaya, project team;
James Gayed, Daniel Baerlecken, Sujit Nair,
Yang Jingwen, Li Zou, sketch design team
Client: Capital Group Holding
Consultants: Ove Arup, engineering
Program: residential development
Total floor area: 95,000 m²

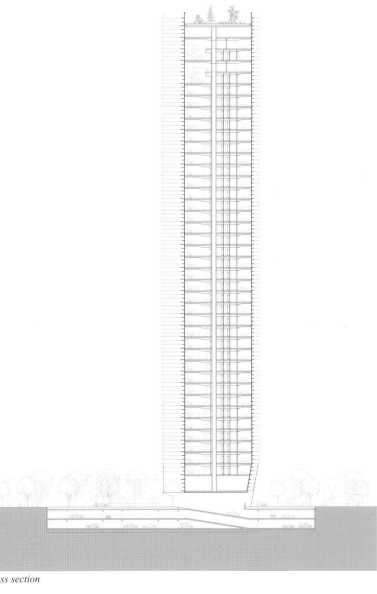

Cross section

CMA CGM HEADQUARTERS TOWER

Marseille, France
Design: 2004– Construction: –2009

The new tower for CMA CGM in Marseille, France rises from the site in a metallic curving arc that slowly lifts from the ground and accelerates to a straight vertical line. The volumes of the tower are generated from a number of gradual, or measured, centripetal vectors that emerge from within the ground datum, gently converge towards each other, and then curve away towards its ultimate coordinate 100 metres above the ground. These vectors trace the structural columns that define, and are enclosed within, a double facade system. The Tower is a tectonic interplay between a fixed structural core and this peripheral array of columns that results in a dynamic symbiosis.

Master Plan

Marseille, the second largest city in France, is a historic Provencale city centred around a centuries-old port, with a rich past of several ancient cultures: Phoenician, Greek and Roman. Because of the city's naval history, there is an opportunity to provide a highly visible landmark building. This new tower will exist as a vertical icon and interact with the vertical landmarks of La Major, the Basilica Notre Dame de la Garde, the Fort St. Jean, and the Chateau d'If in the urban city fabric of Marseille.

Urban Strategy

The immediate vicinity of the Mirabeau site reveals a field of indeterminate medium to lowrise post-war buildings. At an urban scale, flowing past the site on both sides is an elevated viaduct that bifurcates at the western edge of the parcel. A new off-ramp proposed where the viaduct splits would provide direct vehicular access to the project site. At a smaller scale of surface streets and pedestrian routes, a multi-modal transport exchange allows pedestrian and mass transit connectivity. Furthermore, the quai and its waterways lie adjacent to the project site. Directly at the confluence of this dynamic urban movement, the new Tower would accentuate its verticality and create a signature feature that would set a commanding new presence.

Taxonomy

In office towers, the standard design protocol creates a uniform plate that is replicated a number of times to minimize construction time and cost. The design focus therefore becomes marginalized to the building envelope and perhaps a sculptural interior atrium/entry. The programme of the CMA CGM Tower building has an inherent division that supports this 'morph': the upper floors are similar office spaces while the lower floors contain spaces that call for a continuous, horizontal arrangement. The lower portion then becomes shaped to allow for more generous accommodation. The columns are also placed on the exterior to minimize disruption while the curving profiles act together with the core to provide a rigid frame and give a sense of movement and freedom to a new typology of tower.

マルセイユにある世界有数の海運グループ，CMA CGMの新しいタワーは，地上からゆっくりと上昇し，真っ直ぐな垂直線へと加速する湾曲する金属の弧を構成して敷地から立ち上がる。タワーのヴォリュームは，土地の基準面から発生する，漸進的なつまり規則的で求心的な多数のベクトルから生まれ，互いに向かって緩やかに収斂した後，地上100mの最も遠い座標に向かって外側にカーブしながら離れて行く。これらのベクトルは，ダブルファサード・システムを規定し，そのなかに包まれている構造柱の軌跡を追う。タワーは，構造コアと周縁部の柱の配列の相互作用で構成され，ダイナミックな共生に帰着する。

〈全体計画〉

フランス第2の大都市マルセイユは，数百年に渡り港を中心として栄えてきたプロヴァンスの古都であり，フェニキア，ギリシャ，ローマなどいくつもの古代文明が交錯する豊かな歴史を持っている。街の海軍との長い関わりから，非常に目立つランドマーク建築を設計する機会に恵まれた。この新しいタワーは，マルセイユの都市構造のなかに垂直のイコンとして現れ，マジョル大聖堂，バシリカ・ノートル・ダム・ド・ラ・ガルド，サン・ジャン要塞，シャトー・ディフなどの垂直のランドマークと互いに呼応するだろう。

〈都市戦略〉

ミラボーにある敷地周辺は，戦後の低層の建物に対する未解決の問題をかかえた環境がひろがっている。都市的なスケールでは，敷地の西端で2つに分岐した高架の自動車道が，敷地の両側に途切れなく続いている。高架橋の分岐点に提案された高速出口により，車はタワーの敷地内へ直接進入できるだろう。地上を走る道路や歩行者のルートなどのより小さなスケールでは，インターモーダル（複合一貫輸送）な交通機関との接続は歩行者と大量輸送を結びつける。さらに，埠頭とその水路が敷地の隣に延びている。この活発な都市の動きの合流点にじかに接して，タワーはその垂直性を強め，人を惹き付ける新たな存在感を示す特徴的なサインをつくりだすだろう。

〈分類法〉

オフィスタワーの世界では，工期とコストを抑えるために，標準的なデザイン・システムが画一的な平面を生み，それは何度となく複製される。したがってデザインのポイントは，建物の外側や，あるいは彫刻的な屋内アトリウム／エントランスに限られる。CMA CGMタワーのプログラムはこの"相反する2つの性質"を支えるオフィスタワー本来の区分を備えている。上階は類似したオフィス空間である一方，下の階には，連続する水平な配置を必要とする空間が入り，同時に，より広い空間構成に対応できるように形づくられる。柱は分断を最小限にするために外側にも設置される一方，湾曲する輪郭はコアと組み合わされて剛接合を構成し，タワーの新しいプロトタイプに動感と自由な感覚を付与する。

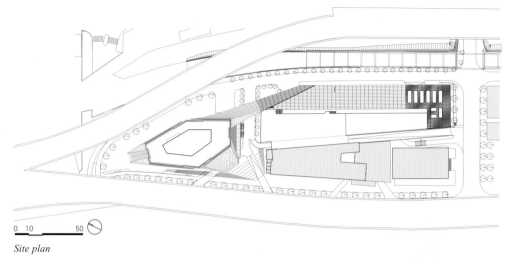

Site plan

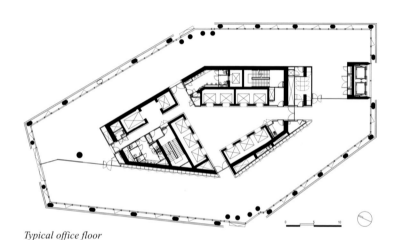

Typical office floor

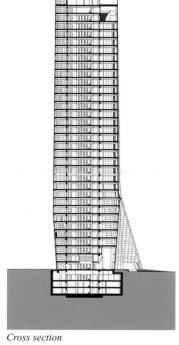

Cross section

Auditorium

Facade study

Architects: Zaha Hadid Architects—Zaha Hadid, design;
Jim Heverin, project director;
Stephane Vallotton, project architect;
Karim Muallem, Simone Contasta, Leonie Heinrich,
Alvin Triestanto, Muriel Boselli, Eugene Leung,
Bhushan Mantri, Jerome Michel, Nerea Feliz,
Prashanth Sridharan, Brigit Eistert, Matthias Frei,
Evelyn Gono, Marian Ripoll, project team;
Jim Heverin, Simon Kim, Michele Pasca Di Magiano,
Viviana Muscettola, competition team
Client: CMA CGM Marseille
Partner architects: SRA –RTA (Paris/ Marseille)
Consultants: Ove Arup & Partners, structural, services
and facade engineering
Total floor area: 64,000 m²
Height: 147 m/ 33 floors

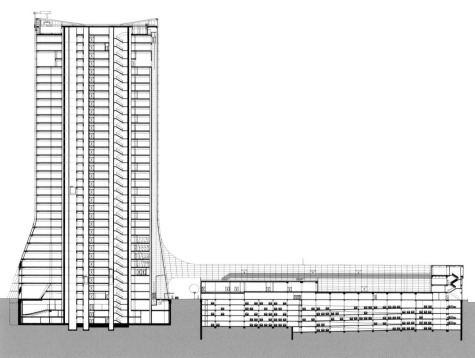

Longitudinal section

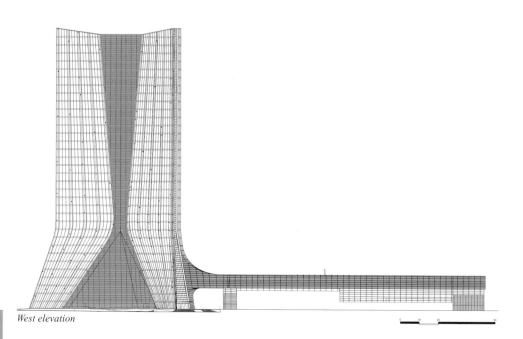

West elevation

GLASGOW MUSEUM OF TRANSPORT RIVERSIDE PROJECT

Glasgow, Scotland, U.K.
Design: 2004–   Construction: –2010

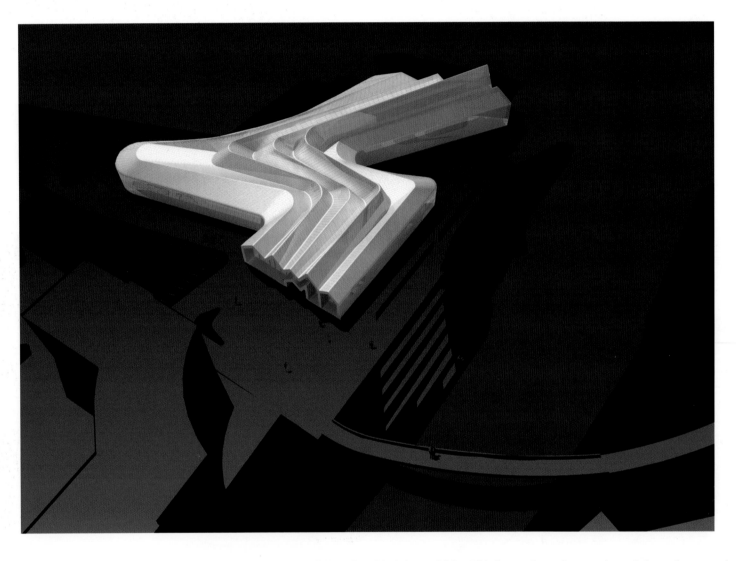

Context

The historical development of the Clyde and the city is a unique legacy; with the site situated where the Kelvin flows into the Clyde the building can flow from the city to the river. In doing so it can symbolise a dynamic relationship where the museum is the voice of both, linking the two sides and allowing the museum to be the transition from one to the other. By doing so the museum places itself in the very context of its origin and encourages connectivity between its exhibits and their wider context.

The building would be a tunnel-like shed, which is open at opposite ends to the city and the Clyde. In doing so it becomes porous to its context on either side. However, the connection from one to the other is where the building diverts to create a journey away from the external context into the world of the exhibits. Here the interior path becomes a mediator between the city and the river which can either be hermetic or porous depending on the exhibition layout. Thus the museum positions itself symbolically and functionally as open and fluid with its engagement of context and content.

Building

The building is conceived as a sectional extrusion open at opposing ends along a diverted linear path. The cross-sectional outline is a responsive gesture to encapsulating a wave or a 'pleated' movement. The outer pleats are enclosed to accommodate the support services and black box exhibits. This leaves the main central space to be column-free and open.

Circulation is through the main exhibition space. Openings are envisaged in the roof and walls as appropriate. It is perceived that there should be views out of the exhibition space. These would allow the visitors to build up a gradual sense of the external context, moving from exhibit to exhibit. All openings would be solar controlled so that total black out could be achieved when required. At the end, with a view of the Clyde and the Kelvin, is the cafe and corporate entertainment space. These also allow access and overflow into the open courtyard. The end elevation is like the front elevation with an expansive clear glass facade.

It has a large overhang to reduce solar exposure to the building interior. It will allow expansive views up and down the Clyde.

Landscape

The landscape is designed to direct the activities surrounding the building. A ring of varying stones slabs creates a shadow path around the building. On the west side the hard surface progresses to a soft landscape of grass to create an informal open courtyard space. A line of trees will be added alongside the existing ferry quay to reduce the exposure of this area to prevailing winds. Along the south side and the east, shallow water pool features are used to give continuity with the river at quay level.

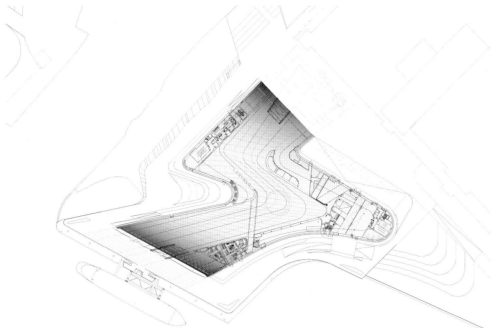

Ground floor

Night view from south

Architects: Zaha Hadid Architects—Zaha Hadid, design;
Jim Heverin, project director;
Johannes Hoffman, project architect;
Matthias Frei, Agnes Koltay, Malca Mizrahi,
Tyen Masten, Gemma Douglas, Johannes Hoffmann,
Daniel Baerlaecken, Achim Gergen, Christina Beaumont,
Markus Planteu, Claudia Wulf, Alasdair Graham,
Rebecca Haines-Gadd, Brandon Buck, Naomi Fritz,
Liat Muller, Elke Presser, Hinki Wong, Michael Mader,
project team;
Malca Mizrahi, Michele Pasca di Magliano,
Viviana R. Muscettola, Mariana Ibanez, Larissa Henke,
competition team
Client: Glasgow City Council
Consultants: Capita Symonds, project management and
costing; Buro Happold, services and acoustics
Program: exhibition space, cafe, retail, education
Total floor area: 10,000 m² (7,000 m², exhibition area)

Sections

Interior view

〈コンテクスト〉
クライド川と街の発展の歴史はグラスゴー固有の遺産である。敷地はケビン川がクライド川に流れ込む場所にあり、建物は街から川へと流れるように構成できる。そうすることで博物館は街と川のダイナミックな関係を象徴する。博物館は街と川、双方を代弁し結びつけ、一方から他方への移行の場所となり得る。そうすることで、博物館は、その生まれて育った場所であるコンテクストのなかに自らを置き、その展示品とより広いコンテクストとの結びつきを促進させる。

建物は、先端がクライド川に、反対側の端が市内に向けて開いたトンネルのような小屋となるだろう。その結果、両側がそのコンテクストに向けて多孔性のものとなる。しかし、一方から他方への接続は、外のコンテクストから離れて展示の世界への旅をつくりだすために建物が方向転換する場所である。ここで、内部通路は都市と川の間の仲介者となり、展示構成に応じて、密封された場所にも多孔性の場所にもなる。こうして、博物館は、象徴的にも機能的にも、そのコンテクストと中身の組み合わせと共に、オープンで流動的なものとして自らを位置づける。

〈建物〉
建物は途中で進路を変える線形の通路に沿って、相対する2つの端部が開き、区分された押し出し成型とみなして構成されている。横断面の輪郭は、波あるいは "ひだをとった" 動きをカプセルに包むことへ応答したジェスチャーである。外側のひだは、サポート・サービスとブラックボックスによる展示に対応するために囲まれている。これによって主要な中央空間は無柱のオープン・スペースとして残される。

動線は主要な展示空間の端から端まで通っている。開口は、屋根と壁の適切な位置にとられ、展示空間の外の眺めの存在を感知することができるだろう。来館者は、展示から展示へと進みながら、外部のコンテクストに対する漸進的な感覚を組み立てて行くだろう。すべての開口では太陽熱が制御され、必要な時は全面的な暗転が可能となる。クライド川とケビン川が見える終端には、カフェと企業のエンタテイメント・スペースが置かれる。これらのスペースも、開いたコートヤードへ通じ、そこに流れ込む。終端部の立面は正面と同じような、大きな透明ガラスのファサードである。

ファサードには建物内部への陽射しの侵入を抑えるために広い張り出しが付けられる。そこからはクライド川の上流や下流に広がる眺めが見える。

〈ランドスケープ〉
ランドスケープが、建物周囲での諸活動を誘導するようにデザインされる。様々な石のスラブで構成された環が建物の周りに影の落ちる通路をつくりだす。西側に面しては、堅い石の面は草の柔らかなランドスケープへと進み、形式張らない開放的なコートヤードをつくりだす。木々が既存のフェリー埠頭のそばに一列に植えられ、卓越風からコートヤードを守る。南側と東側に沿って、特徴のある浅いプールが、川岸のレベルとの連続性をつくりだす。

NEUES STADT-CASINO

Basel, Switzerland
Design: 2004–   Construction: –2009

Urban Concept

The Neues Stadt Casino is an L-shaped volume which encloses the existing music hall, and connects with the adjacent Hans Huber Hall, giving a new identity to the Stadt-Casino.

The facade of the old music hall and the Hans Huber Hall create the main facade along the Steinenberg. The continuation of the two buildings, highlighted by a cut or slice, allows the front surface of the new building to become cohesive whilst the new volume remains sufficiently distanced from the existing building.

Around the corner in the main public square of Basel, the Barfuesserplatz, the situation changes with a dramatic cantilever that sets an unmistakable indication into the urban space. With a generous view underneath the cantilevering volume, we create a new urban connection from the Barfuesserplatz to the Theaterplatz with the new main entrance to the Stadt-Casino.

The surface of the square flows underneath the floating volume of the new building and folds upwards over a ramp. This allows the different levels of the square to be a continuous landscape. The terraced surface of the form of the landscape, and the undersurface of the floating volume, create a generous entrance hall.

Architectural Concept

The main design feature is the idea of a homogeneous, plastic volume, which is differentiated and articulated by bulging the surface, by inverting the surface (new concert hall), by enclosing "foreign bodies" (old music hall), and by hollowing out the volume (entrance hall). The old music hall is surrounded in an L-shape by the new solidium. However, the old concert hall is set in contrast in such a way that it is possible to perceive the historical volume. The cut also expresses a second entrance to the foyer and music hall at the Steinenberg. The dramatic cantilever offers a further architectural attraction—monolithically, the sculptural new building floats over the artificial topography of the square.

Through the architectural stylistic device of an inversion in the main facade, a strong connection between the interior space and the public space of the Barfuesserplatzes is achieved. The stage of the new concert hall is designed as a large window over the Barfuesserplatz. The view into the festively illuminated concert hall

Site plan

will enrich the scene of the place and waken the desire to attend the concert. Underneath the new concert hall the large entry space opens as a direct continuation of the square. The building appears to float and is hollowed-out by the pedestrian traffic.

The modulated entrance hall connects the different levels of the site by manipulating and terracing the ground. Two large cores grow out of this modulated, flowing surface and raise the floating volume. The floating volume presents itself as a large sculptural form. The sculptural appearance is supported by a continuous surface organization, which continues in the roof area and in the undersurface. This "skin" consists of casted, partly perforated aluminium panels. The perforation creates an interesting visual effect: the volume, completely covered with aluminium panels, appears during the day—under certain points of view—as homogeneous. At night, when the exposure conditions are reversed, it shows its spatial depth and transparency.

The grid of the facade is derived from the fa-

cade of the old concert hall and is subtly transferred into a differentiated, horizontal composition. The old facade organization is interpreted in a new way. The horizontals of the structure of the new building are distorted in a curvilinear manner in the places in which it is functionally necessary. Thus, for example, fields with larger transparency become visible because of this distortion of the facade. The facade is a single-layered construction in the areas of the roof and the lower surface, and changes into a double-layered construction in the area of the vertical front, which is partitioned in such a way that all openings are concentrated on a large, continuous band. Here the climatic layer of the facade inverts itself to the inside, and the layer is veiled with a perforated screen. From the multi-layered facade results an effect of iridescence. The depth of the facade guarantees a refined visual attraction.

Functional Concept

That which presents itself outwards as a unitary solidium and as an institutional unit, is sepa-

rated into two functional parts on the inside: the part for the public (including the concert halls), and the part for the musician/management. The Hans Huber Hall, along with the narrow side of the new building, contain all institutional support functions for musicians, instruments, administration and is connected to the concert halls.

Directly underneath the concert hall is the main entrance and the terrace of the restaurant. Beneath this space is located the retail areas, which are accessible through two topographic interventions in the ground floor. Here we use the different levels of the topography, in order to ensure the natural exposure for this storey of the building, and to create the possibility of a direct entrance at street level.

There are two scenarios of circulation, which result in a concept of two entrances: in the first scenario visitors experience the generous shopping landscape and the entrance hall as one continuous space; in the other, each of these functional units can be used separately from the other. The separation of the concert range from the shopping area can be easily removed, so that a mixing of the users is favoured. Starting in the entrance hall, the visitor permeates the skin of the floating volume by climbing a generous staircase, which leads to the level of the new concert hall. The second level of the entrance hall surrounds the new concert hall. The visitor is able to reach the balcony level of the old music hall comfortably from here, by means of three bridges. After each performance, visitors can easily reach the bar on the second level, which offers spectacular views over the mediaeval city of Basel.

Architects: Zaha Hadid Architects—
Zaha Hadid with Patrik Schumacher, design;
Jim Heverin, project architect;
Daniel Baerlecken, Matthias Frei, Naomi Fritz,
Rebecca Haines-Gadd, Paul Peyrer-Heimstaett,
Helmut Kinzler, Judith Reitz, project team
Client: Casino-Gesellschaft
Local architect: Burkhardt + Partners AG
Consultants: Adams Kara Taylor, structural;
Max Fordham, mechanical; Ove Arup & Partners Ltd.,
acoustic; Theatre Projects Consultants, theatre consul-
tant; PPE Engineering, facade engineer
Program: concert hall
Total floor area: 13,723 m²

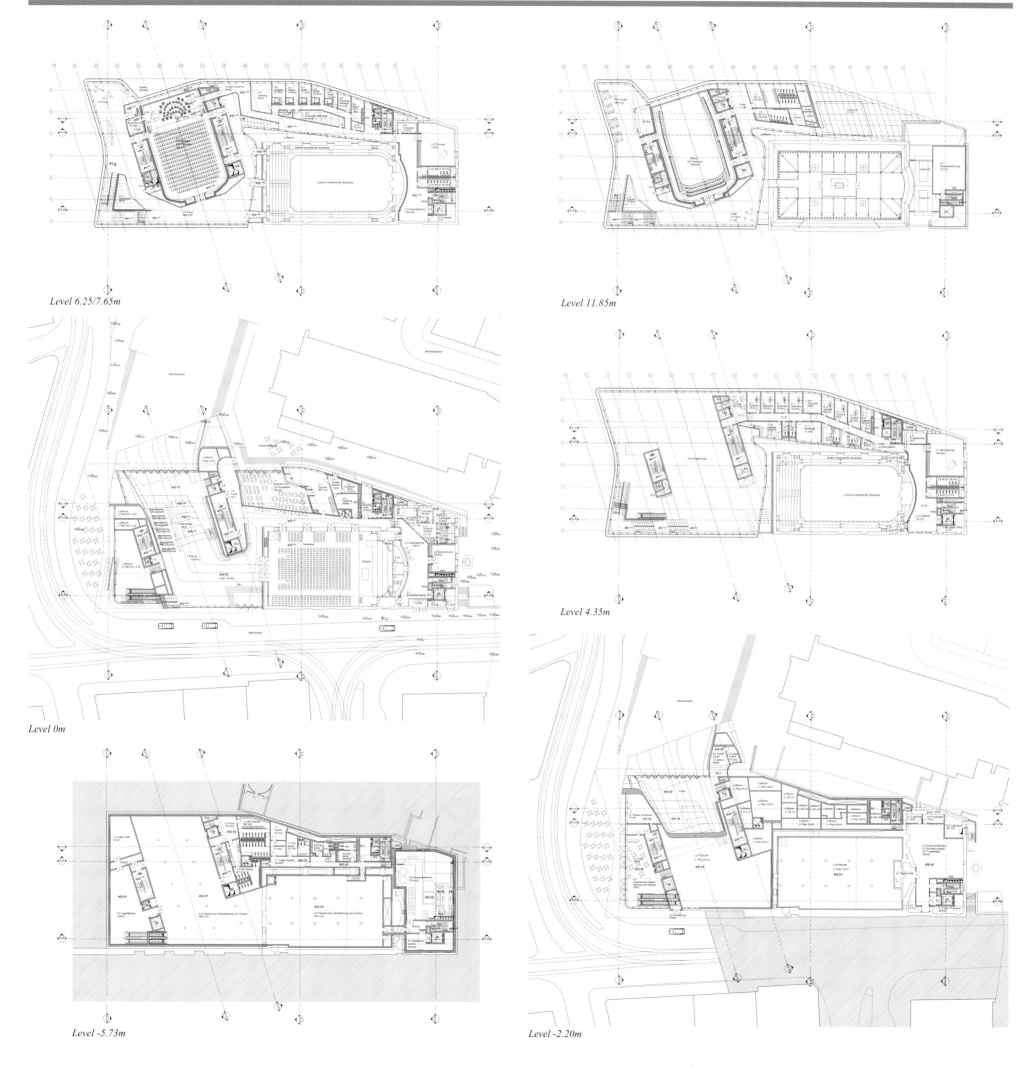

Level 6.25/7.65m

Level 11.85m

Level 0m

Level 4.35m

Level -5.73m

Level -2.20m

Night view from north

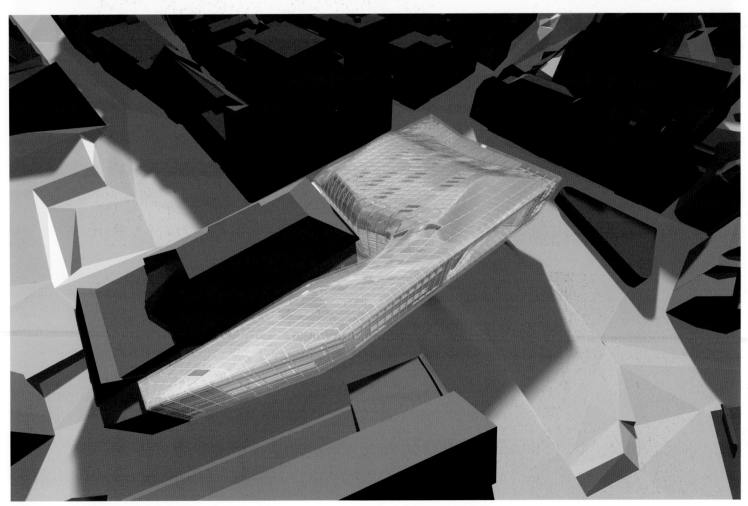

Sequencial diagram

〈都市のコンセプト〉

ノイエス・シュタット・カジノは既存の音楽ホールをL形に囲み、隣接するハンス・フーバー・ホールと結合して、シュタット・カジノに新しい性格を付与する。

旧音楽ホールとハンス・フーバー・ホールのファサードはシュタイネンベルクに沿ってメイン・ファサードを構成する。ヴォリュームを切り取り、あるいは薄く切り分けることで強調された新旧の建物の連続性は、2棟のあいだを十分に引き離しながらも、新棟のファサードに全体をまとめあげる力を与える。

バーゼルの主要な公共広場であるバルフューザー広場のコーナーを回って、都市空間へ向けて明快な意志を表明する劇的な片持ちの張り出しによって周辺状況は一変する。片持ちになったヴォリュームの下に広がるゆったりした眺めと共に、シュタット・カジノの新しいメイン・エントランスと、バルフューザー広場から劇場広場に至る、都市との新たな結びつきが生まれる。

広場は、新しい建物の片持ちで浮かんだヴォリュームの下を流れ、スロープを超えて上方に折り込まれる。これによって、段差のある広場は連続するランドスケープとなる。ランドスケープを構成する段状の面は、浮かぶヴォリュームの下面と共に広いエントランス・ホールをつくりだす。

〈建築のコンセプト〉

デザインを特徴づけているのは、均質で、彫塑的なヴォリュームというアイディアであり、表面を膨らますこと、表面を内側に折り曲げること（新コンサート・ホール）、"異質なボディ"（旧音楽ホール）を囲むこと、ヴォリュームを繰り抜くこと（エントランス・ホール）によって、各領域を差異化し分節する。旧音楽ホールは新しい建物によってL形に囲まれるが、その歴史のあるファサードがはっきりと知覚できるように新棟との対比のなかに置かれる。また、切り取られた開口がシュタイネンベルクに面して、ホワイエと音楽ホールへの2番目のエントランスを表示する。劇的な片持ちは、さらに、広場のつくられた地形の上に浮かぶ新しい建物に、彫刻的でモノリスのような建築的魅力を与える。

メイン・ファサードの、反転という建築文体上の仕掛けを通して、内部空間とバルフューザー広場の公共空間のあいだに強いつながりが生まれる。新コンサート・ホールの舞台はバルフューザー広場を見下ろす大きな窓のように構成されている。窓越しに見える、祝祭にふさわしく照明されたホールの眺めは広場を華やかに彩り、コンサートを聴きたいという気持ちにさせるだろう。新コンサート・ホールの下側には、大きなエントリー・スペースが広場からそのまま続いて開いている。建物は浮かぶように現れ、歩行者の流れがそれを繰り抜いて行く。

敷地状況に合わせて、エントランス・ホールは地表面を巧みに処理し、段状に構成することで異なる高さを連結する。この抑揚をつけられた、流れる面から2つの大きなコアが生まれ、浮かぶヴォリュームを持ち上げる。浮かぶヴォリュームは自らを大きな彫刻的な形態として提示する。彫刻的な外貌は、屋根から下側面へと続く、連続的な面によって支えられる。この"被膜"は部分的に孔をあけた成型アルミパネルで構成される。孔は面白い視覚効果をつくりあげる。アルミパネルで完全に覆われたヴォリュームは、昼間は、ある視点から見ると均質なものとして現れ、夜になり、露出面の状況が逆転すると、その空間的深度と透明性が現れる。

ファサードを構成するグリッドは、旧コンサート・ホールのファサードから引き出され、差異化された水平構成へと微妙に変形させたものである。旧ファサードの構成は新たな方法で翻訳される。新しい建物の水平性には、機能的に必要とされる箇所で、曲線を用いて歪みが与えられる。こうして、たとえばより大きな透明性を持つ領域はこのファサードの歪みによって見えるようになる。ファサードは、屋根の部分と低い方の面は1枚の層、垂直の正面部分は2枚の層による構成へ変化する。すべての開口は大きな連続する帯へと収束するように仕切られる。ここで、ファサードの、気候を配慮したレイヤーは自身を内側へ向かって反転させ、有孔スクリーンのベールに覆われる。幾重にも重なるファサードは、陽射しの変化や見る角度で虹のように色調を変える。ファサードの深度は洗練された視覚的魅力を確かなものにする。

〈機能上のコンセプト〉

外に向けては、まとまりのある凝固体として、そして単一の組織体として自らを表現する建物の内部は、機能によって2つに分割される。公的な領域（コンサート・ホールを含む）と音楽家/管理者のための領域である。ハンス・フーバー・ホールは、新棟の幅の狭い側と共に、音楽家、楽器、事務管理を支える施設としての機能をすべて納め、コンサート・ホールに接続される。コンサート・ホールのすぐ下にメイン・エントランスとレストランが配されたテラスがある。この下には店舗エリアがあり、1階に加えられた2つの地形的介入を通って入る。この介入では、建物のこのレベルが自然に曝され、道路レベルから直接入れるエントランスをつくるために、地形のレベル差を利用している。

動線には2つのシナリオがあり、2つのエントランスというコンセプトに帰結する。一つ目のシナリオでは、訪れる人がゆったりとした店舗風景とエントランス・ホールを一つの連続空間として体験する。もう一つのシナリオでは、これらの機能的ユニットのそれぞれが互いに分離したものとして使うことができる。店舗領域からのコンサート・ホール領域の分離は簡単に解消できるので、それぞれの利用者を混入させることも容易である。エントランス・ホールに始まり、訪れる人は広い階段を上りながら浮かぶヴォリュームの被膜を抜け、新コンサートホールのレベルへ導かれる。エントランス・ホールの2階は新コンサート・ホールを囲んでいる。3つのブリッジによって、ここから気軽に旧音楽ホールのバルコニー・レベルに出られる。

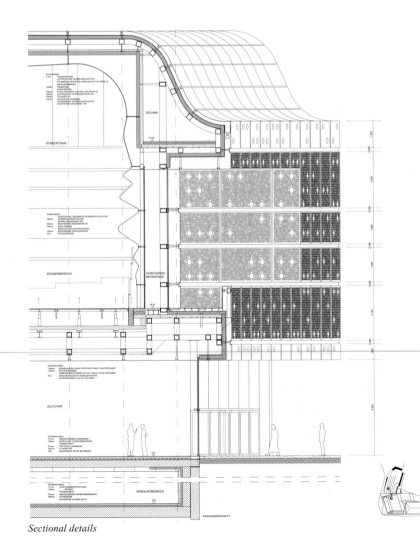

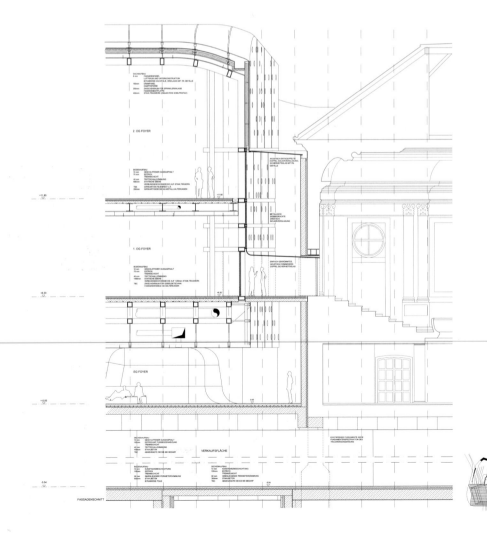

Sectional details

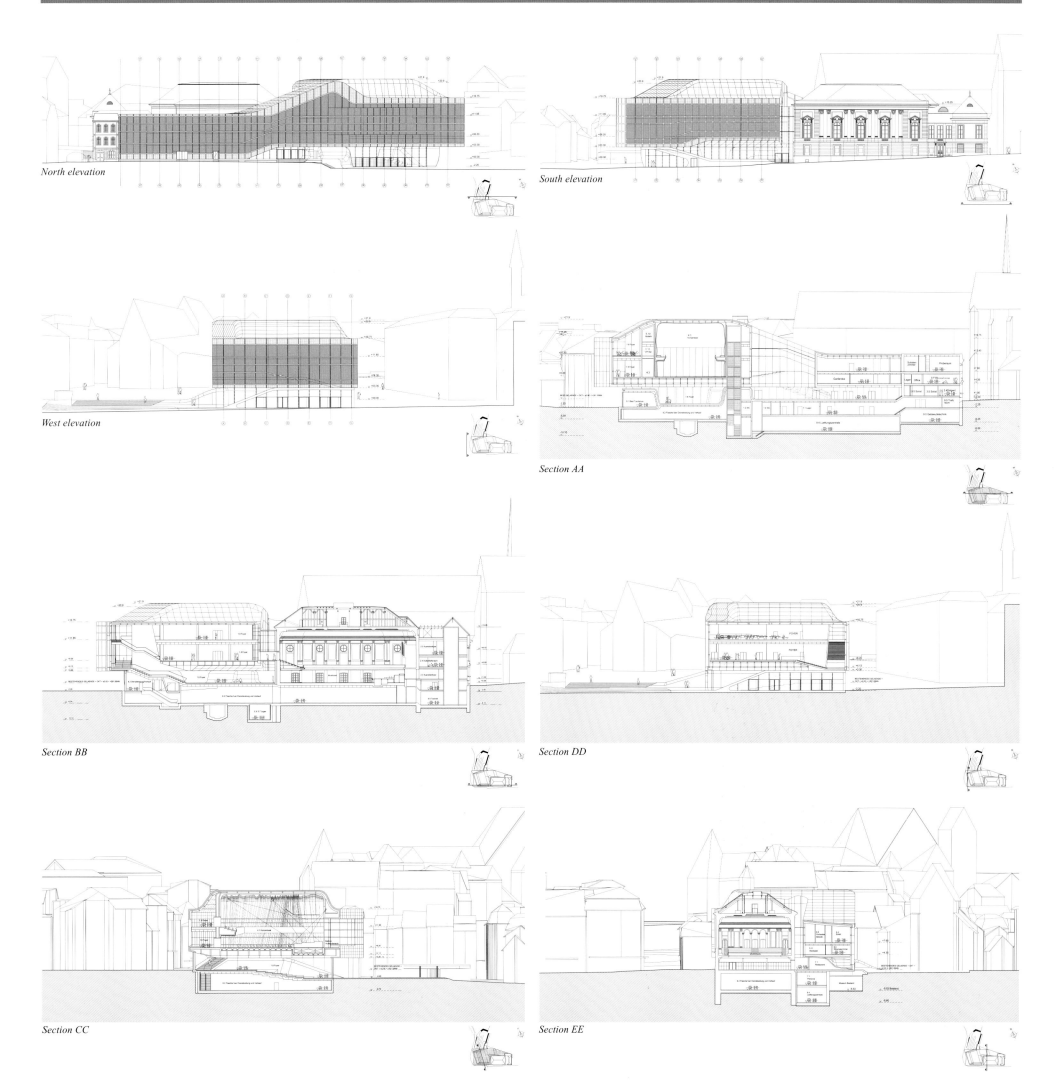

North elevation

South elevation

West elevation

Section AA

Section BB

Section DD

Section CC

Section EE

CITYLIFE PROJECT

Milan, Italy
Design: 2004– Construction: –2014

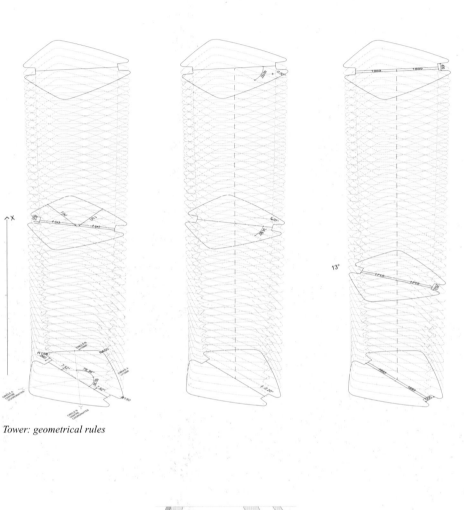

Tower: geometrical rules

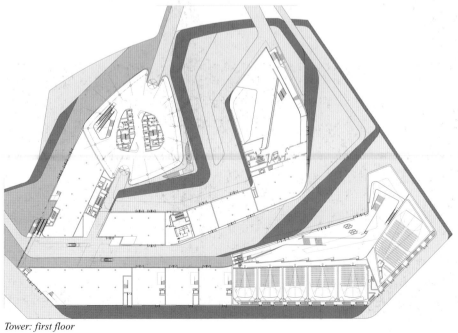

Tower: first floor

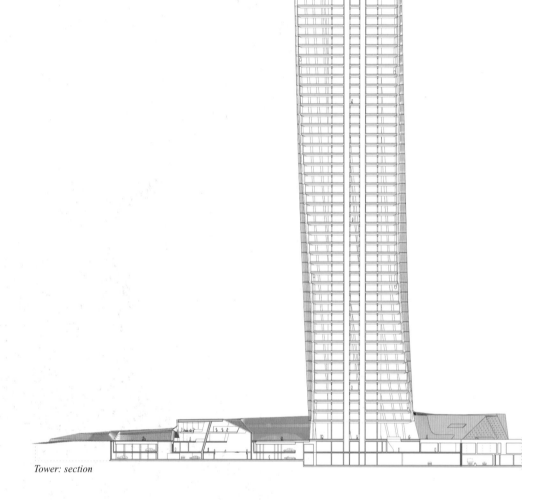

Tower: section

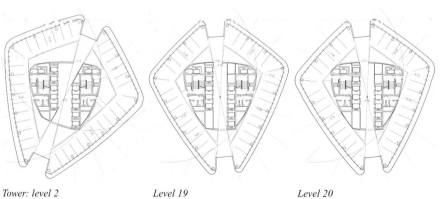

Tower: level 2   *Level 19*   *Level 20*

Towers designed by Z. Hadid (left), D. Libeskind (center) and A. Isozaki

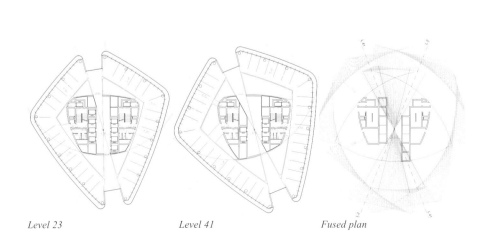

Level 23   *Level 41*   *Fused plan*

Residential building

Our concept for the master plan from the beginning had to do with the idea of a building in parkland and a building which had a high rise entity and also a horizontal entity. In a way what we developed was about these two qualities: the tower has a dynamic form, spiralling upward, a strong optimistic icon, contributing to the new skyline of Milan. The articulation of the split of the tower, because of the split that separate those, shows the light of the building and the core, the tower also brings light and use to the central space, and also connect to the lobby and the retail area on the ground. So there is a continuous line on the ground moving through retail and going up to the building.

The feature of the glazed cut emphasises the entrance into the tower also to make a connection with the retail mall that spans on the base of the tower, another spiralling move, this corresponds between the vertical and horizontal gesture and the seamingless transition between the two as the main concept or characteristic of our design.

The residential area has been designed with meandering lines across the park, one of buildings that transform the park into a series of intimate semi-public gardens for the use of the residents.

We had from the very beginning a very clear way to read the project and I think that the dynamic of this goes between the three towers with their different height also the whole central area very exciting and offers an interesting discourse between the tall buildings and the entire skyline.

全体計画に対するコンセプトは，当初から，緑に包まれた風致地区の建物であるということと，高層棟の独自性と水平性の強い低層棟の独自性を並び備えた建物であるという考え方をどう解くかであった。ある意味で，私たちが展開したのはこの2つの特質についてである。タワーはダイナミックな形を持ち，螺旋状に巻き上がり，楽観的な力強いイコンであり，ミラノの新しいスカイラインの構成に寄与する。タワーの裂け目がつくりだす分節は，建物の照明とコアを外に見せる。中央スペースには外光を送り，空間の有用性を高め，そしてまた，1階のロビー，店舗エリアを連結する。その結果，店舗エリアを通り抜け，建物へと上がって行く連続する道筋が1階に生まれる。

ガラスが嵌め込まれた特徴のある開口は，タワーのエントランスを強調する。またタワーの基部に延びる，小売店が並ぶモールとの連結によってもう一つの螺旋状の動きが生まれる。これは，私たちのデザインの中心的なコンセプト，あるいは特質となっている，垂直と水平のジェスチャー，そして両者の間のなめらかな移行に対応する。

住居棟は蛇行する線を描きながら公園を横断し，住民が使うセミパブリックな一連の小さな庭に公園を変貌させる。

ごく最初から，私たちにはプロジェクトを読む明快な方法があった。その動的な力強さは，高さの違う3本のタワーの間に，また非常に刺激的な中央エリア全体に行き渡り，高層の建物とスカイライン全体の間に，興味深い会話が始まるだろう。

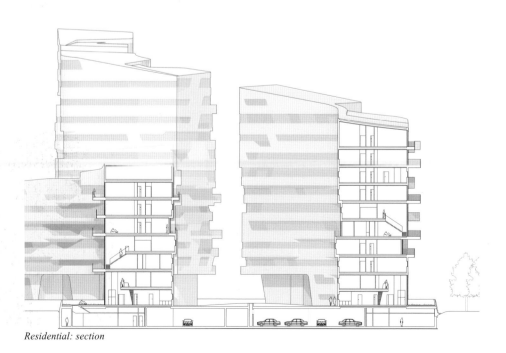

Residential: section

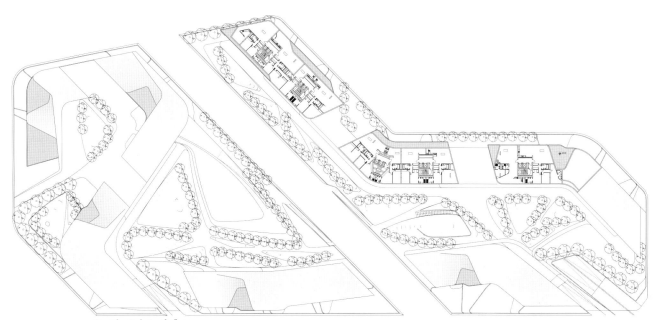

Residential: tenth floor

Architects: Zaha Hadid Architects—
Zaha Hadid with Patrik Schumacher, design;
Gianluca Racana, project architect;
Paolo Zilli, team leader of tower and retail;
Giuseppe Morando, Andrea Balducci Castè,
Annarita Papeschi, Matteo Pierotti, Mario Mattia, de-
sign team of tower and retail;
Maurizio Meossi, team leader of housing;
Samuele Sordi, Vincenzo Barilari, Massimiliano Piccinini,
Giacomo Sanna, Mario Mattia, Paolo Matteuzzi,
Alessandra Belia, design team of housing;
Simon Kim, Yael Brosilovski, Adriano De Gioannis,
Graham Modlen, Karim Muellem, Daniel Li,
Yang Jingwen, Tiago Correia, Ana M Cajiao,
Daniel Baerlecken, Judith Reitz, competition team
Client: CityLife Consortium-Milan
Consultant: Adams Kara Taylor, MSC, structural engi-
neers; Max Fordham Partnership, MilanoProgetti, me-
chanical + environmental

Program: the site will encompass a large park, three office towers and retail buildings, 4 different sites for residential development, one to each of the 4 architects
(Zaha Hadid, Arata Isozaki, Daniel Libeskind, Pier Paolo
Maggiora), educational and social facilities and a museum. Zaha Hadid's design includes a 190 meter office
tower of 43 storeys, totalling 65,000 m² connected to a
3-storey retail galleria of 25,000 m² and on a site opposite a housing complex of 6 buildings ranging from 3
to14 stores totaling nearly 45,000 m² and 300 units.

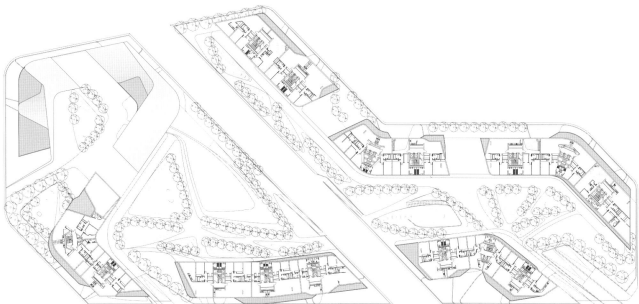

Residential: third floor

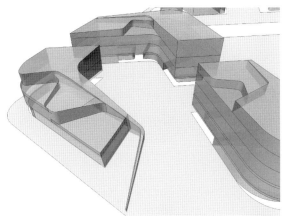

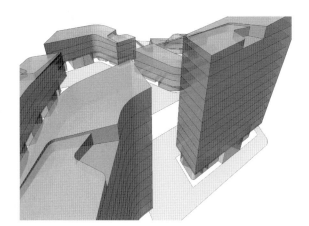

Residential: 3D study

NORDKETTENBAHN CABLE RAILWAY STATIONS

Innsbruck, Austria
Design: 2005–   Construction: –2007

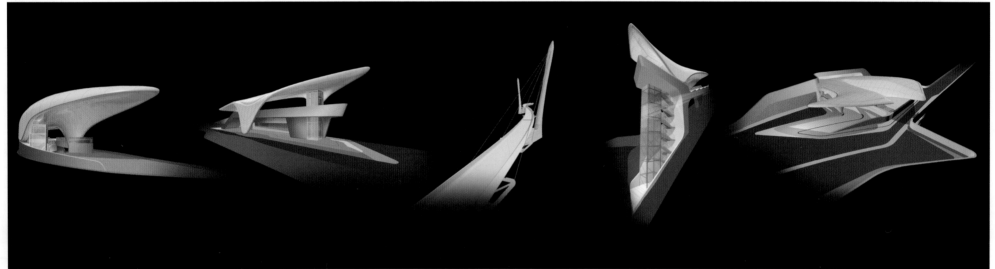

Four stations and bridge: overall view

The project contains the design of four stations along the cable railway tracks leading up to Innsbruck's northern chain of mountains. Adaptation to the specific site conditions in various altitudes while articulating a coherent overall architectural language is critical to this design approach.

Two contrasting elements "Shell & Shadow" generate each station's spatial quality. A lightweight organic roof structure floats on top of a concrete plinth. The artificial landscape functions as a relief in which various movements and circulations are inscribed. Looking at the Roof Shell's fluid shapes and soft contours, one might be reminded on natural phenomena such as glacier movements.

New production methods like CNC milling and thermoforming guarantee a very precise and automatic translation of the computer generated design into the built structure. The resulting aesthetics might be reminiscent of streamlined Industrial Design pieces (Car Bodies, Aeroplane Wings, Yachts etc.).

Each station has its context, its topography, its altitude, its movements. The track's inclination and ratios are dominant technical parameters. A high degree of flexibility enables the shell structures to adjust to these various parameters while still being part of the same formal family. The concept of lightness is explored. Large cantilevers and small touch down areas underline a floating appearance of the shells.

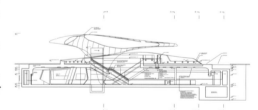

Congress station: section

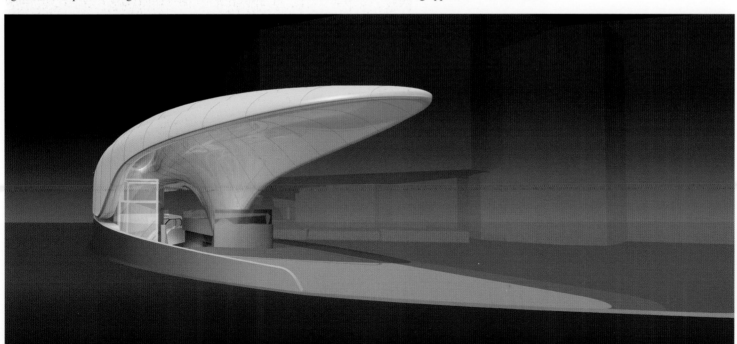

Congress station

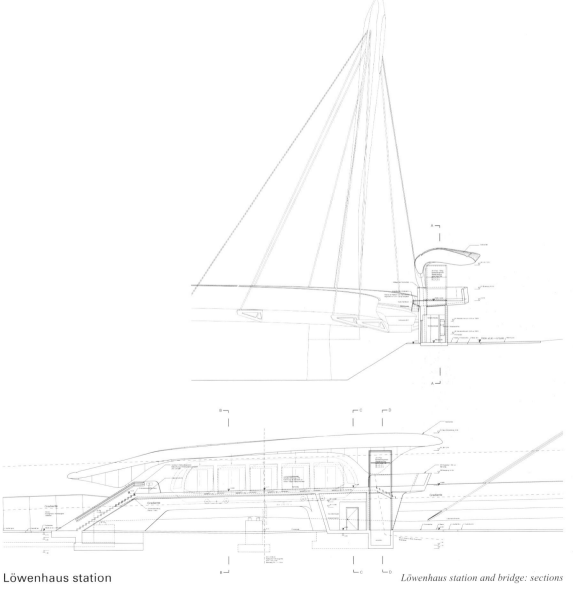

Löwenhaus station

Löwenhaus station and bridge: sections

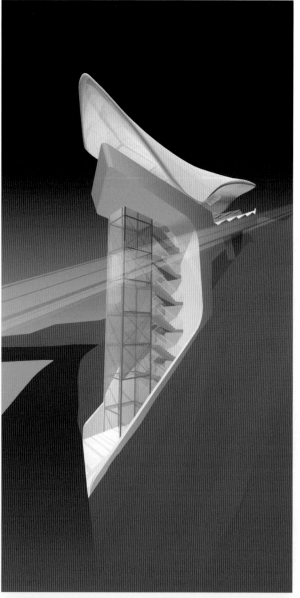

インスブルックの北部連峰に登るケーブル鉄道の軌道沿いに4つの駅をデザインする。4つの駅の建築言語に一貫性をもたせながら、高度の違うそれぞれの敷地状況に適合させることが、このデザインを進めるには不可欠である。

2つの対比的な要素、"シェルとシャドー"から各駅の特徴が生まれている。軽量の有機的な屋根構造がコンクリートの基壇の上に浮かぶように現れる。人工のランドスケープが、そのなかに様々な動きや動線を刻印したレリーフとしての役割を果たす。屋根を構成するシェルの流麗な形態と輪郭は、氷河の流れのような自然現象を想わせる。

CNCフライス盤による切削加工や熱形成などの新しい工法は、コンピュータを駆使して制作されたデザインを、非常に精確かつ自動的に実際の建物へ転換することを可能としてくれる。ここから生まれた審美的表現は、流線型の工業デザイン製品（自動車の車体、航空機の翼、ヨット等々）を連想させるだろう。

4つの駅は、それぞれに固有の文脈、地形、高度、動きを備えている。軌道の傾斜と比率が技術的な規定要因を支配している。シェル構造はその非常に高い柔軟性によって、同じ形態ファミリーの一部にとどまりつつ、これらの多様な規定要因に適応することが出来る。ここでは軽さ、というコンセプトが探求されている。キャンチレバーの大きさに対するにその着地面積の小ささがシェルの浮遊するような外観を強調する。

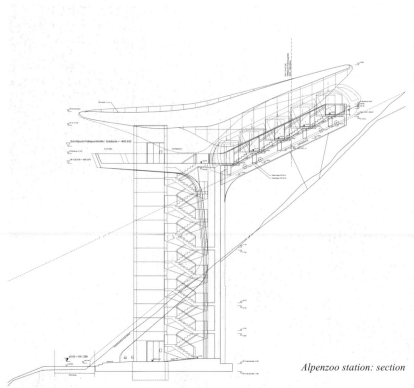

Alpenzoo station: section

Alpenzoo station

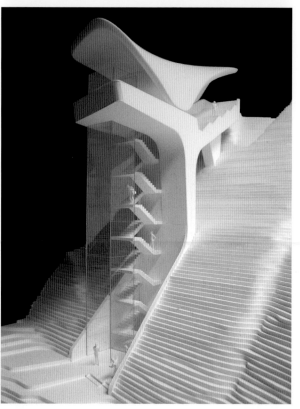

Architects: Zaha Hadid Architects
Zaha Hadid with Patrik Schumacher, design;
Thomas Vietzke, project architect;
Jens Borstelmann, Markus Planteu, design team;
Caroline Andersen, Makakrai Suthadarat,
Marcela Spadaro, Anneka Wagener, Adriano di Gionnis,
Peter Pichler, Susann Berggren, production team
Local architect: Malojer Baumanagement
Client: Strabag, City of Innsbruck
Consultants: Baumann & Obholzer, structural
Program: 4 cable railway stations, 1 bridge
Size: 2,750 m², roof structure

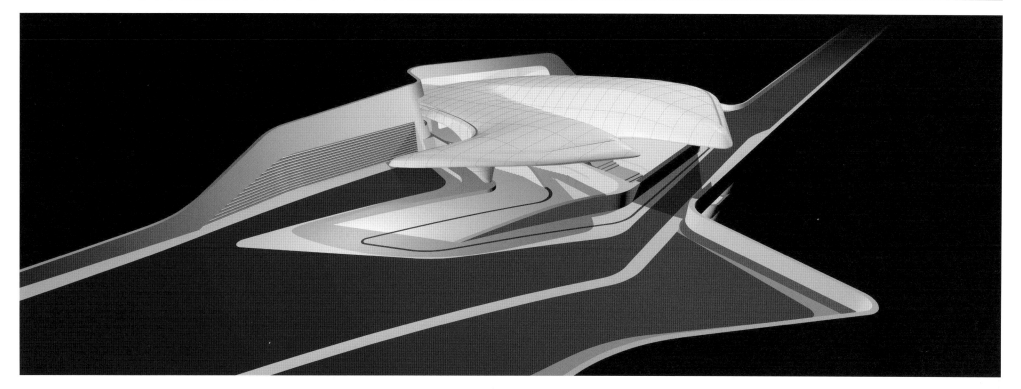

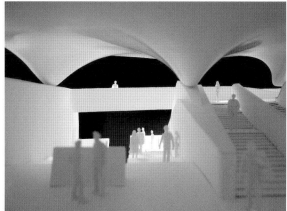

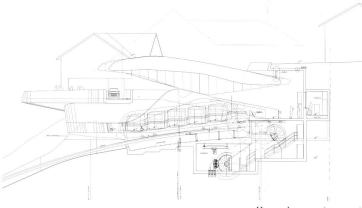

Hungerburg station: section

Hungerburg station

Photos of construction site: ©Roland Halbe Fotografie / 2007

LONDON AQUATICS CENTRE

London, U.K.
Design: 2005–   Construction: –2011

Overall view: Olympic mode

Overall view

Interior: Olympic mode

Interior

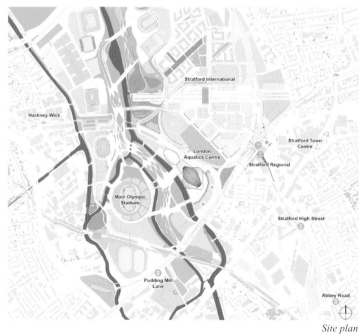

Site plan

Design Concept

The architectural concept of the London Aquatic Centre is inspired by the fluid geometry of water in motion, creating spaces and a surrounding environment in sympathy with the river landscape of the Olympic Park. An undulating roof sweeps up from the ground as a wave—enclosing the pools of the Centre with its unifying gesture of fluidity, whilst also describing the volume of the swimming and diving pools.

The London Aquatic Centre is designed to have the flexibility to accommodate the size and capacity of the London 2012 Olympic Games whilst also providing the optimum size and capacity for use in Legacy mode after the 2012 Games.

Site Context

The London Aquatic Centre is situated within the Olympic Park Masterplan. The site is positioned on the south eastern edge of the Olympic Park with direct proximities to Stratford. The new pedestrian access from the east-west bridge called the Stratford City Bridge which links the Stratford City development with the Olympic Park will cross over the LAC. This will provide a very visible frontage for the LAC along the bridge. Several smaller pedestrian bridges will connect the site to the Olympic Park over the existing canal.

The Aquatic Centre addresses within its design the main public realm spaces implicit within the Olympic Park and Stratford City planning. These are primarily the east-west connection of the Stratford City Bridge and continuation of the Olympic Park space alongside the canal.

Layout

The Aquatic Centre is planned on an orthogonal axis perpendicular to the Stratford City Bridge. Along this axis are laid out the three pools. The training pool is located under the bridge whilst the competition and diving pools are within a large volumetric pool hall. The overall strategy is to frame the base of the pool hall as a podium by surrounding it and connecting it into the bridge.

This podium element allows for the containment of a variety of differentiated and cellular programmatic elements into a single architectural volume which is seen to be completely assimilated with the bridge and the landscape. From the bridge level the podium emerges from underneath the bridge to cascades around the pool hall to the lower level of the canal side level.

The pool hall is expressed above the podium level by a large roof which is arching along the same axis as the pools. Its form is generated by the sightlines for the spectators during the Olympic mode. Double-curvature geometry has been used to create a structure of parabolic arches that create the unique characteristics of the roof. The roof undulates to differentiate an internal visual separation inside the pool hall between the competition pool volume and the diving pool volume. The roof projects beyond the base legacy pool hall envelope to extend the roof covering to the external areas of the cascades and the bridge entrance.

The roof projection over the bridge entrance announces the London Aquatic Centre's presence from the approach from either Stratford City or the Olympic Park. Structurally the roof is grounded at 3 primary positions. Otherwise the opening between the roof and the podium is in-filled with a glass facade.

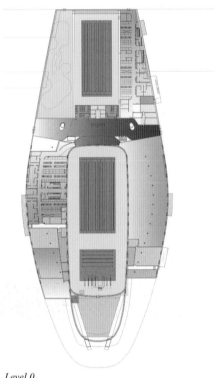

Level 0

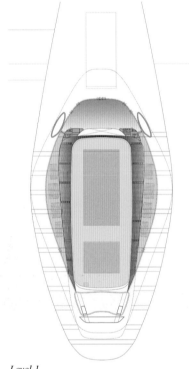

Level 1

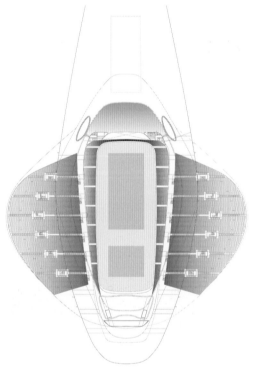

Level 1: Olympic mode

〈デザイン・コンセプト〉

ロンドン・アクアティック・センター（LAC）の建築コンセプトは，水の動きがつくりだす流麗なかたちに触発されたもので，オリンピック・パークの水辺の風景と調和した空間や周辺環境をつくりだす。起伏する屋根が波のように地上から裾を大きく引いて広がり，センターの各プールをその流れのなかに一つに包み込みながら，水泳プールと飛び込みプールのヴォリュームを表現する。

アクアティック・センターは，2012年のロンドン・オリンピック競技に求められるプールの規模と観客収容能力に適合すると同時に，2012年の競技終了以降の運用にも適切に対応できるよう柔軟に設計されている。

〈敷地のコンテクスト〉

LACはオリンピックパーク全体計画内に配置される。敷地はオリンピックパークの南東端にあり，ロンドン近郊のストラトフォードの街に直接面している。ストラトフォードの開発地区とオリンピックパークを東西に結ぶストラトフォード・シティー・ブリッジから入る新しい歩行者専用路が，LACの敷地上に架け渡される。これはブリッジに沿って非常に目立つ正面構成をLACに提供することになるだろう。いくつかの小さな歩道橋が既存の運河を越えて敷地をオリンピックパークへ結ぶ。

LACのデザインには，東西を結ぶストラトフォード・シティー・ブリッジとの接続や，運河沿いのオリンピックパークエリアの延長など，オリンピックパークとストラトフォードの都市計画に内在する主要な公共空間が取り込まれている。

〈配置構成〉

アクアティック・センターはストラトフォード・シティー・ブリッジに直交する軸線上に計画されている。この軸線に沿って，3つのプールが並ぶ。練習プールはブリッジの下にあり，競技プールと飛び込みプールは大きな容積を持つプールホールのなかにある。全体のコンセプトは，プールホールの基部を囲み，ブリッジへ連結することで基壇として組み立てることである。

基壇は，差異化され，細分化された様々なプログラム要素を，完全にブリッジと風景に同化しているように見える単一の建築ヴォリュームへと封じ込める。ブリッジ・レベルから見ると，基壇はブリッジの下面から現れ，プールホールの周りを段々になって低い運河側のレベルへと下がって行く。

プールホールはプールと同じ軸線に沿って弧を描く大屋根によって，基壇レベルの上にかたちを表す。その形態はオリンピック開催中の観客の視線を考えて構成されている。屋根を独特なものとしているパラボリック・アーチを構成するために二様の曲率が使われた。屋根の起伏は，プールホール内の競技プールと飛び込みプールのヴォリュームを視覚的に識別させてくれる。屋根は基部に続くプールホールの外皮を越えて突き出し，階段状に広がる外部エリアとブリッジ・エントランスまで覆うように延びる。

ブリッジ・エントランスの上に張り出した屋根は，ストラトフォードあるいはオリンピックパーク，どちらの進入路から近づいても，LACの存在を知らしめるだろう。屋根は，構造上，3つの主要な位置で着地している。それ以外は，屋根と基壇の間の開口はガラスのファサードでみたされる。

Architects: Zaha Hadid Architects—
Zaha Hadid with Patrik Schumacher, design;
Jim Heverin, project architect;
Sara Klomps, Hannes Schafelner, project team;
Saffet Bekiroglu, Mariana Ibanez, Marco Vanucci,
Karim Muallem, Kakakrai Suthadarat, Sujit Nair,
Feng Chen, Agnes Koltay, Gemma Douglas, competition
team
Client: London 2012 Olympics, London Development
Agency
Consultants: Ove Arups & Partners, London, structural
Program: Aquatics Centre for 2012 Summer Olympics
and future use
Total floor area: 24,000 m²

Jumping tower

Interior

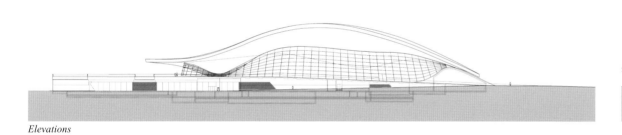
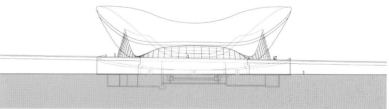

Elevations

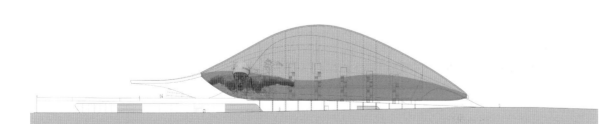
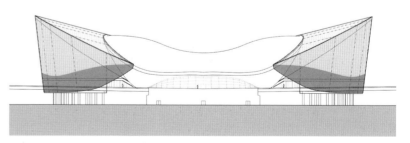

Elevations: Olympic mode

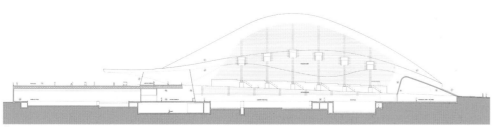
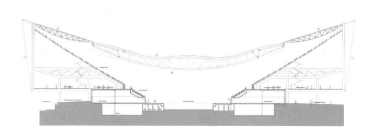

Sections

BRIDGE PAVILION FOR ZARAGOZA EXPO 2008

Zaragoza, Spain
Design: 2005–   Construction: –2008

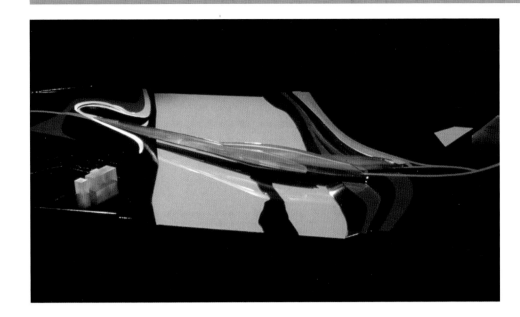

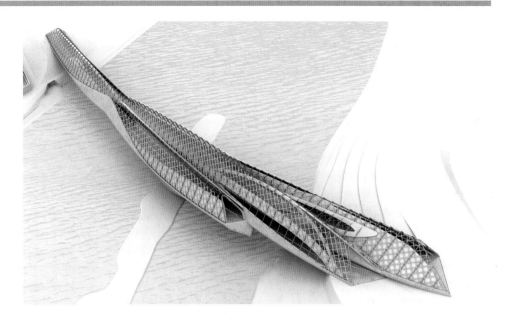

Under construction 2007.08.13.

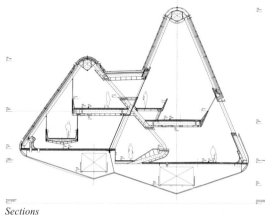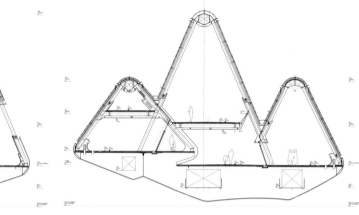

Sections

Zaha Hadid Architects' proposal for the Bridge Pavilion is organized around 4 main objects, or "pods" that perform both as structural elements and as spatial enclosures. Floors inside them are located at the Expo principal levels: +201.5 (the soffit of the bridge is at +200 m, flood protection minimum level), +203 m and +206, +207.5 for the upper level. The inception of our design for the bridge pavilion stems from the examination of the potential of a diamond-shaped section.

The "Diamond Section" works out perfectly on several levels.

As employed in the case of space-frame structures, it represents a rational way if distributing forces along a surface. Underneath this floor plate, a resulting triangular pocket space can be used to run utilities. The diamond section has been extruded along a slightly "Curved Path". The extrusion of this rhombus section along different paths generated four different "PODS".

The "Stacking" and "Interlocking" of these truss elements, or "pods" has two specific reasons: it optimises the structural system and allows for a natural differentiation of the pavilion interiors, where each pod corresponds to a specific exhibition space. Trusses/pods intersect bracing each other and loads are distributed across the four of them instead of a singular main element, with the result of reducing the size of load-bearing members.

The pods are stacked according to precise criteria, aimed at reducing the section of the bridge as much as possible where the span is longer (approximately 185 m from river island to right bank), and enlarging it where the bridge needs to span less (85 m from river island to Expo side). One long pod spans from the right riverbank to the island, where the other three are grafted in it, spanning from island to left bank.

The interlocking has had unforeseen but extremely interesting effects on our design. Interiors become exciting complex spaces, where visitors move from pod to pod though small in-between spaces that act as filters or buffer zones, tuning-down sound and visuals from one exhibition space to the next, therefore allowing for a clearer understanding of the art installation content. The identity of each pod remains thoroughly readable inside the pavilion, almost performing as a three-dimensional orientation device.

Spatial concern is one of the main drives of this project: each zone within the building is endeavoured of its own spatial identity, their nature varies from sheer interiors focused on artwork or open spaces with strong visual connection to the Ebro river and the Expo. Natural surfaces have been investigated when designing the Pavilion's "Skin".

Shark scales are fascinating paradigms both for their visual appearance and for their performance. Their pattern can easily wrap around complex curvatures with a simple system of rectilinear ridges. On a building scale, this proves to be performative, visually appealing and economically convenient.

The building's envelope plays an essential role in defining its relation to the surrounding environment and its atmospheric variation. The project has been designed imagining that its interior could be thoroughly enlivened by the effect of atmospheric agents, such as the Tramontana wind blowing along the Ebro and Zaragoza's sun. At Expo stage, a single weathering layer that protects it from rain will enclose the building. This skin will be generated by a complex pattern of simple overlapping shingles.

Some shingles can rotate around a pivot, allowing for temporary opening or closing of part of the façade. Levels of light range from rays through tiny punctual apertures to wide full size openings, via several degrees of aperture due to the way shingles overlap within each pattern. Large apertures are located on the lower level, in correspondence with either end of the bridge, allowing for full visual contact with Ebro and the Expo.

ブリッジ・パビリオンは，4つの主要素，すなわち構造としても空間を包み込むものとしても機能する"ポッド"を中心に構成されている。ポッド内の各階はエクスポの主要レベルに位置している：＋201.5m（ブリッジの底面は＋200m，洪水から守る最低レベル），上層は＋203m，＋206m，＋207.5m。ブリッジ・パビリオンのデザインは，ダイアモンド形断面の部材が持つポテンシャルを調べることから始まった。

"ダイアモンド・セクション"はいろいろなレベルで見事に役割を果たす。

スペースフレーム構造に使われている場合，それは表面に沿って力を配分する合理的な方法に対応する。この床版の下に生まれる三角形のポケット・スペースは，電気・ガス・水道の配管を通すのに使える。ダイアモンド・セクションはわずかに"湾曲する通路"に沿って押し出される。異なる通路に沿ったこの菱形部分の突出は，4つの異なる"ポッド"をつくりだす。

これらのトラス状の要素，すなわち"ポッド"を"積み重ね"，"噛み合わせる"ことには2つの明確な理由がある。構造システムを最適化すること，そしてパビリオン内部の自然な差異化を許し，ポッドをそれぞれ特定の展示空間に対応させることである。トラス/ポッドは互いに筋交いを交差させ，荷重を単一の主要素の代わりに4つのトラス/ポッドを横断して分散させる結果，耐力壁の部材の大きさを縮小できる。

スパンの長い側（川の島から右岸まで約185m）は出来るだけ橋の断面を減じ，短い側（川の島からエキスポ側まで85m）では拡大させることを意図して，ポッドは精確な規準に従って重ねられる。一つの長いポッドが右岸から島を架け渡し，他の三つのポッドは，そのなかに継ぎ足され，島から左岸を架け渡す。

この噛み合せは見えないが，デザインに非常に面白い効果を与える。内部は好奇心をかきたてる複雑な空間となり，訪れた人はポッドからポッドへと中間にある小さな隙間を通って移動する。ここは，フィルターあるいは緩衝地帯として働き，一つの展示空間から隣の展示空間への音や映像の伝達を弱めるので，アート・インスタレーションの展示内容をよりはっきりと理解できる。各ポッドの特質はパビリオンの中で完全に読み取れるように残り，ほとんど三次元の方向指示装置に近い役割を演じる。

空間への関心が，このプロジェクトを推進させる主要素の一つとなっている。建物内の各領域は，自らの空間特性を獲得しようと努め，その特徴はアートワークに照準を合わせた純然たるインテリアからエブロ川とエクスポ会場に視覚的に強くつながるオープン・スペースまで多様である。"パビリオンの外皮"をデザインするにあたっては，自然界にある表皮にヒントを探した。

鮫の鱗は，その視覚効果と操作性の両面において魅惑的なパラダイムである。そのパターンは建物の湾曲を，直線構成の畝を持つ単純なシステムで簡単に包むことが出来る。建物のスケールでも，有効であり，視覚に訴える魅力があり，経済性もあることが実証されている。

建物の外皮は，周辺環境とその大気の変化との関わりを遮るのにきわめて重要な役割を演じる。このプロジェクトでは，その内部が，エブロ川に沿って吹き寄せる北風，トラモンターナやサラゴサの陽射しのような大気の作用の影響によって全面的に活気づけられることを想像しながらデザインを進めた。エクスポ開催時には，雨から守る耐候性の一枚の層が建物を包み込むことになる。この外皮は単純に重ね合わされたこけら板がつくる複雑なパターンによって生成されるだろう。

いくつかのこけら板は旋回心軸の周りを回転させて，ファサードの一部を一時的に開いたり，閉ざしたりできる。光の強さや量は，小さな点のような孔から射し込む一筋の光線から，各パターン内でのこけら板の重ね方による様々な度合いの切れ目を通る光，広いフルサイズの開口から入る光まで多岐にわたる。大きな開口は下のレベルに，橋の両端と対応した位置にあり，エブロ川とエクスポ会場が広く見渡せる。

Architects: Zaha Hadid Architects—
Zaha Hadid with Patrik Schumacher, design;
Manuela Gatto, project architect;
Matthias Baer, Federico Dunkelberg, Fabian Hecker, Maria José Mendoza, José Monfa, Marta Rodriguez, Diego Rosales, Guillermo Ruiz, Lucio Santos, Hala Sheikh, Marcela Spadaro, Anat Stern, project team
Consultants: ARUP, engineering
Program: interactive exhibition area focussing on water sustainability, integrating a pedestrian bridge to perform as gateway for the Zaragoza Expo 2008
Total surface: 6,415m² (3,915m², exhibition surface; 2,500m², pedestrian bridge)

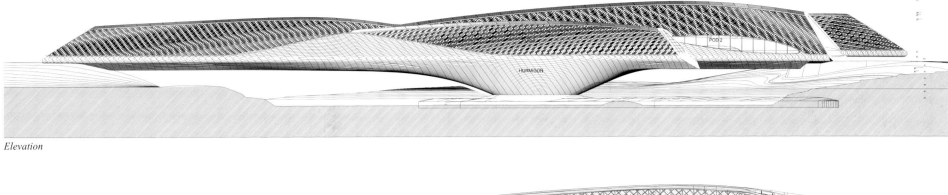

Elevation

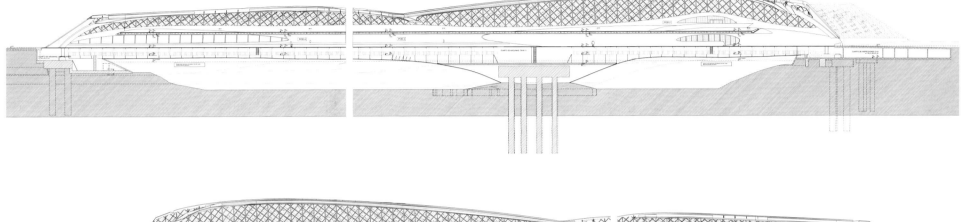

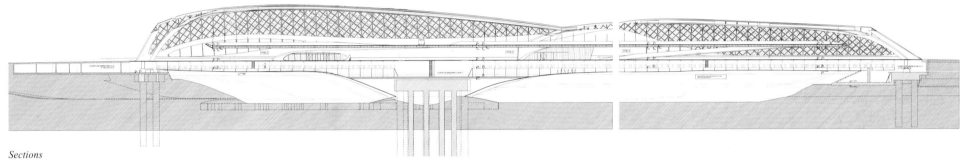

Sections

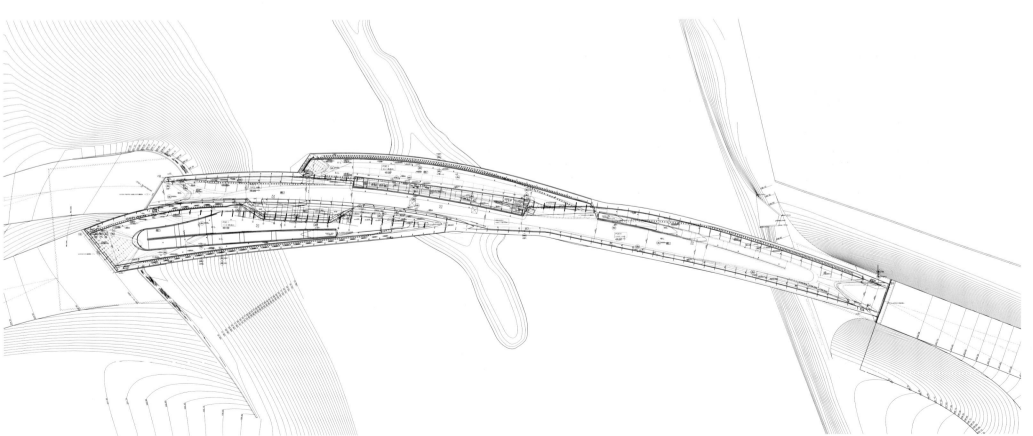

Plan S=1:1200

RESIDENCE IN BARVIKHA FOREST

Moscow, Russia
Design: 2006–

The project is located on the north-face hillside in Barvikha, Russia, where natural vegetation such as pine and birch trees grow up to 20 m high. Within this stunning location the programme of the villa is divided into two main components. The first one is strategically placed to be merged with the sloped landscape, while a separate volume floats, 22 meters above the ground to benefit from the dynamic views of the Barvikha forest over the trees.

The form for the villa comes from the natural topography. With its fluid geometries, the building emerges from the landscape, remaining partially embedded in the hillside, in order to articulate the existing surroundings with the artificial landscape.

The program is organized vertically on four levels. The lower level or basement is envisioned as leisure space; the programme in this level includes a living room, massage and fitness areas as well as sauna and hamman baths. One level up, main living room, dining, kitchen, entertainment, indoor swimming room and parking spaces are located on the ground floor. The main entrance lobby, study/library, guest room and children's room are distributed on the first floor while the master bedrooms and a lounge with exterior terrace occupy the upper level.

The two main components of the house are articulated by three legs. These concrete columns establish a strong dialogue between both levels while functioning as structural elements. Within the interior space of the legs are the vertical shafts required to place all mechanical elements and services connecting to the upper level. Incorporated within the space between the legs is the vertical circulation of the house where a transparent glass elevator and staircase are situated, providing a direct connection between the lower and the upper levels.

The main entrance to the house is located on the first floor. Within this space, the three concrete columns intersect the main roof, proposing skylights and a double-high space. The view from the living room, following the grand staircase located in the entrance lobby, is framed by two-curved in-situ cast concrete structures. These concrete structures serve both a structural purpose and the function purpose creating of the divisions between main living room, dining room and indoor swimming pool.

The major materials proposed for this project are pre-cast and in-situ cast concrete, steel and glass. To give the interior spaces a sense of fluid continuity, these materials are repeated throughout the whole villa.

The general concept for the design of the villa responds to a strategy that extends the exterior topography to the interior of the building, while its geometrical definition is derived from the surrounding environment of flowing terrain levels that are stretched to generate the new landscape, proposing a continuous integration between interior and exterior spaces.

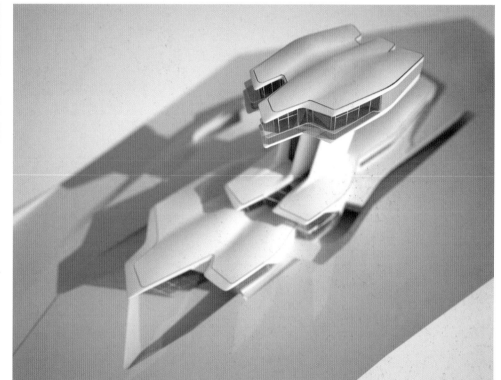

敷地は，ロシア，モスクワ近郊の保養地バルヴィーハの北斜面の丘にあり，周囲には高さ20mに達するマツやカバの自然林が広がる。このような非常に魅力的な敷地の中で，このヴィラは二つのヴォリュームに分かれて配置される。一つは斜面を利用してその風景に溶け込むように置かれ，もう一つの分離されたヴォリュームは，バルヴィーハの森の広大な眺めをほしいままに，地上22mの高さに浮かぶ。

建物の形は地形から引き出されたものである。その流体的な幾何学形態は，周囲の自然と人工の風景を明確に区別するために，一部，丘の斜面に埋め残したまま風景から浮かび上がる。

プログラムは，4つのレベルに分けられる。一番下のレベル，地下階はレジャー・スペースを想定したもので，居間，マッサージとフィットネス・エリア，サウナ，ハンマーム・バス。ここから1階上がると，メインの居間，食堂，台所，娯楽室，室内プール，駐車場が1階にある。メイン・エントランス・ロビー，書斎／ライブラリー，ゲストルーム，

子供の部屋はすべて2階にあり，さらにその上に主寝室，外にテラスの付いたラウンジが置かれる。

2つのメイン・コンポーネントは3本の脚によって明確に区分されている。これらのコンクリート柱は主要構造材でありかつ，各レベル間に強い関係性を生み出す。脚の内側は，上階につながるすべての機械設備が配置された垂直のシャフトである。脚の間は垂直動線で，透明なガラスのエレベータと階段が組み込まれ，下階と上階をダイレクトにつなぐ。

メインエントランスは2階にある。この広い空間で3本のコンクリート柱がメイン・ルーフと交差し，スカイライトと2層の吹抜けスペースをつくりだす。エントランスロビーの大階段の先に続く居間からの眺めは，現場打ちコンクリートの躯体がつくる二重の曲面で枠取られる。コンクリートの躯体は，構造としての役割と同時に，居間，食堂，室内プールを分ける役目も果たす。

主な構成材は，プレキャスト・コンクリート，現場打ちコンクリート，スティールとガラスを予定。

内部空間に流れるような連続性を付与するために，これらの材料は建物全体に連続して用いられる。

全体的なコンセプトは，外の地形を屋内にまで引き伸ばすことを目指したもので，幾何学的な輪郭が，様々なレベルの地層が流れるように続く周囲の環境から引き出され，内外のスペースを切れ目なく一体化する。

Architects: Zaha Hadid Architects—
Zaha Hadid with Patrik Schumacher, design;
Tetsuya Yamazaki, Helmust Kinzler, project architect;
Daniel Fiser, project designer; Anat Stem,
Daniel Santos, Thomas Sonder, Mariana Ibanez,
Marco Vanucci, Lourdes Sanchez, Ebru Simsek, project team
Consultants: Ove Arup & Partners, structural

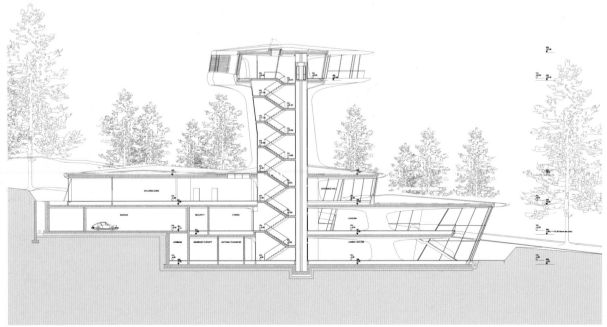

Section

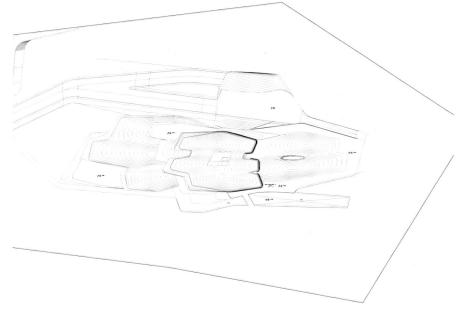

Site plan

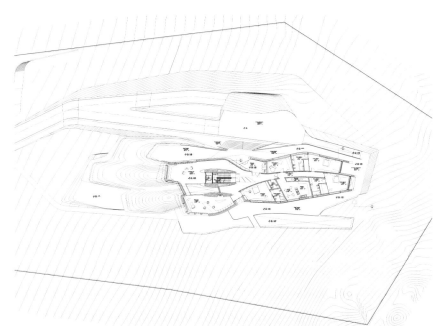

Level 2

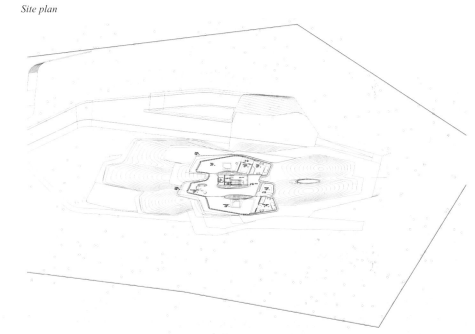

Level 3

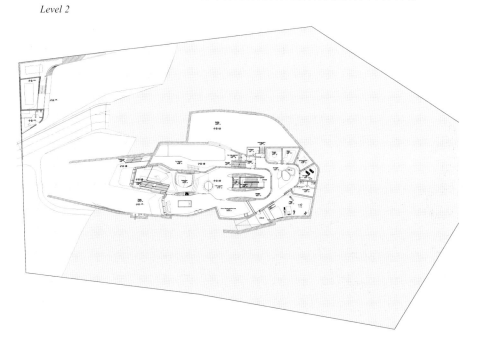

Level -1

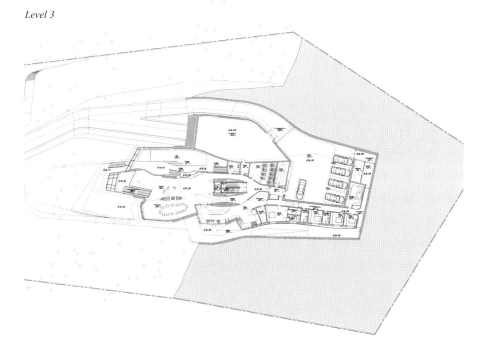

Level 1

DUBAI BUSINESS BAY – SIGNATURE TOWERS

Dubai, United Arab Emirates
Design: 2006–

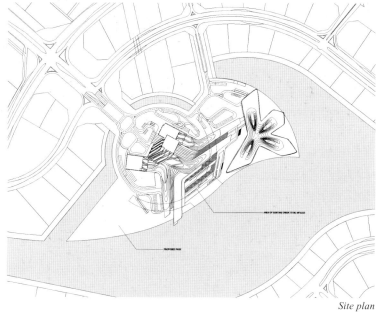

Site plan

Zaha Hadid's design for the Signature Towers confirms the role of Business Bay Development at the very forefront of Dubai's rapidly changing future. The three towers rise above the creek and project themselves as an icon for the surrounding developments and for the gulf region. The tower's striking design creates a new presence that punctures the skyline with a powerful recognizable silhouette. The fluid character of the towers is generated through an intrinsically dynamic composition of volumes. The towers are inter-twined to share programmatic elements and rotate to maximize the views from the site towards the creek and neighbouring developments. The design quality of the towers to act as a symbol and icon extends beyond their scale and location. These qualities are derived from the boldness of the architectural concept, from the 'choreographed' movement that combines the three towers in one overall gesture and 'weaves' with a series of public spaces through the podium, the bridges and the landscape beyond.

Context

There will, in the future, be a silhouette of towers, whose pinnacles will represent the hearts of the new districts within the greater metropolitan area of Dubai. On the ground, the Business Bay development site will become stitched into the proposed extended road and infrastructure network of the enlarged metropolitan area. The new pedestrian routes and roads passing under and around the Towers' development will extend across the creek, bringing people directly from Sheikh Zayed Road via a grid of major and minor thoroughfares and boulevards.

Connectivity and Public Space

The site is composed by 4 different parts: (A) central circular plot, (B) an elongated park plot, (C) the surface of the creek on axis of plot A and (D) a rectangular plot across the creek at the west margin. Connectivity between these parts becomes therefore central to the project; in order to produce an articulated design that encompasses both the scale and the different qualities of each of the parts, transforming them into a coherent scheme. The circular shape of the plot and attached vehicular circulation layout creates a barrier of vehicular traffic around the site, generating an island that detaches the plot from the waterfront promenade. By incorporat-

ing the design of two new link bridges and a new ground the project effectively multiplies the potential and connectivity of the site, linking the park at the East—via the towers with the water's edge at the West margin of the creek.

Programme

Programming of public and private life is an active tool to inject life into the space, integrating new layers of activity and landscape, creating a network of synergetic uses that can develop a new urban ecology.

The programme was addressed as a whole with the three towers corresponding directly to the three main functions: offices, hotel and residential. Together, the towers generate a critical mass of sustainable programmatic relationships. The towers share a common base/podium, designed as a materialized shadow of the towers and programmed with retail, restaurants and amenities that support the demand from the tower's population. The three towers are conjoined two by two, the Offices and the Hotel at the base and the Hotel and the Residential at the top. Through these adjacencies, the towers are strategically organized in a symbiotic relation, sharing certain segments of the programme. The advantage of joining the three towers in one organism, allows the development to be lived in a full day cycle: anchored in it's residential population, it reaches the peak of activity during office hours and it mutates through the diversity of the ever-changing population of the hotel. The heterogeneous population mix creates a cosmopolitan urban environment, constantly energized and renovated through it's own life.

ダンシング・タワーに対するザハ・ハディドのデザインは、ドバイの急速に変貌する未来に対する最前線としてのビジネス・ベイ開発の担う役割を立証している。3本のタワーはドバイ・クリークを見下ろして立ち上がり、周囲の開発地区及び湾岸地域のイコンであることを明快に表現する。タワーの強く人目を引くデザインは、力強く、すぐに判別できる輪郭によってスカイラインを穿つ新たな存在となる。流体のような性格は、ヴォリュームに本来備わっているダイナミックな構成に由来する。タワーはプログラムを共有するために捻り合わされ、クリークと近隣の開発地区がよく見通せるように向きを変える。シンボルやイコンとして振る舞う、独特なデザインの影響は、そのスケールや位置を越えて広がるだろう。これらの特徴は、建築コンセプトの大胆さ、つまり3本のタワーを一体化したジェスチャーとしてまとめ上げ、基壇、ブリッジ、前方のランドスケープ全体に一連の公共空間を"織り上げる"、舞踊のように"振り付けられた"動きから生まれている。

〈コンテクスト〉

将来、3本のタワーは見事なシルエットを描いて立ち、その尖塔はドバイ大都市圏の新しい地区の中心を示すものとなるだろう。地上では、ビジネス・ベイ開発地区の敷地は、拡大した大都市圏に計画されている道路の延長部やインフラ網と縫い合わされ、タワーの足下や周囲を抜ける新しい歩行者専用路と道路がクリークを横断して延び、人々はシェイク・ザイード通りから直接、格子状に広がる大小の街路や広い並木道を通ってここに導かれるだろう。

〈接続性と公共空間〉

敷地は4つの異なる部分で構成されている。（A）中央の円形の区画。（B）細長い公園の区画。（C）区画Aの軸線上にあるクリークの水面。（D）クリークを渡った西端の長方形の区画。従って、これらの区画間のつながりはプロジェクトの中心的課題となる。それぞれの区画のスケールや異なる性格を包括し、有機的に関係づけられたデザインを生み出すために、統一性のある構成へと変形される。円形の区画と付随する車線配置は敷地周りの車両交通を遮り、この区画を水辺の遊歩道から引き離すアイランドをつくりだす。2本の新しい接続ブリッジと新しく開発された土地のデザインを合体することで、東側で公園を、クリークの西端でタワーを経由して水辺と連結させながら、敷地の潜在力と接続性を効果的に高める。

〈プログラム〉

公私の生活の場をプログラムすることは、空間に生命を注入する有効な手段であり、さまざまな活動とランドスケープがつくりだす新たな階層を結合させ、新しい都市エコロジーの展開が可能な共同使用のネットワークをつくりだす。

プログラムは、オフィス、ホテル、住宅の3つの主要な機能にそれぞれ対応する3本のタワーを一体化したものとして構成される。3本のタワーはまとまって、持続可能なプログラムに基づいた結びつきをつくるのに十分な人の数と施設を生み出す。タワーは共通の基部／基壇を共有する。基壇はタワーの影を具体化したものとしてデザインされ、タワーに生活し利用するすべての人の要求を支える店舗、レストラン、アメニティが組み込まれる。3本のタワーは、オフィス棟とホテル棟が基部で、ホテル棟と住宅棟が頂部で、2本ずつ結合されている。こうした近接によって共生的関係を戦略的に組み立て、プログラムの一定部分を共有する。3本のタワーを一つの有機的組織体に接合する利点は、この開発地区を、24時間サイクルで生きる場にできることである。住宅棟によって確保されるタワーの人口は、オフィスアワーで頂点に達し、ホテルの常に変動する人々の多様性によって変化する。異種の人々の混在はコスモポリタンな都市環境をつくりだし、人それぞれの生活パターンによって常に活性化され、革新される。

Architects: Zaha Hadid Architects—
Zaha Hadid with Patrik Schumacher, design;
Chris Lepine, project architect;
Lars Teichmann, project director;
Chris Lepine, Stephan Wurster, Eren Ciraci, Alessio Constantini, David Campos Hoda Nobakhti, Chryssanthi Perpatidou, Bowornwan May Noradee, Nahed Jawad, Hussam Chakouf, Bassam Al Shiekh, Daniel Norell, Tomas Rabl, Chiara Ferrari, Erhan Patat, poject team; Tiago Correia, project architect (competition); Ana Cajiao, Saleem Abdel-Jalil, Sophie Le Bienvenu, Hooman Talebi ,Mathias Reisigl, Diego Rosales, Tyen Masten, Daewha Kang, Renos Constantino, Graham Modlen, design team (competition)
Client: Dubai Properties, Dubai, United Arab Emirates
Program: offices, hotel, residential, retail, bridge, waterfront park and promenade
Total floorl area: 500,000 m²

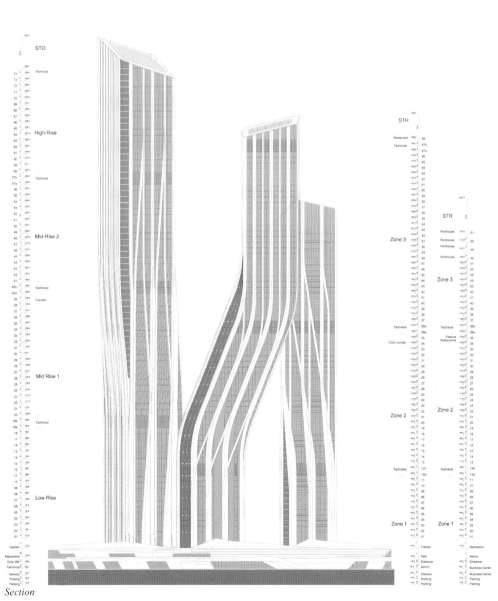

Section

ISSAM FARES INSTITUTE FOR PUBLIC POLICY & INTERNATIONAL AFFAIRS, AMERICAN UNIVERSITY OF BEIRUT

Beirut, Lebanon
Design: 2006–

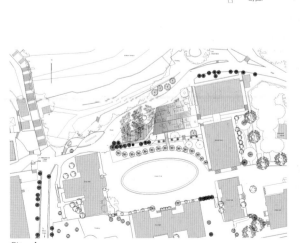

Site plan

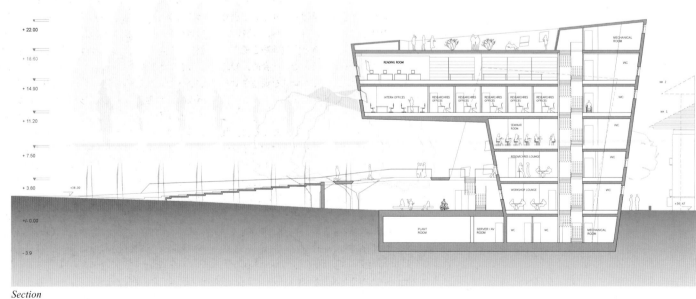

Section

Introduction

The Issam Fares Institute for Public Policy and International Affairs at the American University of Beirut is designed not only to attract students and academics but also to draw local, regional and international researchers, thinkers and policy makers. Their work projects and strategizes current and future policy decisions in Lebanon and the Middle East. Our proposal aims to reflect and facilitate that social and intellectual program.

Urban and Site Strategy

The design approach accommodates the existing site landscape conditions which allow the IFI to function in a harmonious fashion. The building emerges fluidly from the geometry of the surrounding network of public paths as opposed to sitting on the land as an isolated object.

The form of the building flows as an undulating extension of the site moving up to create different dynamic spaces and then vanishes back into the terrain. The gesture extends beyond the limitations of the site, creating a structure that is open and spacious—two qualities that rarely result from the construction of a confined building in a small site.

Programme and Circulation Strategy

After having carefully analysed the pedestrian flow through and around the site in relation to adjacent and existing buildings at the AUB campus—and after examining the programmatic requirements we propose the following architectural solution:

The IFI is to be accessed from two main public entrances. The West entrance gently ramps up to the second floor from grade level where the Directors office, Administration and Researchers Lounges are located. The East entrance leads to the first floor where the Conference/Workshop, break-out rooms and lounge spaces are situated. The Researchers' offices and seminar rooms are located on the third floor and fourth floor. The entire fifth floor is the Reading Room and above that is a roof terrace that allows one to look out on to the surrounding landscape.

The Auditorium and its related amenities are located underground creating a comfortable and quiet academic space. The third and fourth floors are connected via bridges through the atrium leading clearly to an escape core at each end of the building.

Spatial Character

The two opposite entrances, partly interwoven, are strategically situated at the nexus of several primary circulation paths, one leading directly from the east while the other gently slopes cutting through the main atrium hall to the west. Thus, the atrium blurs the line between building and landscape. On the western side of the site, the sloping up of the ramp and stairs provides new outdoor spaces for AUB students to relax within the shaded confines of the existing preserved trees. These areas are magnified by the welcoming double height feature which in turn preserves and emphasises the lines of sight from

the oval towards the sea to the north.

Facing the interior of the building atrium are two glass walls that visually connect and physically bind the building together. This merging of the building further encourages the main social strategy of the project which is to enable the users to gather, interact and then disperse.

The roof garden offers an exclusive scenic view towards the lower campus and the sea to the north as well as the oval and the surrounding area to the south. Plantings for the reduction of heat gain and the preservation of rainwater for site landscaping use are located on the roof.

Materiality

The main structural elements are built from in-situ concrete. Exterior walls are structural with fenestrations to allow for pleasant and cool interior conditions. One cantilever beam and wall supports the third floor and above. The clear floor to floor height is three meters with an additional nine centimetres depth for the placement of services and use of floors finishes.

The local ground conditions are thought to consist of voided limestone overlain by sand. Therefore, shallow strip foundations will bear onto the rock. A soil nailing method will allow steeper excavation sides, thus reducing the excavation area required and diminish the impact made on the adjacent buildings and trees.

Waterproofing and a drained cavity will be used together to provide suitable dry basement conditions, as the rock in the area is highly permeable.

Furthermore, the IFI building site lies within 20 kilometres of a major fault line. Therefore, a seismic analysis of the area will be carried out to inform the design and determine the load conditions and necessary precautions for the construction of a building on the particular site.

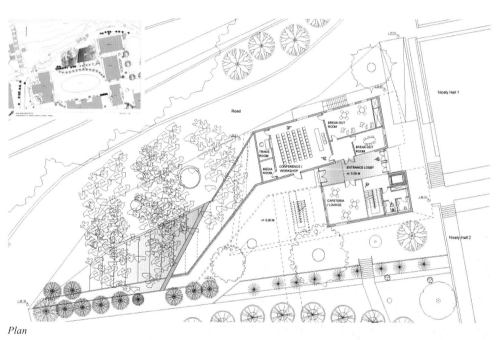

Plan

〈概要〉

ベイルート・アメリカ大学付属イッサム・ファーレス公共政策国際問題研究所には，学生や学者ばかりでなく，地元や地方，さらには世界各国の研究者，思想家，政策担当者をも惹き付けるデザインが求められる。彼らの仕事は，レバノンや中東に於ける，現在及び未来の政策決定の立案と実施戦略を練ることである。このプロポーザルは，その社会的，知的プログラムを反映させ，そうした研究を促進させる施設とすることを目標に設計される。

〈都市と敷地に関わる戦略〉

IFIが周囲と調和を保ちながら機能するように，敷地の既存風景に適合させることを考えてデザインが進められた。建物は，孤立したオブジェクトとして土地の上に置かれるのとはまったく逆に，周囲の公共通路のネットワークから流動体のように現れる。建物の形態は，起伏する土地の延長のように流れ出て，それぞれに異なるダイナミックなスペースを構成するために上昇し，次に，地中に再び戻り消えて行く。こうした身振りの影響は敷地の境界を越えて広がり，オープンで広々とした空間を持つ構造体を

つくりだす。この2つの特徴を，狭い敷地の小さな建物で実現できるのは稀なことである。

〈プログラムと動線に関わる戦略〉

AUBキャンパスの，隣接する建物や既存建物との関わりのなかで，敷地を通り抜け，あちこちと回る歩行者の流れを慎重に分析し，さらにプログラム上の要求を検討した後，以下の建築構成を提案した。

IFIには2つの主要なパブリック・エントランスが必要である。西エントランスは地上レベルから，所長室，管理部門，研究者のラウンジのある2階へゆるやかなスロープとなって上がる。東エントランスは会議室／ワークショップ，休憩室，ラウンジ・スペースが配置された1階へ導く。研究者のオフィスとセミナー室は3，4階にある。5階はすべて閲覧室で，その上には屋上テラスがあり，周囲の風景が見晴らせる。

講堂とその関連施設は地下にあり，快適で静かな，学研生活に相応しい空間である。3階と4階は，アトリウムに架け渡されたブリッジで結ばれる。ブリッジは建物の各端部にある緊急時の避難用コアへ分かりやすい経路で通じている。

〈空間の特徴〉

互いに向き合い，部分的に絡み合う2つのエントランスはいくつかの主要動線を構成する通路の連結地点に戦略的に配置される。通路の一つは東から直接延び，他方は緩やかなスロープとなってメイン・アトリウム・ホールを貫いて西に向かう。この結果，アトリウムは建物とランドスケープの間の境界線を曖昧にする。敷地の西側には，上がって行くランプと階段が，保存された木立がつくる日影のなかでAUBの学生が憩えるように新しい戸外スペースをつくりだす。これらのエリアは，人を喜んで迎えるような2層の高さを持つ構成によって大きく見え，また，敷地に隣接するグリーン・オーヴァルから北の海に向かう見通しを守り，強化する。

アトリウム内で向き合う2枚のガラス壁は，建物を視覚的に結び，物理的に束ねて一つにする。この，建物全体の合流によって，プロジェクトの重要テーマである，建物の利用者が集い，話を交わし，そしてまた散らばって行く場という交流のための戦略はさらに促進される。屋上庭園からは，足下のキャンパス，北には海，そしてオーヴァルと南に広がる周辺領域など，広々とした景色が見晴らせる。屋上には熱取得を抑えるための植栽を行い，敷地の造園に使う雨水の貯水層を設置する。

〈建設〉

主構造は現場打ちコンクリート。外壁は構造壁で，屋内を快適で涼しくするような窓割りを行う。1本の片持ち梁と1枚の壁が3階とその上の階を支持する。床から床までの正味高さは3mで，配線配管の設置と床材のために9cmの深さが付加される。

この地域の土壌の組成は，砂に覆われた有孔の石灰石であることについて検討が行われた。従って，浅い帯状基礎を岩の上へ押し入れることになるだろう。鉄筋補強工は，地盤の側面を急勾配で根切りができる結果，必要な根切りの面積を減少させ，隣の建物や木々への影響を小さくする。

この地域の岩は非常に水が浸透しやすいので，防水と排水溝を併用することで，地下階を適度に乾燥した状態に置く。

さらに，IFIの敷地は大断層線から20kmの範囲内にある。従って，設計，荷重条件の決定，この特殊な条件下にある土地への建設に必要な事前対策に情報を提供するために，この地域の地震についての分析が行われるだろう。

Architects: Zaha Hadid Architects—
Zaha Hadid with Patrik Schumacher, design;
Saleem Abdel Jalil, project architect;
Graham Modlen, Karim Muallem, Human Talebi,
Brandon Buck, Miya Ushida, project team
Client: AUB American University of Beirut
Consultants: ARUP—Paul Nuttal, Kathy Beadle, structural; ARUP —Francisco Aguirre, Daniel Kelly,
Simon Reynolds, mechanical & electrical; ARUP and
Marshall Day Acoustics—Dr. Harold Marshall,
Peter Fearnside, Peter Exton, Frank Butera, acoustics;
Gross Max, landscape

SZERVITA SQUARE

Budapest, Hungary
Design: 2006–   Construction: –2010

The new building on Szervita Square will enhance Budapest by providing a new landmark. Both building and square are an iconic attraction for the inner city of the contemporary Budapest.

Our goal is to give the inner city an injection of contemporary elegance. A state of the art building with high quality work spaces would strengthen the multifunctional character and urban vitality of Budapest's city centre. We perceive the need to balance divers' requirements: keeping the importance of the cultural heritage in mind the issue is to reconcile the functional, economic and historic preservation needs of the city centre. We feel that aesthetic and atmospheric rejuvenation is always an essential part of preservation—preserving the vitality of a historic city centre.

One can perceive distinguished architectural periods in the development of Budapest's inner city fabric. Szervita Square itself is an interesting example with high quality architecture from different periods being gathered around the square. We have an important opportunity now to continue this series with another significant piece of architecture that can represent the architectural thinking of our time.

Continued Urban Vitality

The historic city must maintain its function not only as a cultural centre, retail centre and provider of tourist destinations, but equally as a central business location that provides top value work and business communication spaces.

The continued importance as a business hub is dependent upon, the provision of appropriate space for expansion purposes. State of the art spaces should be provided within the city centre to prevent the rush to the outskirts. Such space provision can not easily be achieved in historic buildings. The historic substance might therefore be supplemented with carefully inserted new elements.

European city centers run the risk of loose their function as an economic center if the provision of attractive central space is not succeeding. Here at Szervita we have a nice possibility to bring innovative business into the centre of the city, contributing to the vitality of the centre and of Szervita Square in particular. Our proposal is intended to contribute the city's ambition to stay at the heart of innovative economic life.

Animation of the Square

Conservation and the care of the historical squares and piazzas are an important contribution to the image and life of the city. Our proposal provides an underground car park in order to reduce parking spaces on the surface of the square. The square can thus be fully utilized as public relaxation space, aesthetically enhanced by the new building and animated by the provision of retail, a cafe etc.

Work and Leisure

Apart from shops in the basement level, we suggest to have leisure areas as a restaurant and nightclub or a gym as a complement to the offices in the upper floors. As a means of increasing leisure activities those will serve not only the users of the building but also the neighborhood. It will increase the fluctuation in circulation so that a high level of activity in the lower floors can be guaranteed outside the normal working or shopping hours.

A stunning bar that takes advantage of the astonishing view over the city at the top of the building will help to keep the area busy at night.

Landmark Building—Iconic Piazza

The whole ensemble is composed of two components merging into one unity: The building and the square.

The building itself embraces the square and at the same time constitutes its vertical frame. Vice versa the piazza as the horizontal element in front of it complements the building as by providing an outdoor space to the functions of the interior.

The buildings height is lower close to the low rising baroque building on its north and rising higher towards the other side of the square opposite to the tower of the baroque Szervita church, hence communicating with its surrounding and incorporating the existing urban forces into its form. The fluid shape bends around the square and provides different views from all sides—an ever changing silhouette. From the south-west we perceive it as a very slim body and from the south and north views we see the form dramatically rising up.

The facade of the building melts into the skin of the square. The square itself is a dish, an urban sink that provides different qualities of atmosphere as well as distinct public areas.

In its continuous movement the skin of the composition becomes first a facade that fades into the piazza and finally sweeps up at the end to become a canopy that will provide not only sun shading but an intimate area protected from the noise of the inner city.

The components of the building are layered on top of each other, but generated from the same dramatic principle and therefore correspond to one another structurally, aesthetically and formally: core, structure, skin and brise soleil. The result is a composition that serves as a single iconic figure.

As an additional unique feature we added the brise soleil to the facade. It is not only aesthetic but also a functional purpose to serve as sun shading and guarantees for a comfortable climate in the office spaces above… The form of the brise soleil is projected to the piazza where it becomes urban furniture, either as pads that can be used to rest on or the pits that can be used as an outdoor space for the restaurant/cafe and some of them even become skylights to provide daylight for areas underneath. In their arrangement this urban furniture produces a soft urban landscape.

The brise soleil is partially subdivided into smaller elements; their depth is defined by the angle of the sun. The density of the brise soleil is perceived differently from each angle of the pedestrian. The movement of the pedestrian in turn animates the brise soleil.

The structural skin, together with the concrete core, forms the load bearing system. This minimizes the columns required, leaving us with open spaces to be separated as desired.

The piazza has two main entrances, one from the north and one from the south both leading to the sunken main entrance of the building. We provide another secondary entrance from the rear of the building as a convenient access from the ground level. The lower main entrance on the basement level is 2 levels high and is not only visually but also physically connected to the secondary entrance above. It is an inviting gesture and the spaces created by this way allow the activity of the square to take place in the inside as well.

Parking is provided under ground to serve not only the inhabitants of the building but the surrounding as well.

Sustainability

The roof of the building is covered with transparent photovoltaic solar panels. Together with other renewable sources such as geothermal energy to support power supply, it will provide a major amount of the energy. It is important to achieve a sustainable design especially with regards to energy efficiency; a thoughtful, innovative building design with solid construction forms a basis for that.

A new generation of office buildings should be a place that people enjoy, providing optimized comfort conditions and a bright and inviting environment. The goal is to create a high level of comfort while minimizing energy consumption.

Our sustainable approach aims to provide an environment of the highest quality with a minimal ecological footprint, setting an example for contemporary building design.

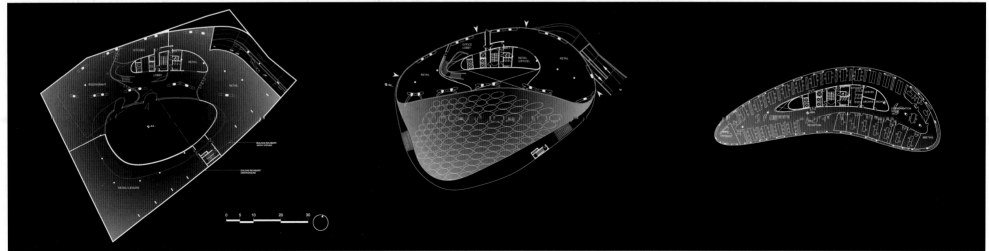

Basement: retail, -4.0m   Ground level: +0m   Level 5: office, +20m

セルヴィータ広場に計画されている建物は新しいランドマークとなり，ブダペストの真価を高めるだろう。建物と広場は共に，現代のブダペスト旧市街に人を引きつけるイコンのような存在となる。

　目標は旧市街に現代的な優美さを注入することである。質の高いワークスペースを持つ最先端の建物は，ブダペスト中心部の多機能的な性格と都市の活力を高めるだろう。私たちは多様な要求を均衡させる必要があることを理解している。問題は，文化遺産の重要性を心に留めながら，都心の機能，経済，歴史的保存，それぞれの面でのニーズを融和させることである。美しさや，雰囲気を若返らせることは保存に――つまり，歴史ある都心の活力を保持することに不可欠な部分であると思う。

　ブダペスト旧市街の発展の歴史には，一際目立つ建築の時代があることに気づかされる。セルヴィータ広場そのものが，異なる時代に建てられてきた優れた建築をその周りに集めた，興味深い例証である。現代の建築思考を表現できる，もう一つの意義深い建築作品によってこのシリーズを継続させる重要な機会を私たちは今，持つことになった。

〈都市の活力を維持する〉
この歴史ある都市は，文化の中心地，ショッピングの中心地，ツーリストの目的地の提供者としてだけでなく，同様に，最高レベルの，仕事やビジネスのコミュニケーション・スペースを提供する中心的なビジネスの場所として，その機能を維持する必要がある。

　ビジネス・ハブとしての存在感の維持は，拡大する用途に対する適切なスペースの供給に左右される。都市周縁への需要の殺到を防ぐために，最先端のオフィス・スペースが都心に提供されなければならない。こうしたスペースの供給は，歴史的な建物のなかでは簡単ではない。従って，歴史的建築は，慎重に挿入された新しい要素によって補完されるだろう。

　ヨーロッパの都心は，魅力的な中心スペースの供給が成されなければ，経済の中心としてのその機能を失う危険に陥るだろう。セルヴィータには，街の中心に革新的なビジネスを運び込み，中心部，特に

セルヴィータ広場の活力に貢献できる十分な可能性がある。計画案は，革新的な経済生活の中心に留まろうという街の野心に応えることを意図している。

〈広場を活気づける〉
歴史的な広場や小広場の保存や管理はこの街のイメージや生活に対する重要な貢献である。ここでは広場の駐車スペースを減らすために地下駐車場の設置を提案している。広場はこうして，人々が憩う場所として全体を使えるようになり，新しい建物で美しさが強化され，小売店やカフェなどが加わることで活気づくだろう。

〈仕事と余暇〉
地下階の店舗の他に，上階のオフィスを補足するものとしてレストランやナイトクラブ，ジムなど，余暇のためのエリアの設置を提案する。増加する余暇活動に対処する方法として，これらは，建物のユーザーのみならず，近隣の人々にも役立つだろう。それは人の流れを大きく変動させ，低層階の活発な動きを，通常の勤務時間やショッピングアワー以外でも保証するだろう。最上階の，市街の素晴らしい眺めを生かした，目の覚めるような位置にあるバーは，夜もこの界隈を賑やかにしてくれるだろう。

〈ランドマーク・ビルディングとイコンのような広場〉
一つに溶け込んで行く2つの要素，建物と広場が全体的な効果をつくりあげる。建物は，広場を囲み，同時にその垂直のフレームを組み立てる。反対に，広場はその前に広がる水平要素として，屋内の機能に対し戸外スペースを提供することで建物を補足する。

　建物の高さは，北にある低層のバロック建築に近づくにつれて低くなり，背の高いバロックのセルヴィータ教会と向き合う，広場のもう一方の側に向かって高くなる。これによって，その周囲と対話を交わし，既存の都市のエネルギーをその形態のなかに合体させる。流体のようなかたちは，広場を囲んで曲がり，どの側面から見ても異なる姿，変化し続ける輪郭を見せる。南西からは非常にスリムなボディーに気づき，南と北からは，劇的に上昇する形態を見ることになる。

建物のファサードは広場の被膜のなかに溶解して行く。広場そのものは，一枚の皿，都市のシンクでもあり，様々な性格の雰囲気，明確な公共空間を提供する。その連続する動きのなかに，合成材でつくられた被膜は最初に，広場のなかに消えて行くファサードとなり，最後に，終端で掃くように上昇しキャノピーとなる。キャノピーは，日影ばかりでなく，旧市街の騒音から守られたエリアを提供するだろう。

　建物の構成要素は互いに上に重ねられて行くが，同じドラマチックな原則から生まれ，それゆえに互いに，構造的にも，美的にも，形態的にも調和する――コア，構造，被膜，ブリーズソレイユ。この結果，一つのイコンのような姿が現れる。

　特徴のある付加的要素として，ファサードにブリーズソレイユを加えた。美的理由からだけでなく，日除けとして働き，上方のオフィス・スペースに快適な気候を保証する機能的な目的がある。ブリーズソレイユは広場に突き出し，腰を下ろせるパッドなどの都市の家具や，戸外のレストラン／カフェとして使えるピットとなり，そのいくつかは下のエリアに外光を送るスカイライトにさえなる。その配置によって，この都市の家具はしなやかな都市のランドスケープをつくりだす。

　ブリーズソレイユは部分的に小さなエレメントへと細分され，その深さは太陽の角度によって規定される。ブリーズソレイユの密度は，歩行者の見る角度によって異なる。逆に，歩行者の動きはブリーズソレイユを活気づける。

　構造的な被膜は，コンクリート造のコアと共に荷重を受けるシステムを形成する。このシステムは，必要な柱の数を最小限にし，希望により仕切れるオープン・スペースを残してくれる。

　広場には2つの主要な入口がある。一つは北から，一つは南からで，どちらも建物の一段低くなったメイン・エントランスへ導く。1階からの便利なアクセスとして建物の背面から入る2つ目のエントランスがある。地下階に面し，低い位置にあるメイン・エントランスは2層の高さで，視覚的にも物理的にも上の2つ目のエントランスとはつながっていな

い。それは人を誘うジェスチャーであり，ここに生まれたスペースによって，広場での活動は内部でも同様に行える。地下の駐車場は，建物の利用者ばかりでなく近所の人も利用できる。

〈サステナビリティ〉
建物の屋根は透明な光電子ソーラーパネルで覆われる。電力供給を補助する地熱エネルギーのようなその他の再生可能資源と併せて電力の大半を供給するだろう。持続可能なデザインの達成は，特にエネルギー効率の点で重要である。ソリッドな建築形態を持つ，考え抜かれた，革新的なデザインがそのための基礎となる。

　オフィスビルの新世代は，人々が楽しめ，最適化された快適なコンディション，明るく，感じの良い環境を提供する場所であるべきだろう。目標は，エネルギー消費を最小限に抑えながら，高レベルの快適さをつくりだすことである。

　私たちのサステナビリティへの取組みは，コンテンポラリーな建築デザインのための模範となるような，環境への影響を最小にし，最高の質を持つ環境を提供することを目指している。

Architects: Zaha Hadid Architects—
Zaha Hadid with Patrik Schumacher, design;
Ebru Simsek, project architect;
William Tan, Ting Ting Zhang, design team
Client: Orco Property Group
Consultants: Adams Kara Taylor, structural;
Program: office and retail
Total floor area: 35,000 m² (approx.)
Size: 48 m height/11 storeys

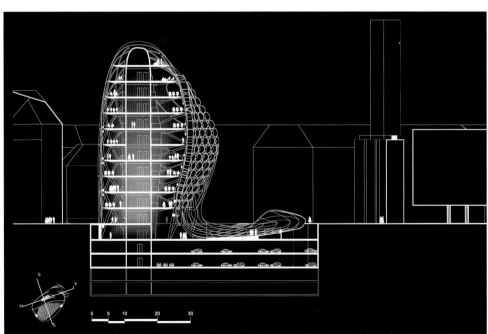

Transverse section

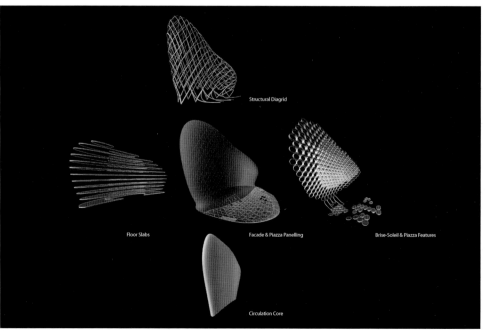

Structural Diagrid

Floor Slabs　　Facade & Piazza Panelling　　Brise-Soleil & Piazza Features

Circulation Core

Diagram: structures

UNIVERSITY OF SEVILLE LIBRARY

Seville, Spain
Design: 2006–   Construction: –2009

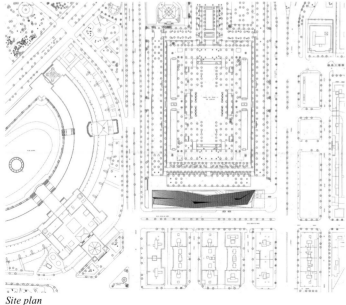

Site plan

The General Library and the Investigative Resources Centre of the University of Seville is conceived as a continuous volume which emerges from the extension of the park. The project expands itself longitudinally to the given site, and progressively rises from a soft material into a stretched sculptural object.

Located on the edge 'el Prado de San Sebastián' park, the 160 m long library is lifted off the ground to float on top of four structures which extend to a very shallow plinth; allowing the introduction of landscape at the entrance level, and producing terraces that in turn defines the public spaces.

This strategy of having a transitory area that attracts and invites the users is mainly to promote cultural, educational and entertaining activities for the students of the university. Therefore, the Library performs as an attractor, not only for the users of the park, but also for the 3,300 researchers; becoming a new centre for the university and the City of Seville.

Lately, the concept for university libraries and specially a library which introduces technology in the process of research have changed. Our design research proposes a reading space hierarchically on top of the other spaces, which will be gradually distinctive. The technology is manifested in smaller spaces, where the user will be informed; more than technical requirements of big scale spaces, the emergent quality of these spaces is about communication and distribution of the information which they generate; in contrast with the reading space, which the user's comfort is given in terms of reading concentration.

In terms of materiality, the architecture of the building is conceived mainly in concrete and a number of glass fenestrations, generating a pleasant temperature in the inside.

Accessibility and Context

The site is delimited clockwise starting north; by a busy avenue which will hold the future Metro station 'Prado de San Sebastián', a residential buildings street, a medium traffic avenue, and the park, which tend to be gradiently quiet. From this point the design premises take place, and so the directionality of the building: north-south pointing to the 'Plaza España'.

The movement is read formally, by means of the facade treatment and through a main skylight which crosses the whole concrete structure from north to south. Therefore, gathering the spaces with more flow of activities in the north, and the main library space with a triple level reading room in the south.

The attending public comprises three groups of users: pedestrians coming from the main university campus and other university centres who cross the park, flow of people using public transport, and users with own vehicle. Therefore, the accesses to the building will be located respectively: in the west facade, as a prolongation of the central plaza and pathways of the park-main entrance, drop-off entrance with pedestrian ramp in the east facade, and entry to the parking from the north road.

Programme

The design scheme is based on a half-basement podium appearing over the level of the street, locating the storage spaces, workshops, parking and plant rooms ventilated and illuminated through tall windows.

On top of the platform the park is extended to form the public spaces which become transition areas between the park and the library located on the top floors. The users access the building through gardens and four nubs which contain the common zones: reception, conference room, exhibition room, cafeteria, and bookshop; all integrated to the adjacent context of 'el Prado.'

Due to the linearity of the plot the cores/lifts have been distributed along the back facade allowing extensive views to 'el Prado' for the waiting and reading spaces.

The main reception hall is defined by a striking twist at the centre of the longitudinal structure. The main triple height area becomes the hub of the General Library and the Investigative Resources Centre which in turn distributes channels towards the two wings on each level. On the first floor we have located the special service zone for the recuperation of scientific and technical information, and also, the zone of assistance to application to the TICS and audiovisual means.

The second floor contains the reference and study zone for students, concluding the lecture room which expects to house 600 readers. A space for 20,000 books is located in the central atrium of a triple height space with three levels of terraces. The atrium is illuminated by a skylight which runs along the north-south axis of the building.

セビリア大学の総合図書館と資源研究センターは公園の延長のように現れる連続するヴォリュームとして考えられている。建物は敷地の長手方向に広がり，柔らかな材料から，引き伸ばされた彫刻的なオブジェクトへと漸進的に立ち上がる。

"エル・プラド・デ・サン・セバスチャン"公園の端に位置し，長さ160mの図書館は，非常に浅い台座の上へ延びる4つの構造体の最上部に，浮かぶように地上から持ち上げられる。それによってエントランス階にランドスケープを導き入れ，反対側に公共空間を縁取るテラスをつくりだす。

利用者を引き付け，招き寄せる移動空間にするという戦略は，主に学生の，文化，教育，エンタテインメントに関わる活動を促進するためである。従って，図書館は公園の利用者ばかりでなく，3,300人の研究者のためのアトラクターの役割を果たし，大学とセビリア市のための新しいセンターとなる。

近年，大学図書館のコンセプトは，特に研究過程にテクノロジーを導入している図書館のコンセプトは変化している。この点についてのデザイン研究の結果，閲覧室は，ヒエラルキーをつけて他のスペースの最上部に置くことを提案した。階層的な差異は徐々に明確になって行く。テクノロジーは，閲覧室より小さなスペースで発揮され，利用者は情報の伝達と配布という性格を持つ環境のなかで，大空間のなかでよりも多くの情報を提供されるだろう。読書への集中という点では，これらのスペースが与えてくれる利用者の快適性は，閲覧室とは対照的である。

材料の点では，建物の構造は主にコンクリート造とし，ガラス張りの数多くの開口が屋内を気持ちのよい温度に保つ。

〈アクセスとコンテクスト〉
敷地は北を起点として時計回りに，将来，地下鉄の"プラド・デ・サン・セバスチャン"駅が出来る予定の賑やかな大通り，住宅の並ぶ通り，中程度の交通量の大通り，静かな公園と順に境界を接している。これがデザインの前提となり，建物の方位は"プラザ・エスパーニャ"に向いた南北軸をとることになった。

人の動きは，ファサードの扱いと，北から南へコンクリートの構造体の全長に渡されたメイン・スカイライトによって形態から判読できる。北側に人の流れを多く集め，3層の閲覧室のある図書館のメイン・スペースは南に置かれる。

利用者は3つのグループで構成される。メインの大学キャンパスから来る歩行者と公園を横切って来る他の大学センターからの歩行者。公共交通を利用する人の流れ，そして自分の車で来る利用者。従って，建物へのアクセスは順次，別々に設置されるだろう。西側ファサードには，中央広場と公園の道の延長としてのエントランス。東側ファサードにはメイン・エントランスと歩行者専用ランプの付いた降車地点にあるエントランス。駐車場へは北側の道路から入る。

〈プログラム〉
デザイン・スキームは，道路レベルの上に現れる半地下の基壇をベースとしている。ここには倉庫，ワークショップ，駐車場，機械室が置かれ，背の高い窓によって換気され，外光が入る。

基壇の上まで公園が延びてきて公共空間を構成し，公園と最上階に位置する図書館の間の移行エリ

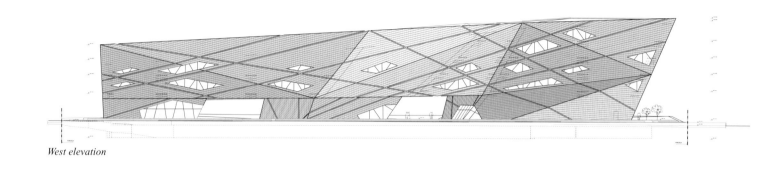

West elevation

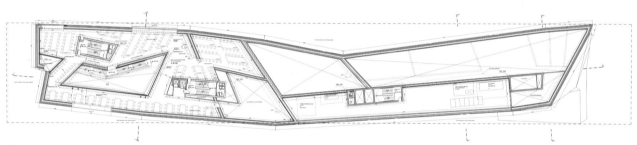

First mezzanine

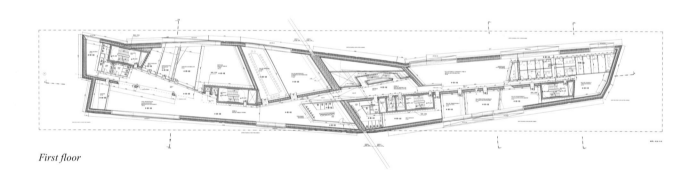

First floor

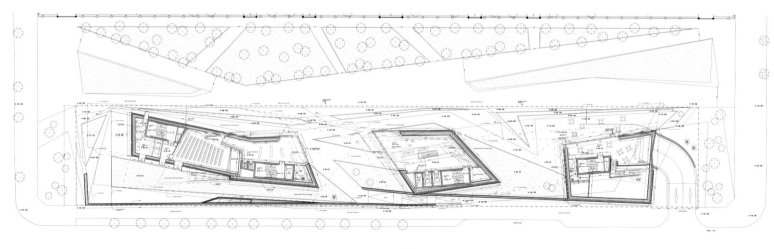

Ground floor

アとなる。利用者は庭園と4つの核を通って建物にアクセスする。4つの核には共有ゾーン，レセプション，会議室，展示室，カフェテリア，ブックショップが入っており，すべて，隣接する"エル・プラド"のコンテクストに統合される。

線形の敷地のために，コア／エレベータは背面に沿って配置されているので，待合室と閲覧室からは"エル・プラド"が遮るものなく見通せる。

メイン・レセプションホールは長く延びる建物の中心に構成された非常に目立つツイストによって境界がつけられている。3層吹抜きとなったメイン・エリアは，総合図書館と資源調査センターのハブとなり，交互に各階で2つのウィングに向かって径路を配分する。2階には，科学技術情報を提供する特別サービス・ゾーン，また，TICS（情報通信技術）やオーディオビジュアル媒体の利用のための支援ゾーンが置かれる。

3階には，学生のためのリファレンスと学習ゾーンがあり，600人の読者の収容が想定される講義室が端部にくる。2万冊の蔵書を収めるスペースは，3つの階それぞれにテラスの付いた，3層吹抜けた中央アトリウムに配置される。アトリウムは建物の北から南に沿って延びるスカイライトからの光で照らされる。

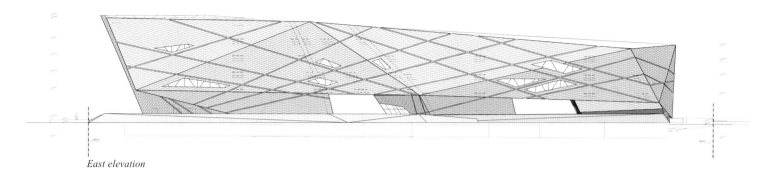

East elevation

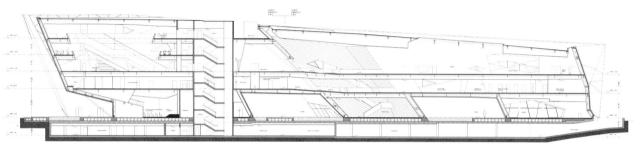

Longitudinal section

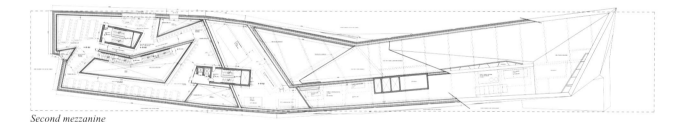

Second mezzanine

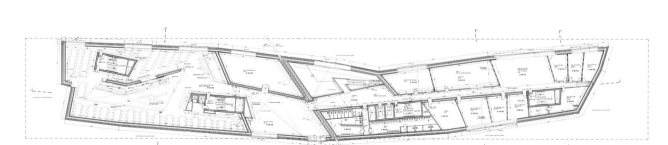

Second floor

Architects: Zaha Hadid Architects—
Zaha Hadid with Patrik Schumacher, design;
Sophie Le Bienvenu, Sara Klomps, Alberto Barba, project architects;
Loreto Flores, Edgar Payán, Keji Majekodunmi, Lourdes Sánchez, Tarek Shamma, Suzanne Berggren, Ben Holland, project team; Sophie Le Bienvenu, Federico Dunkelberg, Tarek Shamma, Ebru Simsek, Fulvio Wirz, Mariagrazia Lanza, Miya Ushida, competition team
Local architect: IDOM Sevilla
Client: University of Seville
Consultants: IDOM Bilbao, structural; IDOM UK, facade and coordination
Program: general library and the investigative resources centre of the University of Seville
Total floor area: 10,499 m²

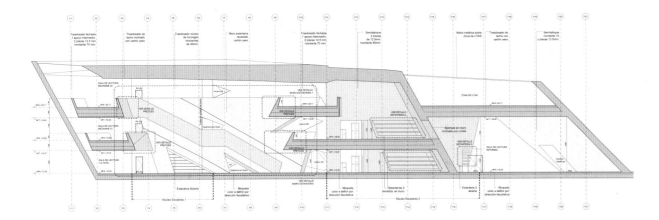

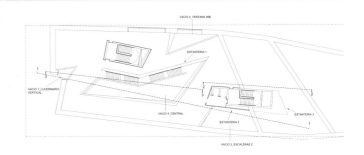

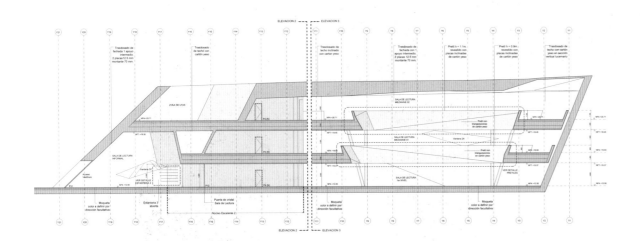

Sections

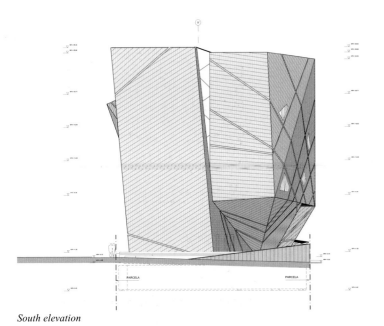

South elevation

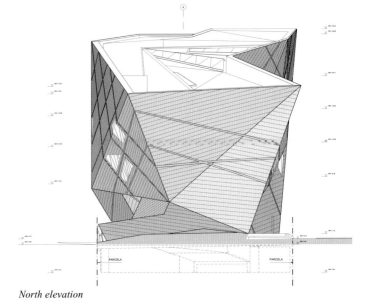

North elevation

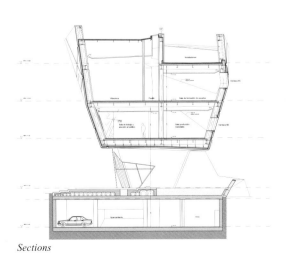 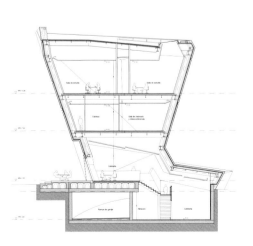 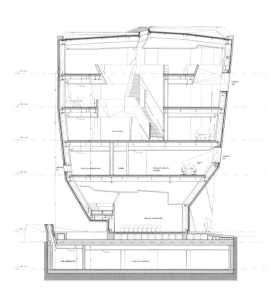

Sections

KARTAL—PENDIK MASTERPLAN

Istanbul, Turkey
Design: 2006–

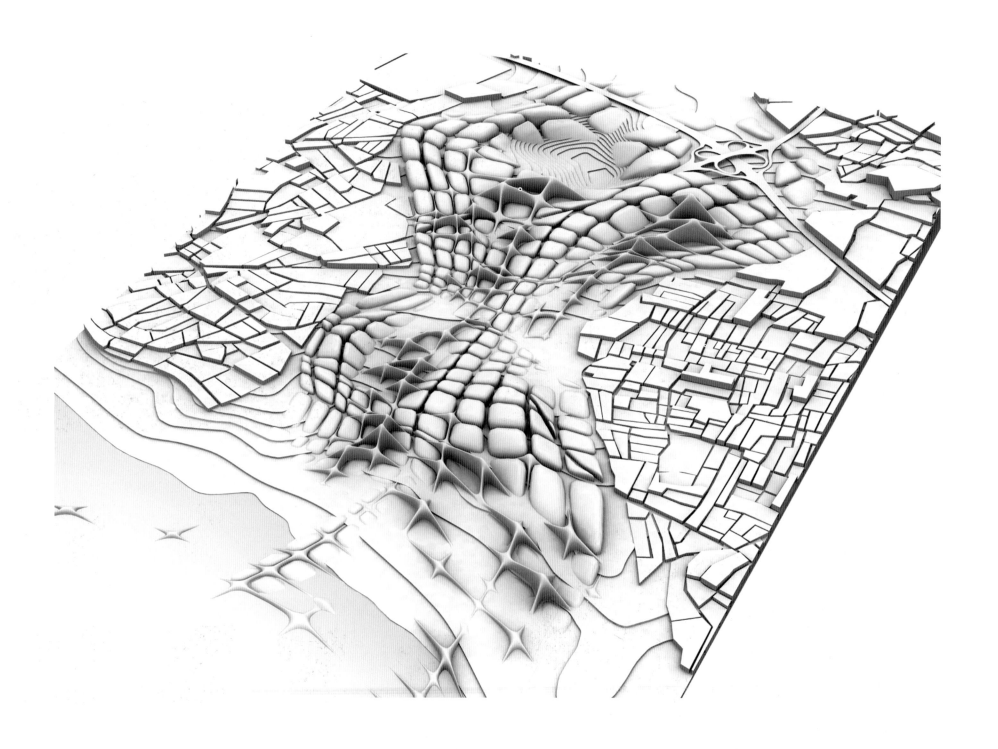

Architects: Zaha Hadid Architects—
Zaha Hadid with Patrik Schumacher, design;
DaeWha Kang and Saffet Bekiroglu, project leaders;
Sevil Yazici, Daniel Widrig, Elif Erdine, Melike Altinisik,
Miya Ushid, project team
Client: Greater Istanbul Municipality
Total project area : 555 hectares/6,000,000 m² con-
struction area

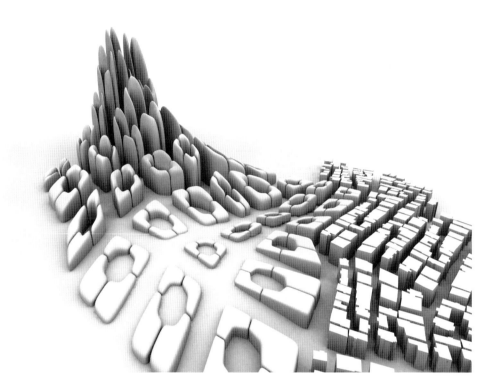

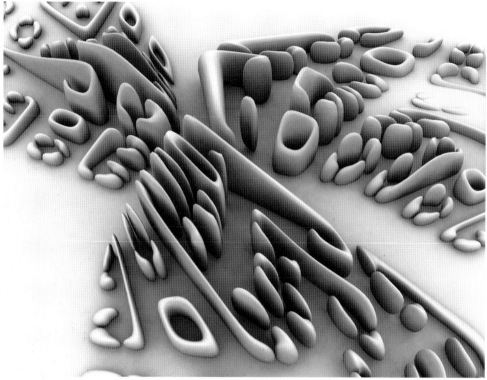

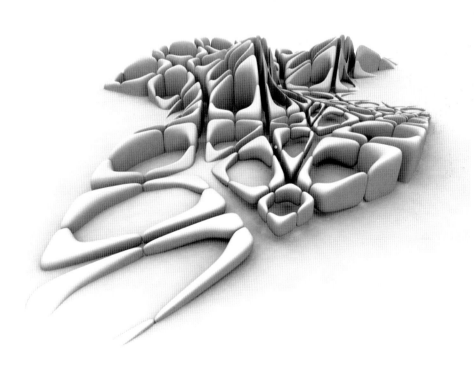

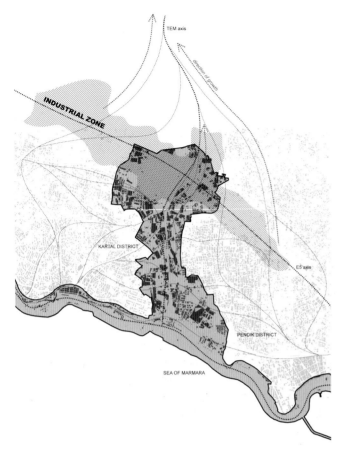

Regional connections and potential growth

Road network studies: stitching across site

Major arteries and soft grid

Height analysis

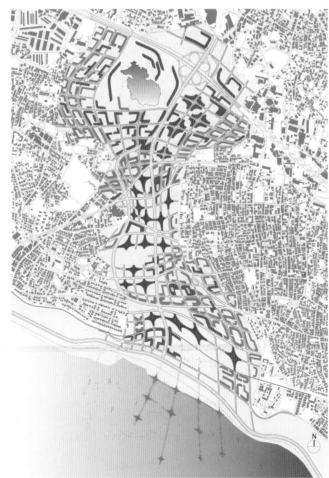

Master plan

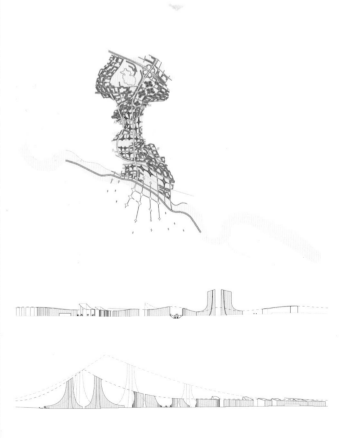

Conceptual sections

The Kartal-Pendik masterplan is a winning competition proposal for a new city centre on the east bank of Istanbul. It is the redevelopment of an abandoned industrial site into a new sub-centre of Istanbul, complete with a central business district, high-end residential development, cultural facilities such as concert halls, museums, and theatres, and leisure programs including a marina and tourist hotels. The site lies at the confluence of several important infrastructural links, including the major highway connecting Istanbul to Europe and Asia, the coastal highway, sea bus terminals, and heavy and light rail links to the greater metropolitan area.

The project begins by tying together the basic infrastructural and urban context of the surrounding site. Lateral lines stitch together the major road connections emerging from Kartal in the west and Pendik in the east. The integration of these lateral connections with the main longitudinal axis creates a soft grid that forms the underlying framework for the project. Locally, this net can be bundled to form areas of higher programmatic intensity as well as a vertical buildup of the city fabric. In certain areas the net rises up to form a network of towers in an open landscape, while in other areas it is inverted to become a denser fabric cut through by streets, and at other times may completely fade away to generate parks and open spaces. Some areas extend out into the water, creating a matrix of floating marinas, shops, and restaurants.

The fabric is further articulated by an urban script that generates different typologies of buildings that respond to the different demands of each district. This calligraphic script creates open conditions that can transform from detached buildings to perimeter blocks, and ultimately into hybrid systems that can create a porous, interconnected network of open spaces that meanders throughout the city. Through subtle transformations and gradations from one part of the site to the other, the scripted fabric can create a smooth transition from the surrounding context to the new, higher density development on the site.

The soft grid also incorporates possibilities of growth, as in the case where a network of highrise towers might emerge from an area that was previously allocated to low-rise fabric buildings or faded into open park space. The masterplan is thus a dynamic system that generates an adaptable framework for urban form, balancing the need for a recognizable image and a new environment with a sensitive integration of the new city with the existing surrounds.

カルタル＝ペンディク・マスタープランはイスタンブールの東河岸に，新たに都市の中心をつくるためのコンペ優勝案である。放棄されていた産業地を再開発し，イスタンブールの新たな副都心にしようというもので，中央ビジネス地区，最高級の住宅開発，コンサートホール・美術館・劇場などの文化施設，マリーナや観光客のためのホテルを含むレジャー関連施設を揃える。敷地は，イスタンブールとヨーロッパ及びアジアを結ぶ幹線道路，海岸道路，シーバス・ターミナル，大都市圏と結ぶ鉄道及びライトレール（路面電車）などいくつものインフラ交通網の合流地点にある。

プロジェクトは，敷地を囲む基本的な交通インフラと都市のコンテクストを一つに結ぶことから始まる。横方向の線が，西のカルテル，東のペンディクを起点とする主要道路の接続を一つに縫い合わせる。これらの横方向の接続と長手方向の主軸線との統合は，プロジェクトの基礎を為す枠組みを形成し，しなやかなグリッドをつくりだす。局地的には，このネットは，プログラムが高度に集中すると同時に都市構成が垂直に展開するエリアを形成するために束ねることができる。あるエリアでは，ネットは広々としたランドスケープの中にタワーのネットワークをつくるために立ち上がり，一方，他のエリアでは，道路に切り通されたより密度の高い都市を構成するファブリックを形成するために内向きに折り曲げられ，そしてある時は，公園やオープン・スペースを生み出すために完全に消え去るだろう。いくつかのエリアは水の中へ広がり，水に浮かぶマリーナ，ショップ，レストランのマトリックスをつくりだす。

都市のファブリックは，各地区の異なる求めに応じて多様な建築型式を生み出す都市の絵図によってさらに分節される。この飾り文字で書かれた脚本は，一戸建ての建物から周縁のブロックへ，そして最後には，都市全体を蛇行する，多孔性の，相互に連結されたオープン・スペースのネットワークをつくれるハイブリッド・システムへと変換可能な，開かれた状態をつくりだす。敷地の一部分から他の部分への微妙な変形やグラデーションによって，脚本化されたファブリックは，周囲のコンテクストから，より高密度の新たな開発へと敷地をスムーズに移行させる。

しなやかなグリッドにはまた，成長の可能性が組み入れられている。たとえば，以前は低層の建物が配置されていた，あるいは広い公園のなかに消えて行ったエリアから高層タワーのネットワークが現れるかもしれない。こうして全体計画は，固有のイメージと新しい環境の必要を，新しい街とその周りの土地との微妙な統合と平衡をとりながら，都市形態のための適応能力のあるダイナミックなシステムとなる。

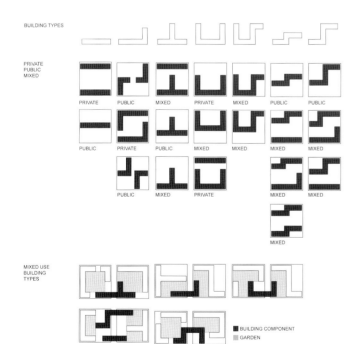

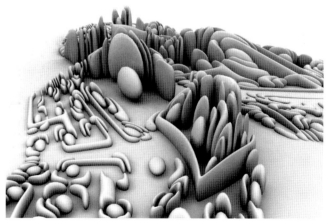

Calligraphy studies

Formal studies

EDIFICI CAMPUS

Diagonal Mar, Barcelona, Spain
Design: 2006–   Construction: –2008

Design and Context

Zaha Hadid's design for the Edifici Campus confirms the role of the 22@ area at the very forefront of Barcelona's changing water edge. The tower's striking design creates a new presence in a territory of transition. The spiralling tower stitches the border of the municipalities of Barcelona and Besòs, creating a new infrastructure that is a joint-venture of the two cities and two clients: El Consorci, Zona Franca de Barçelona y b_TEC, Consorci del Campus Interuniversitari del Besòs. The design articulates the transition between the forum and the campus, between the new equipments and parks waterfront area, in Barcelona, and the requalification of the delta of the river Besòs area, in Sant Adriá del Besòs.

The formal theme of the spiral actively binds the two together with an encompassing movement, stimulating the seamless integration of the city fabric, connecting in a dynamic way, the different surrounding areas.

Synergies and Opportunities

The new node created at the Edifici Campus anchors itself on the functional mix of university and office spaces, establishing a bridge between the world's of education, research and business, promoting new opportunities of interaction between the diverse types of users through its new public spaces, the courtyard and the atrium. Our design proposal takes on the challenge of combining the needs and aspirations of the two clients and creating a symbiosis between their programmes.

Thinking of the two briefs as one single building is the most coherent, efficient, sustainable and cost effective way to fulfill the potential of this great opportunity. This new building form, defined as a combined entity created by fusion, will set a new typology of intervention within the Knowledge City concept.

The critical mass generated at the site will act as a catalyst on the transition between the forum and the campus, creating potential new synergies between the different stake holders and contributing actively to the overall redevelopment of the 22@ area.

Connectivity and Public Space

The fluid character of the tower is generated through an intrinsically dynamic composition of volumes that dissolves the classic typology of the tower and the podium into a seamless piece. The building uses the site's inclined topography to redesign the landscape in order to create seamless accessibility between the new campus and the forum.

Through the use of cantilevers, the building lifts from the street level, releasing the ground to be occupied by civic/public uses. The continuous, 'choreographed', spiral movement 'weaves' a series of public spaces, connecting the campus, through the courtyards and under the cantilevers, to the forum beyond.

Site plan

〈デザインとコンテクスト〉
エディフィシ・キャンパスのデザインは、日々変貌するバルセロナのウォーターフロント最前部にある22@エリアの役割を強化する。タワーの印象的なデザインは、転換期にある地域の新しい魅力的な存在となるだろう。螺旋状のタワーは新しいインフラ施設として、バルセロナとベソス両市の境界を縫い合わせ、2つの市と2つの団体（ソーナ・フランカ・デ・バルセロナ協会，ベソス国際大学キャンパス協会）の共同によって建設される。

デザインは、フォーラムとキャンパス、そして新しい建物が建てられるバルセロナ側にある公園の水際地区とサン・アドリア・デル・ベソスのベソス川デルタの再整備地域、その2つの間の変転を有機的に統合する。

螺旋状の形態が目指すのは、その包囲するような動きによって両者を合体させることで、都市構造のシームレスな統合を促し、ダイナミックな方法で周囲の異なる領域を連結する。

〈協同と好機〉
エディフィシ・キャンパスの新しい結節点は、自らを大学とオフィス・スペースの機能的混合状態に繋留し、教育，研究，ビジネスの世界に橋を架け、そこに生まれる新しい公共空間、コートヤード、アトリウムによって、多彩な分野の人々が交流する新たな機会を増大させる。設計案は、2つのクライアントのニーズと要望を組み合わせ、両者のプログラムの共生をつくりだすことに挑戦する。

2種類の設計概要を一つの建物に統合する考えは、この大きな機会が持つ可能性を実現する，最も統一性があり効率的で，サステイナブルかつ経済的な方法である。融合によってつくられ，連合体として明確に規定されたこの新しい建築形態は，知の都市のコンセプトの範疇に，調停という新しいタイポロジーを創出するだろう。

敷地に生まれる臨界質量は，フォーラムとキャンパス間の推移に触媒として作用し，22@エリア全体の再開発に対する様々な投資者と貢献的な活動の間に，新しい協同の可能性をつくりだす。

〈接続性と公共空間〉
建物の流動体のような性格は，タワーの古典的タイポロジーとポディウムを継ぎ目のない単体へと溶解する，本質的にダイナミックなヴォリューム構成から生まれている。建物は，敷地の傾斜する地形を利用してランドスケープを再構成し，新キャンパスと街の間をなめらかにつなぐ。

片持ち梁を用いて，建物を道路レベルから持ち上げ，その下の土地を市民が使えるように開放する。連続する，"振り付けられた"螺旋状の動きは，一連の公共空間を"縫い合わせ"，キャンパスをコートヤード，片持ち梁の下を通り，その先にあるフォーラムへ結ぶ。

0   100   200   300   400   500

Architects: Zaha Hadid Architects—Zaha Hadid with Patrik Schumacher, design; Tiago Correia, project architect; Aurora Santana, Alejandro Diaz, design team; Fabiano Continanza, Mónica Bartolomé, Raquel Gallego, Victor Orive, Jessica Knobloch, Maria Araya, Hooman Talebi, Ebru Simsek, project team
Client: El Consorci - Zona Franca de Barcelona, Polígon Industrial de la Zona Franca, España Consorci del Campus Interuniversitari del Besòs, b_TEC Barcelona Innovación Tecnològica
Consultants: J/T Ardèvol i Associats SL, technical architect; Ferran Pelegrina Associats SL, local architect; Adams Kara Taylor, BOMA Brufau, Obiol, Moya & Ass. SL, structural; Max Fordham LLP, Grupo JG. SL, mechanical, electrical and plumbing; Ferrés Arquitectos y Consultores.SL, facade engineering; ALS, lighting
Program: offices, university, exhibition Hall, auditorium and retail
Total floor area: 27,650 m² (12,150 m², office; 8,500 m², university; 7,000 m², parking)

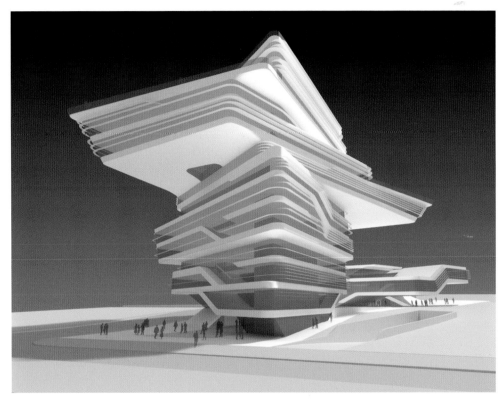

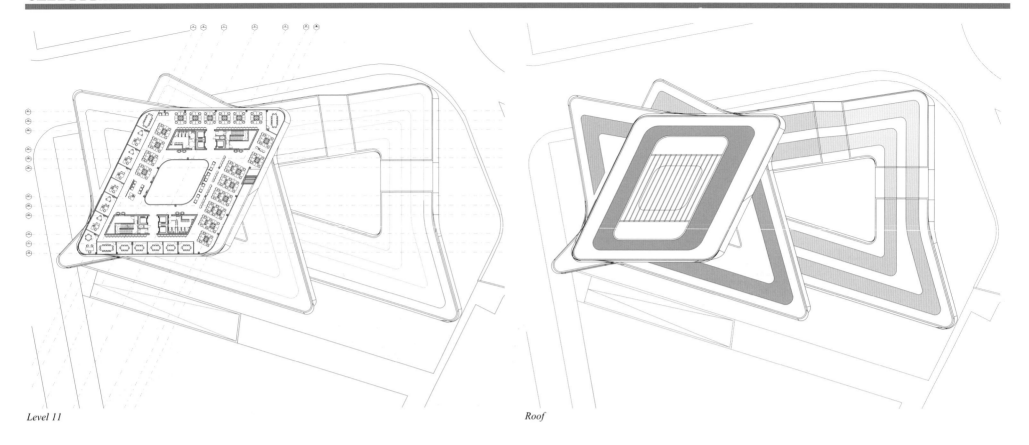

Level 11

Roof

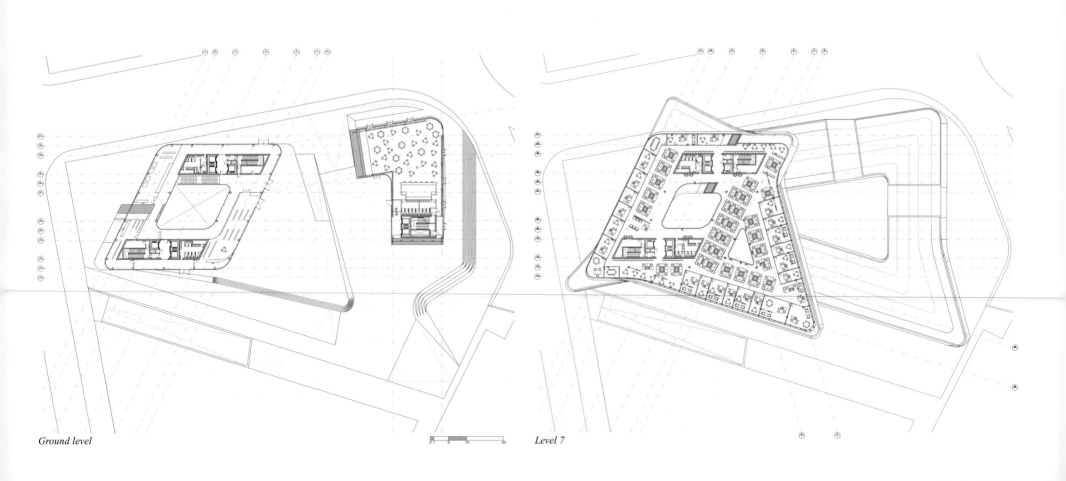

Ground level

Level 7

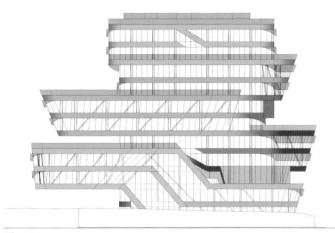
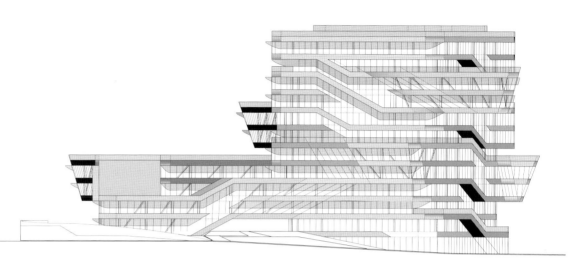

Elevations

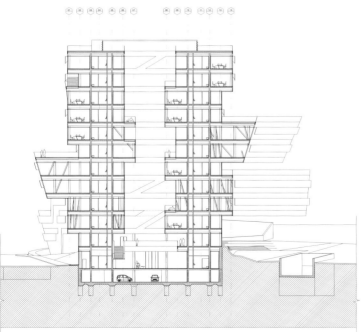
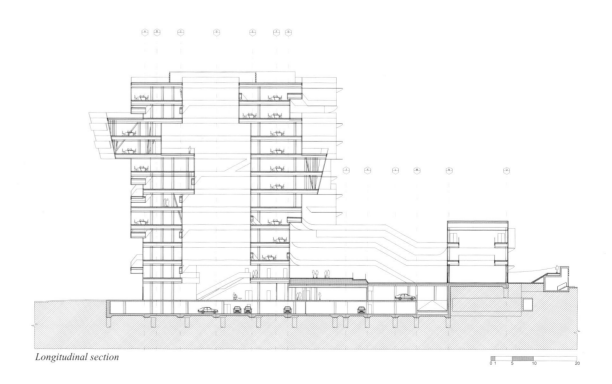

Cross section

Longitudinal section

E.ON ENERGY RESEARCH DEPARTMENT-RWTH AACHEN

Aachen, Germany
Design: 2006–   Construction: 2007–08

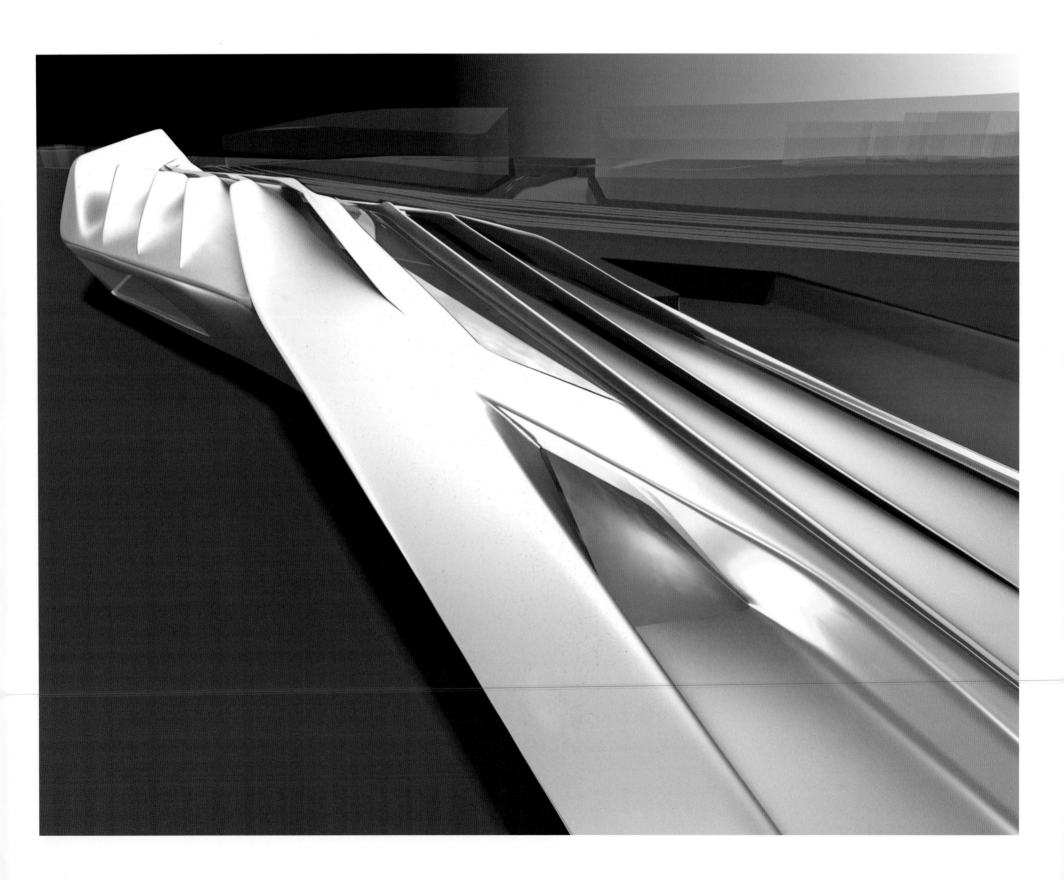

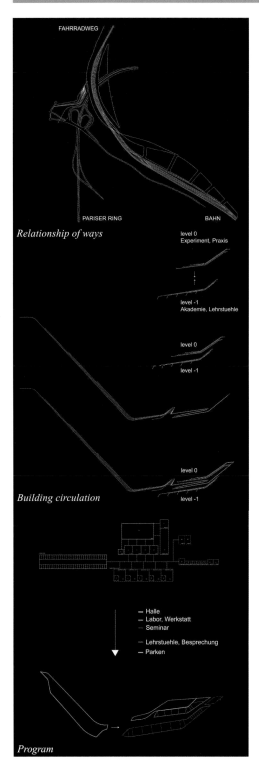

Relationship of ways

level 0
Experiment, Praxis

level -1
Akademie, Lehrstuehle

level 0

level -1

level 0

Building circulation

level -1

— Halle
— Labor, Werkstatt
— Seminar

— Lehrstuehle, Besprechung
— Parken

Program

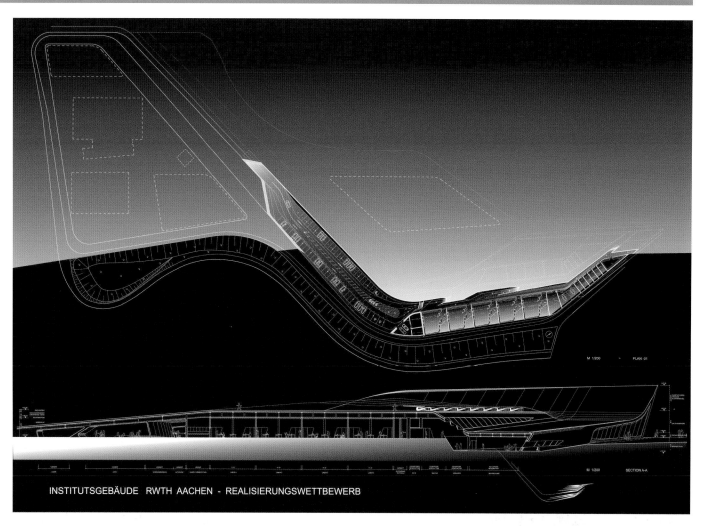

INSTITUTSGEBÄUDE RWTH AACHEN - REALISIERUNGSWETTBEWERB

Architects: Zaha Hadid Architects—
Zaha Hadid with Patrik Schumacher, design;
Gernot Finselbach, project architect;
Philipp Vogt, assistant project architect;
Britta Knobel, Arnoldo Rabago,
Margarita Yordanova Valova, Graham Modlen,
Nils Fischer, Sara Klomps, Helmut Kinzler, competition
team
Client: Building and Real Estate NRW, Aachen
Consultants: Buro Happold Consulting Engineers, structural; Transsolar Energietechnik GmbH, services, mechanical and electrical
Program: E.ON Energy Research Department RWTH
Aachen, 5 faculties, laboratories, exhibition hall
Total floor area: 5,000 m², program; 2,000 m², parking
Costs: 13 million euro

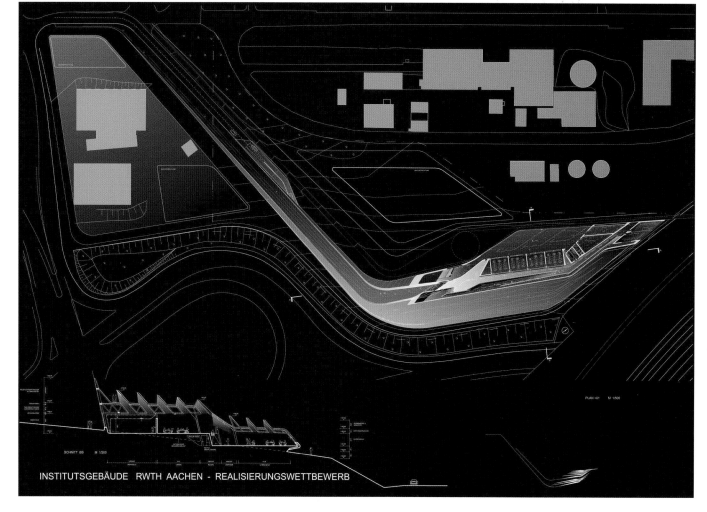

INSTITUTSGEBÄUDE RWTH AACHEN - REALISIERUNGSWETTBEWERB

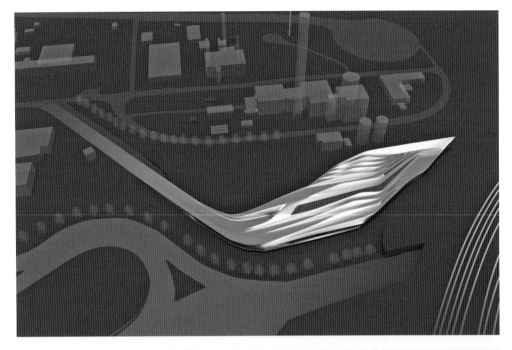
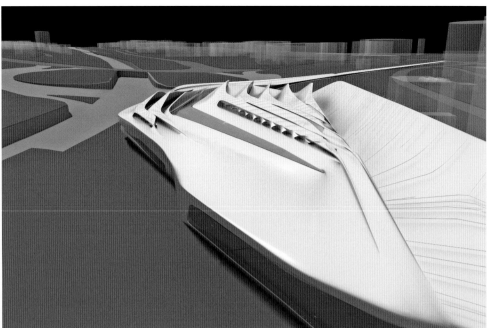
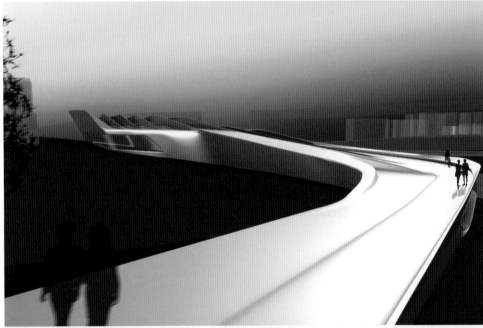
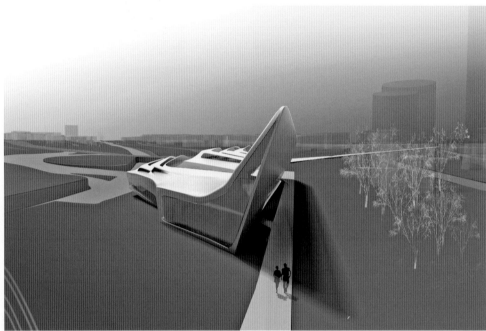

The new E.ON Energy Research Department building at RWTH University in Aachen emerges from between existing rail tracks, grass and tree slopes and a 4-lane arterial road. Our concept translates the direction and contours of the site as a primary form generator for the building and connects the two arms of the university campus into a larger spatial gesture.

There is a close correlation between the structure and form of the proposal to movement within the building and around it; the natural day light and air flow across the site. The structural and aerodynamic fins along the length of the roof-scape allow for the modulation both of daylight and wind stream air flow over the roof, maximising the provision of natural light and ventilation to all parts of the building interior.

A long integrated landscaped path guides people to the main entrance. From here a central corridor continues inside and becomes a circulation passage. A separate drive running parallel to the path descends to a parking garage beneath. The internal passage divides the programme into two clear bands, one practical with laboratories and exhibition space on a raised upper level, orientated towards an open garden. On the lower level, the academic band with 5 departments—including a library and meeting rooms facing the train tracks.

At the far northerly corner of the building, the roof envelope rises, marking a turning point of the internal passage. The 2-storey open gallery, with staircases at each end and a middle ramp that form a circulation loop, generating a constant fluency of movement between the practical and academic volumes.

アーヘン工科大学（RWTH）E.ONエネルギー研究所は，既存の鉄道軌道，草と木に包まれた斜面，4車線の幹線道路の間から現れる。コンセプトは敷地の方位と輪郭を，建物の第一の形態構成要素として解釈し，大学キャンパスの2本のアームをより大きな空間のジェスチャーへ連結するものである。

構造とその形態の，屋内の動きや周りを囲む自然の光と敷地を横切る空気の流れとの間には相互に密接な関係がある。ルーフスケープの全長に沿って延びる構造的で空力的なフィンは，昼光と屋根の上の風や空気の流れを調節し，建物内部のすべての部分へ自然光と大気を最大限に送り込む。

建物に一体化され，景観構成された細長い通路が，メイン・エントランスに導く。ここから中央廊下が屋内に続き，動線通路となる。通路と離れ，平行して走るドライブは下の駐車場へ降りて行く。屋内の通路はプログラムを明快な2本の帯状のスペースに分ける。1本は，実験室と展示室で構成された実務的なスペース，持ち上げられた上のレベルを構成し，広い庭に向いている。低い方のレベルは，図書室，いくつかの集会室を含め5つの部門の置かれたアカデミックな帯で，鉄道軌道の方を向いている。

建物北端のコーナーでは，屋根は軸先を上げ，内部通路の転換点を示す。両端に階段が付き，真ん中ではループ状の動線を形成するスロープのある2層のオープン・ギャラリーは，実務的なヴォリュームとアカデミックなヴォリュームの間に常によどみなく流れる動きをつくりだす。

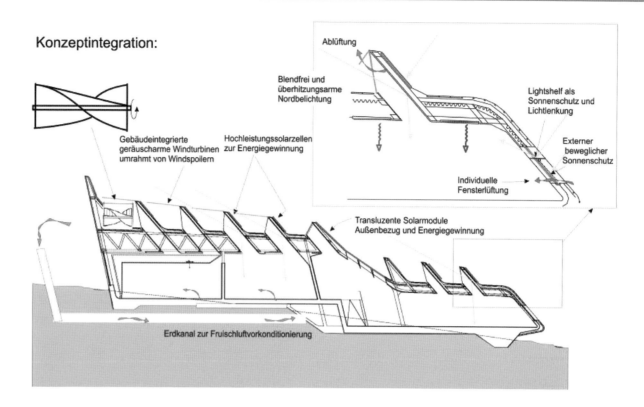

Konzeptintegration:

Ablüftung

Blendfrei und überhitzungsarme Nordbelichtung

Lightshelf als Sonnenschutz und Lichtlenkung

Externer beweglicher Sonnenschutz

Gebäudeintegrierte geräuscharme Windturbinen umrahmt von Windspoilern

Hochleistungssolarzellen zur Energiegewinnung

Individuelle Fensterlüftung

Transluzente Solarmodule Außenbezug und Energiegewinnung

Erdkanal zur Fruischluftvorkonditionierung

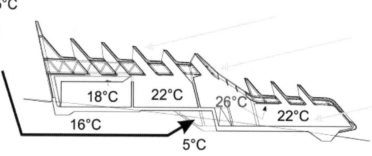

Winter-Modus:

-5°C

Einbindung solarer Gewinne
Zulfutvorwärmung über Erdkanal
Strahlungsheizung
Lüftungsanlagen mit
Wärmerückgewinnung

18°C 22°C 26°C 22°C
16°C
5°C

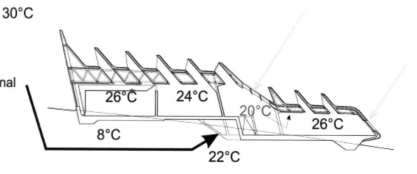

Sommer-Modus:

30°C

Optimale Verschattung
Zuluftvorkühlung über Erdkanal
Strahlungskühlung

26°C 24°C 20°C 26°C
8°C
22°C

Diagram: energy concept

NURAGIC AND CONTEMPORARY ART MUSEUM

Cagliari, Italy
Design: 2006–

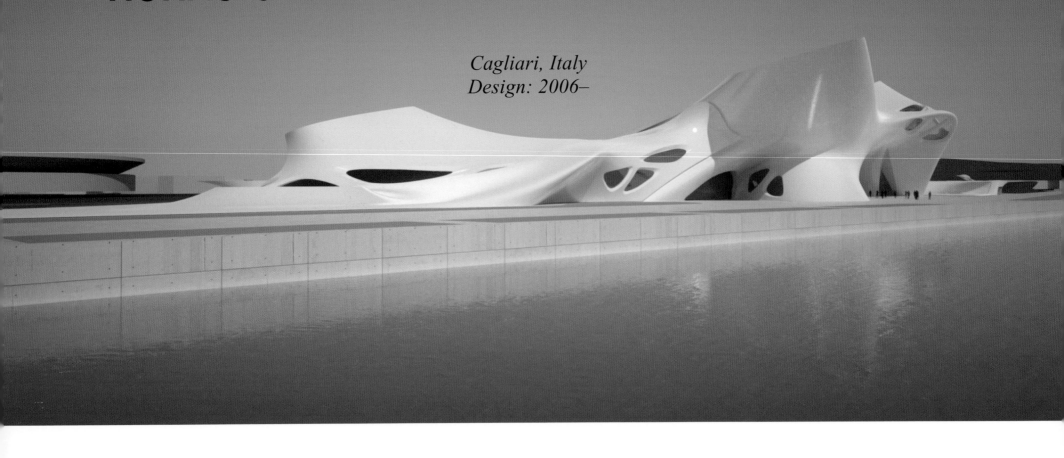

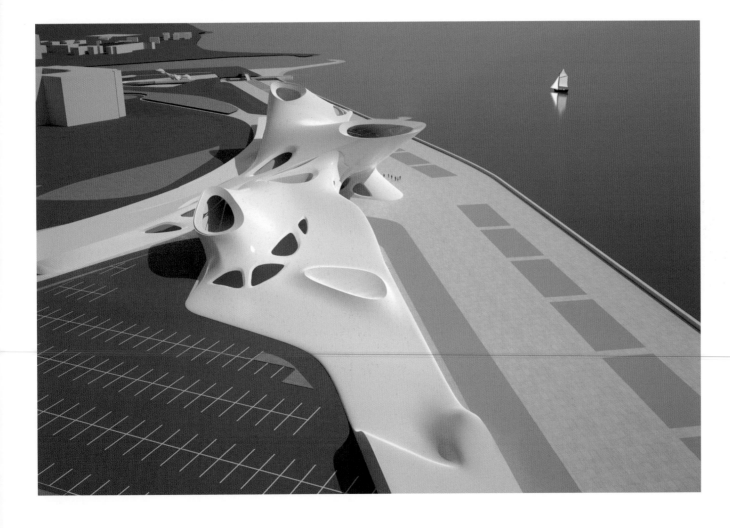

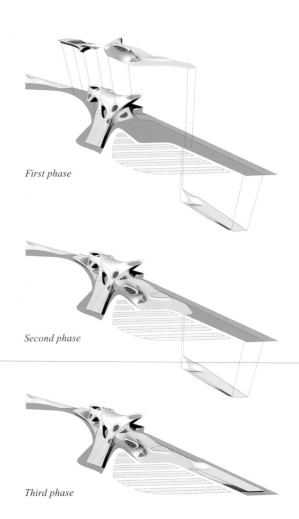

First phase

Second phase

Third phase

Architectural Concept

The new museum is like a coralline concretion, empty inside, hard and porous on the external surface, able to accommodate, in a continuous osmotic exchange with the external atmosphere, cultural activities in a lively and changing environment. At times it assimilates to the ground, creating a new landscape, while at others it acquires a strong mass defining the new skyline.

The open and dynamic quality of the shape is also pursued inside the building, where the circulation of the visitors through the exhibition, information and commercial paths determine the geometry of the spaces.

The erosion that forms a great cavity inside the building articulates the volume in a succession of open spaces for exhibition, places of aggregation and occasions for installation of contemporary art.

Such spaces, visible from a variety of viewpoints, satisfy the perceptive and the aesthetic dialogue between the contemporary and the Nuragic art. The inner cavity allows the genesis of two continuous skins, one contained within the other. The museum program is placed between the "external skin" of the facade system, and the "inner skin", equipped with a flexible serial system of anchorage and electrification, that allows multiple uses of surfaces/ walls for installations or video projections.

Paths

The communication, contemporary and Nuragic exhibitions, and the public paths crossing the building and intercepting each other, create the fluid structure of the building, allowing a variety of uses and configurations. The vertical and oblique elements of circulation create zones of interference and turbulence creating a visual continuity between the different parts of the building.

The Public Path
- The public commercial path lets the visitors cross the building in parallel with the path along the sea. It offers in sequence areas a store, bookshop, bars, restaurants, and the systems of loggie where outdoor pieces of art could be accommodated.

The Exhibition Paths
- The path of the communication area is articulated along the "loggiato" of the ground floor in continuous dialogue with the courts/external cavity.
- The contemporary art exhibition path starts from the ground floor, crossing the building until the open "loggia" of the top floor
- The Nuragic art exhibition path from the ground floor slides between the two skins of the building allowing a more intimate vision of the works of art without sacrificing the view on the great central space.

Phasing—Morphology and Strategy

The growth of the museum will occur in three phases: as with living organisms, the growth of the museum will be self-regulated. It will happen naturally when the conditions of a mature balance between the economic atmosphere and philanthropic and cultural environment are reached.

Site plan

建築コンセプト

新しい美術館は，珊瑚の塊に似ていて，内側は空洞，外側は堅く，多孔性の面で包まれ，外の状況が絶え間なく浸透し，交換し合うなかで，活発に変化する環境での様々な文化活動に対応することができる。建物はときに地面に同化して新しいランドスケープをつくり，一方で新しいスカイラインを刻む強いマッスを獲得する。

この形態の持つ開放的でダイナミックな特質は内部でも追求され，展示場を抜けて行く来館者の動線，インフォメーションとコマーシャルの通路が空間のジオメトリーを決定する。建物内部に壮大な空隙を形成する浸食は，ヴォリュームを，展示のための連続するオープン・スペース，コンテンポラリー・アートのインスタレーションを集め，行える場所に明確に分けている。

様々な視点から展望できるこうした空間は，コンテンポラリー・アートとヌラーゲ芸術（イタリア，サルジニア島で発見された先史時代の塔状石造建築）の間の直感的で美的な対話の条件を満たすに十分である。内側の空隙は，1枚がもう1枚の中に包み込まれた連続する2枚の被膜を生成させる。美術館のプログラムは，ファサード・システムである"外側の被膜"と"内側の被膜"の間に配置される。内側の被膜は，固定と充電のためのフレキシブルな一連のシステムを装備し，その表面／壁をインスタレーションやビデオ映写など，多目的に使える。

通路

コミュニケーション，コンテンポラリー・アート，ヌラーゲ芸術の展示，そして建物内を横断し，交差する公共通路が，建物の流体のような構造をつくりあげ，多彩な使い方と配置構成を可能とさせる。動線を構成する垂直や斜めの要素は互いに干渉し合う乱流するゾーンを形成し，建物の異なる部分間に視覚的連続性が生まれる。

〈公共通路〉

商業ベースの公共通路は，来館者を，海沿いの通路と平行して，建物内を進むように導く。そこには店舗，ブックショップ，バー，レストランが並び，戸外での作品展示のための柱廊を提供する。

〈展示通路〉

・コミュニケーション・エリアの通路は，中庭／外部の空隙と連続する対話をする"ロッジャート（長い回廊）"に沿って分節される。

・コンテンポラリー・アートの展示通路は1階を起点として，最上階のオープンロッジアまで建物を横断して行く。

・1階から始まるヌラーゲ芸術の展示通路は建物の2枚の被膜の間を進み，壮大な中央空間の眺めを犠牲にせずに，芸術作品を間近に見せてくれる。

段階的な形態構造とストラテジー

美術館は3段階を経て成長する。生きている有機体として，美術館の成長は自己調整される。経済状況と文化的環境が成熟した均衡に達したとき，美術館は自然に成長して行くだろう。

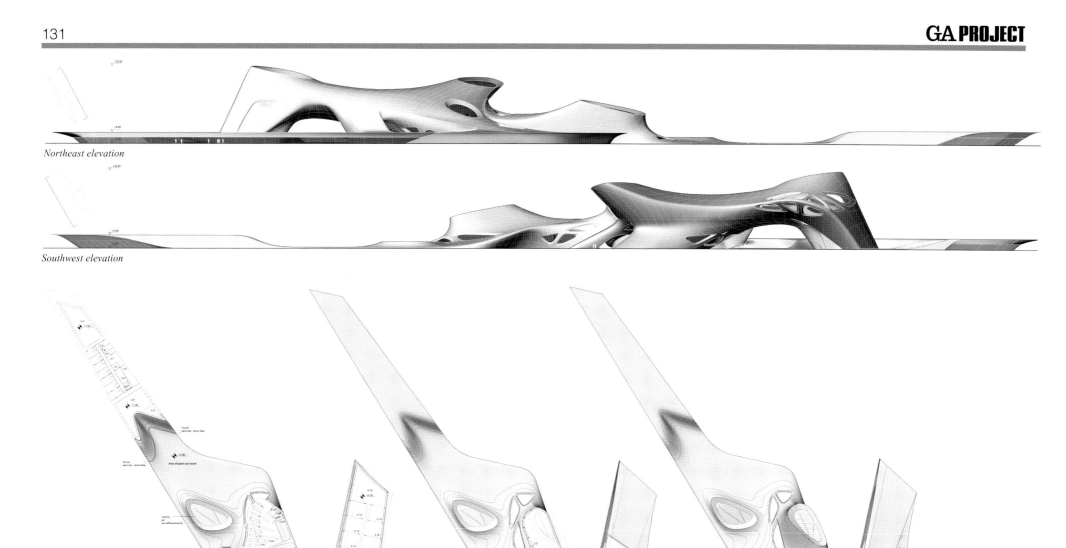

Northeast elevation

Southwest elevation

Architects: Zaha Hadid Architects—
Zaha Hadid with Patrik Schumacher, design;
Paola Cattarin, project architect; Paolo Matteuzzi,
Federico Bistolfi, design team; Michele Salvi,
Serena Pietrantonj, Vincenzo Barilari, Samuele Sordi,
support team
Local architect: Luca Peralta
Client: Regione Autonoma della Sardegna, Assesso-
rato Pubblica Istruzione
Consultants: Elisabetta Alba, Nuragic Art Consultant;
Max Fordham LLP—Neil Smith, environmental sus-
tainability, mechanical, electrical;
Adams Kara Taylor—Hanif Kara, structural;
Building Consulting—Pasquale Miele, quantity surveyor
Total floor area: 12,000 m²

Level 0   *Level 1*   *Level 2*   *Level 3*

Southeast elevation

Northwest elevation

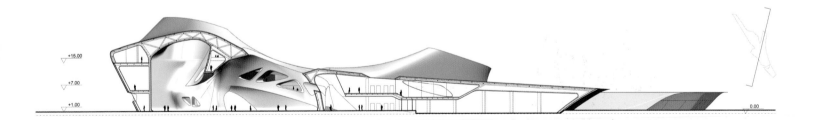

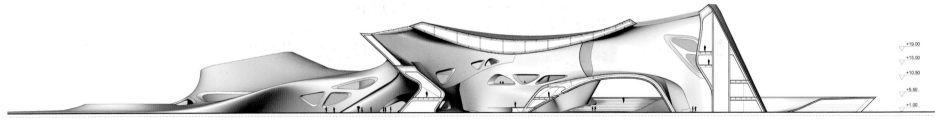

Sections

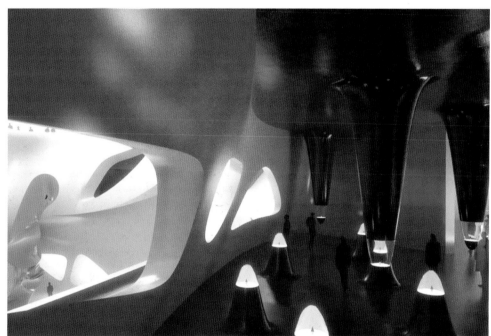

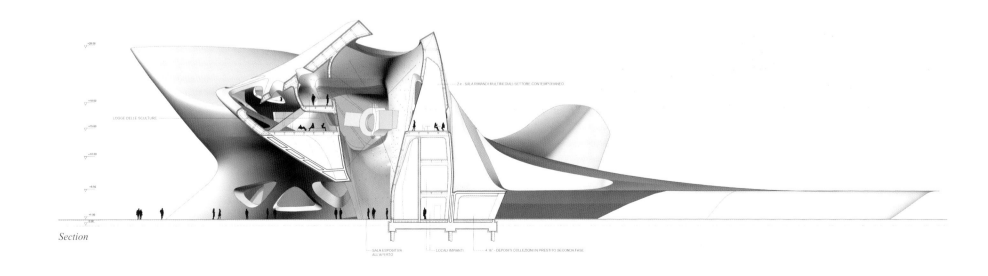

Section

DUBAI FINANCIAL MARKET

Dubai, United Arab Emirates
Design: 2007–

The aim of the design is to create a strong sculptural element that will be prominent from the waterfront, but also has a distinctive roof form when viewed from the adjacent dancing towers as well as the high-rise developments around Business Bay. The financial exchange is lifted above the ground with the heavier sculptural solid hovering over a light volume of glass. The major challenge of the financial exchange is to accommodate a large perimeter of stockbroker shop fronts onto a single trading floor area while economizing on the overall area of the building and maintaining overall coherence of the central space to the broker's shops on the perimeter. Our approach was to begin articulating the plan into a series of petals, allowing us to maximize the amount of shop frontage for any given area covered on the site. Each of these petals could then engage the site in a different way—for example establishing the main entry to the site, reaching out to the most prominent corner overlooking the creek and the bridge. From the interior point of view this organization creates a strong communal central space, while also establishing more private areas for trader's lounges as well as a women's trading area. For the stockbroker's offices the focus is inward towards the trading and the action, cantilevering over the waterfront, or connecting back into the retail centre.

Each office has a glazed shop front on the trading floor and an overlook from its mezzanine level. On the upper level the administrative and back of house offices also have balconies looking down into the trading area. The balconies and bridges on the first and second levels form a continuous ribbon skimming the perimeter of the space, emphasizing the large number of shops sharing the single space. Stock tickers will be projected horizontally around the areas of the balconies that face directly into the trading space, further emphasizing the main trading floor. To bring light into this unbroken perimeter of space a series of domed skylights draw light in from the roof. The large oculi shine over the main trading space through the course of the day, flooding it with light from the east with the first rays of morning at the opening of trading and closing the day with the sun's last light from the western skylight.

デザインの目標は，ウォーターフロントからすぐ目に付くのはもちろん，隣のダンシングタワーから，また同様にビジネス・ベイを取り巻いて開発されている高層ビルから見たときもすぐ分かる独特の屋根を持つ，強く，彫刻的なエレメントをつくることである。証券取引所は，ガラス張りの軽快な1階の上を舞うように地上から持ち上げられ，堅く密度のある彫刻のような連続するヴォリュームを構成する。最大のチャレンジは，株式仲買人のオフィス・ブースが大きく取り囲む周縁部を，一室空間を構成する立会い場の上へ配置する一方，建物全体の面積を節減し，中央空間とその周縁部との一体感を維持することである。このために，どのエリアにもブースの数を最大限に配置できるように，数枚の花びらが連なる平面構成へと明快に区分し，次に，これらの花弁を，それぞれ異なる方法で敷地と結びつけている。たとえば，1枚は敷地のメイン・エントリーにつながり，1枚はクリークとブリッジを見晴らす最も目立つコーナーへ向かって伸びる。内部の視点からは，この構成は強い存在感を持つ中央の共有空間をつくりだす一方，仲買人のラウンジのある私的なエリアや女性専用の立会い場も設置されることになる。株式仲買人のブースのために，焦点は取引の行われている内側に向かい，そしてまた，ウォーターフロントの上に片持ちで張り出し，再び取引場へと接続する，動きに向かう。

立会い場に面して前面がガラス張りになったオフィス・ブースは，メザニン・レベルにあり，場内がよく見える。上階は管理事務部門のオフィスで，同じように立会い場を見下ろせるバルコニーが付いている。2階と3階のバルコニーとブリッジは，この中央空間の周縁部すれすれを滑るように進む連続する帯となって，一室空間を共有する多数のブースの存在感を強める。取引状況を自動的に表示するチッカーは立会い場に直接面したバルコニー・エリアを囲んで水平に突き出され，中央空間をさらに際立たせる。閉ざされた周縁部へ外光を運ぶため，一連のドーム形のスカイライトが屋根から外光を引き入れる。大きな丸窓が，一日中，立会い場を照らし，取引の始まりには，東から入る朝の最初の光線で満たし，西側のスカイライトから入る太陽の最後の光が一日を閉めくくる。

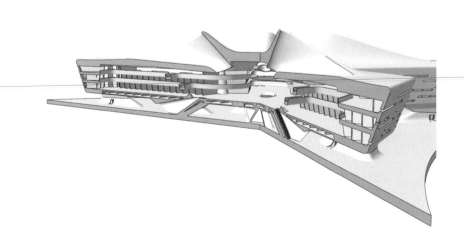

Architects: Zaha Hadid Architects—
Zaha Hadid with Patrik Schumacher, design;
Raymond Lau, project leader;
Lars Teichmann, project director;
Raymond Lau, Aturo Lyon, Aturo Revilla,
Chikara Inamura, Bessy Tam, Renato Pimenta,
Amalthea Leung, project team;
DaeWha Kang, Simone Fuchs, Andrea Caste,
Tariq Khayyat, Maria Eva Contesti, Jesse Chima, de-
sign team
Client: Dubai Properties
Consultant: Gross.Max, landscape
Program: financial market
Total floor area: 42,000 m²

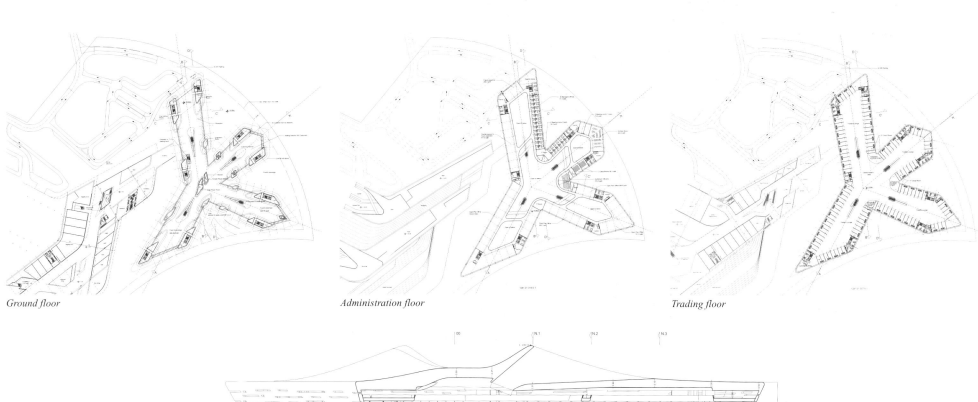

Ground floor   *Administration floor*   *Trading floor*

Section

MOSCOW EXPOCENTER

Moscow, Russia
Design: 2007–

Architects: Zaha Hadid Architects—
Zaha Hadid with Patrik Schumacher, design;
Inanc Eray, design leader;
Yevgeniy Beylkin, Melike Altinisik, Erhan Patat, design
team
Client: BCI Construction Limited
Program: exhibition halls, hotel and residential tower
Floor area: 26,340 m², exhibition halls

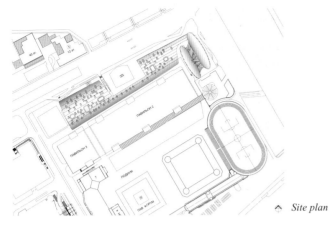
△ *Site plan*

Site Location

Closely located to the Moscow International Business Center (MIBC), the largest investment and construction project in Russia, and Europe as a whole, the Expocenter Project offers the city a new exposition venue, hotel, and residential development.

The realization of the MIBC development has turned Moscow into a strong focal point of business activity, as MIBC is providing a more effective utilization of city territories, and raising the market cost of the land areas of the city. The Expocenter project will be the finishing keystone in this development, defining the northern edge of the Expocenter site.

The introduction of this new landmark will expand the current usage as a business zone, into a 24 hour living and events space.

Design

The project realizes the possibility of integrating the vertical urban space with the existing horizontal urban fabric of the site. Consequently, the proposal envisions the unification of vertical and horizontal elements to become a major landmark on the site.

The main function of the horizontal space is to house the exposition and conference halls. Lifted above the ground, the exposition halls are large volumes designed for versatility, able to cater to exhibitions ranging from boutique high-fashion catwalk shows to world trade shows, from Russian art to International Events. Lifting these large volumes leaves the ground floor free to function as social, public space, to be occupied by offices, restaurants and bars. The exposition halls cantilever to the sides at the upper levels, providing for a snow-free outdoor event space; and concealing the traffic at the southern part of the building. Such a venue with 26,340 sqm net exhibition space, which is located in the center of the Moscow, will be in high demand for such high-class exhibitions and events.

The conference halls, located at the Eastern side of the first floor horizontal space, accommodate 3 auditoriums of different sizes, which can also combine to create one large hall of 1,500 seats. The flexibility of the spaces allow for everything from smaller corporate meetings to large public conferences. The auditoriums are linked to the tower complex via a fly through bridge for convenient access to smaller meeting rooms and other associated facilities.

The residential tower is designed as an elegant continuation of the Moscow City skyline (first a drop and then a rise), with a large vertical volume divided into two smaller shapes in order to sustain its overall slenderness. The elliptical form provides an elegant edge. The urban vertical space between these volumes is structured with fluid passages, sky lobbies, and the larger volumes of a flat and a gym.

This verticality of the urban space swoops to the ground to create a main lobby that serves both as a grand social meeting space, and allows for separate entrances for the residence blocks and the hotel. The hotel rises to the 26th floor of the Western tower, with beautiful views to the Moscow City development. The 2nd and 3rd floors of the hotel complex contain a gym, a spa, and many specialized restaurants, bistro cafes and shops.

The residences are located in the Eastern tower and on the top floors of the Western tower. The project is comprised of a variety of 1 to 4 bedroom units varying in size and design. The design allows for 4 remarkable corner units in each floor. The ability of the residents to utilize the hotel facilities gives a unique character to these high-end dwellings.

The intersection of the horizontal and vertical volumes creates the main public plaza which serves as the central focus point of the project.

Moscow is a thriving and constantly expanding business and cultural center, and it is a necessity to have an Expocenter which is capable of housing the high-class exhibitions and events that a city of Moscow's calibre attracts. When constructed, the easily accessible central location of the complex will not only make it the natural choice for large events, but will also create an influx of new activity and opportunity.

〈敷地〉

モスクワ国際ビジネスセンター（MIBC）に近接して建てられるエクスポセンターは，ロシアはもちろんヨーロッパ全体で最大の建設投資プロジェクトであり，モスクワ市に博覧会場，ホテル，住戸棟を新たに提供する。

MIBCの実現は，都市域のより効果的な活用をもたらし，市の土地価格の市場価値を高め，モスクワをビジネス活動の強力な中心地に変えた。エクスポセンター計画はこの開発を仕上げる要であり，敷地の北端部の境界を定めるだろう。この新しいランドマークの導入は，ビジネス・ゾーンとしての現在の状況を，24時間稼働の生活とイベント・スペースへ拡大する。

〈デザイン〉

プロジェクトは，垂直の都市空間を，水平に広がる既存の都市構成と統合する可能性を具体化する。したがって提示案では垂直と水平要素の統合が敷地の重要なランドマークになることを想定している。水平なスペースの主要な機能は博覧会場と会議場を提供することである。地上から持ち上げられた博覧会場は多角的に使えるように設計され，高級ファッションのキャットウォーク・ショーから世界交易展，ロシア芸術から国際的イベントまで広く対応できる。持ち上げられたこれらの大きなヴォリュームは，1階を自由に残し，オフィス，レストラン，バーなど，公共的なスペースとして使えるようにする。博覧会場は上階の側面が片持ちで張り出し，その下に雪を避けられる戸外のイベント・スペースを提供し，建物の南側の車両交通を隠す。モスクワの中心に位置し，正味面積26,340平米の展示空間のある，こうした，行為の発生地には，一流の展示やイベントが強く求められるだろう。

2階の水平に広がるスペースの東側に位置する会議場には，大きさの違う3つのホールがあり，つなげると1,500席の大ホールになる。フレキシブルな空間は，会社の小規模な集まりから大規模な公的会合まですべてに対応できる。各ホールはブリッジでタワー・コンプレックスに連結され，小集会室やその他の関連施設へ簡単にアクセスできる。

住戸タワーは，モスクワ市のスカイライン（まず下降し次に上昇する）に優雅に連続し，その大きな垂直のヴォリュームは，すらりとした全体像を維持するために2つのより小さな形に分割される。タワーを構成する楕円形は優美なエッジを提供する。2つのヴォリュームの間に生まれる垂直の都市空間は，流れるような通路やスカイロビー，そして住居

フラットとジムを納めたより大きなヴォリュームで組み立てられる。この都市空間の垂直性は，地上に向かって急降下してメイン・ロビーを形成する。ここは人が集まり交流するのに相応しい広いスペースで，住戸棟とホテル棟に別々のエントランスを提供する。ホテルは西タワーの26階までを占め，発展するモスクワ市の美しい眺めを望める。ホテル・コンプレックスの2，3階にはジム，スパ，様々な専門レストラン，ビストロ，カフェ，ショップが入る。

住戸は東タワー全体と，西タワーの最上階を占める。大きさやデザインの違う，1〜4寝室の多様性に富んだユニットで構成される。デザインによって，各階に4つのコーナー・ユニットを配置する，例外的な構成が可能となった。住民がホテル施設を利用できる点は，これらの最高級の住宅にユニークな性格を与える。

水平と垂直のヴォリュームの交差部には公共広場が生まれ，プロジェクトの中心となる焦点の役割を果たす。モスクワは今，繁栄し，常に拡大を続けるビジネスと文化の中心であり，市の優れた魅力を伝える一流の展示とイベントを行うことのできるエクスポセンターを必要としている。

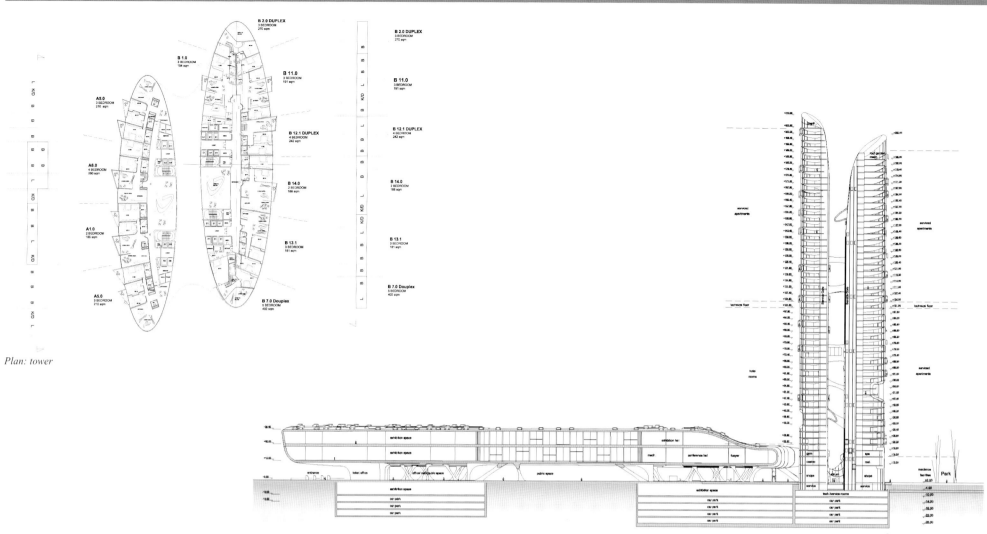

Plan: tower

Section

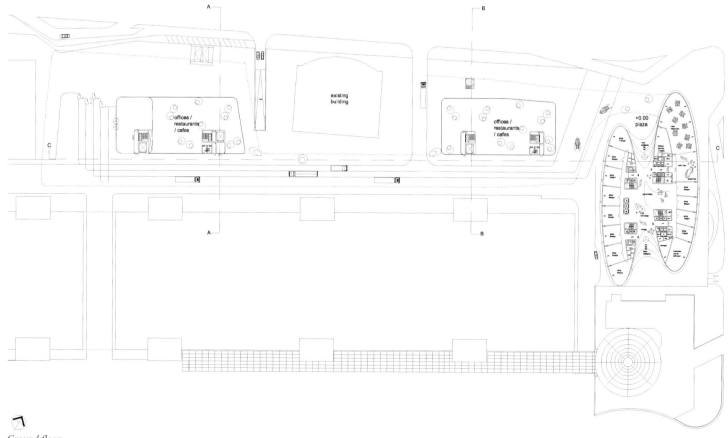

Ground floor

ABU DHABI PERFORMING ARTS CENTER

Abu Dhabi, United Arab Emirates
Design: 2007–

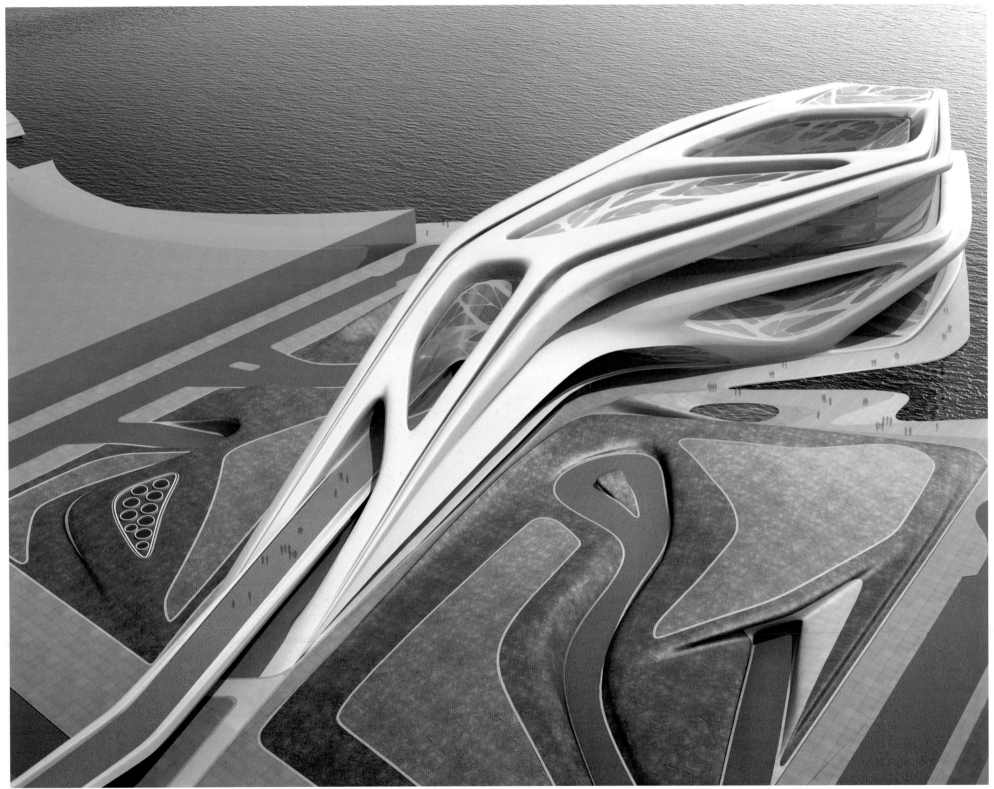

Overall view from east

North elevation

Concert hall

Overall view from northwest

Architects: Zaha Hadid Architects—
Zaha Hadid with Patrik Schumacher, design;
Nils-Peter Fischer, project director;
Britta Knobel, Daniel Widrig, project leader;
Jeandonne Schijlen, Melike Altisinik, Arnoldo Rabago,
Zhi Wang, Rojia Forouhar, Jaime Serra Avila,
Diego Rosales, Erhan Patat, Samer Chamoun,
Philipp Vogt, Rafael Portillo, project team
Client: The Tourism Development and Investment
Company of Abu Dhabi (TDIC)
Consultants: AMPC Anne Minors Performance Con-
sultants, theatre; Sound Space Design (Bob Essert),
acoustics; WSP Group, structural, fire, traffic & build-
ing services

Program: Performing Arts Centre proposing to house
five theatres—a music hall, concert hall, opera house,
drama theatre and a flexible theatre with a combined
seating capacity for 6,300. The centre may also
house an Academy of Performing Arts.
Size: 62 m; height; 135 m; width; 490 m; length incl.
bridge; 10 floors, above; 4 floors, underground
Built area: 25,800 m² (excl. bridge)
Total floor area: 62,770 m²

Design Concept

Analytical studies of organizational systems and growth in the natural world lead to the set of topologies that are the framework of the Performing Art Centre's distinct formal language.

These natural scenarios are formed by energy being supplied to enclosed systems, and the subsequent decrease in energy caused by development of organized structures.

The 'energy' of the Performing Art Centre is symbolized by the predominant movements in the urban fabric along the pedestrian corridor and the Cultural Centre's seafront promenade— the site's two intersecting primary elements.

Branching algorithms and growth-simulation processes have been used to develop spatial representations into a set of basic geometries, and then superimposed with programmatic diagrams and architectonic interpretations in a series of iteration cycles. The primary components of this biological analogy (branches, stems, fruits and leaves) are transformed from abstract diagrams into architectonic design.

The central axis of Abu Dhabi's Cultural District is a pedestrian corridor that stretches from the Sheikh Zayed National Museum toward the sea. This central axis interacts with the seafront promenade to generate a branching geometry where islands are formed, isolated, and translated into distinct bodies within the structure to house the main spaces of the centre.

This diagram of the interacting paths becomes the primary organization system for the building, making the movement of the public through the structure an integral feature of the design.

The sculptural form of the Performing Arts Center emerges from this linear movement, gradually developing into a growing organism that sprouts a network of successive branches. As it winds through the site, the architecture increases in complexity, building up height and depth and achieving multiple summits in the bodies housing the performance spaces, which spring from the structure like fruits on a vine and face westward, toward the water.

The building, which reaches a height of sixty-two meters, becomes part of an inclining ensemble of structures that stretch from the Maritime Museum at its southern end to the Abu Dhabi Contemporary Art Museum at the northern tip.

With its center of mass at the water's edge, the Performing Arts Center focuses its volume along the central axis of the site. This arrangement interrupts the block matrix, at the Arterial Road, opening views to the sea and the skyline of Abu Dhabi.

Spatial Arrangement

The concert hall is above the lower four theatres, allowing daylight into its interior and dramatic views of the sea and city skyline from the huge window behind the stage. Local lobbies for each theatre are orientated towards the sea to

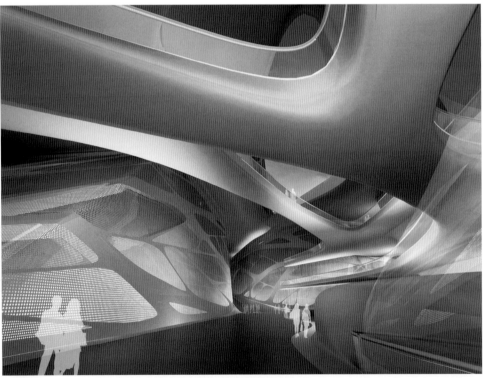

Interior

give each visitor a constant visual contact with their surroundings.

On the north side of the building, the restaurant offers a wide, shaded roof terrace, accessible through the adjacent conference centre above the lyrical theatre.

The Academy for Performing Arts is housed above the experimental theatre to the south, whilst in the eastern tail of the sculpture, retail areas take advantage of the pedestrian traffic using he bridge connecting the Performing Arts Centre with the central pedestrian zone.

〈デザイン・コンセプト〉

自然界の有機的な組織システムと成長についての分析的研究から、舞台芸術センターの独特な形態言語の枠組みとなる一連の位相幾何学に導かれた。

これら自然界のシナリオは、閉鎖系に供給されるエネルギーによって形成され、引き続く有機的な構造の成長によってエネルギーは減少する。舞台芸術センターの"エネルギー"は、敷地上で交差する2つの主要素、歩行者回廊に沿った都市構造を支配する動きと文化センターの海辺の遊歩道に象徴される。

分岐アルゴリズムと成長シミュレーションの方法を使って、空間表現を基本的な幾何学形態一式へと展開させ、次に、プログラムに基づいたダイアグラムと構成的な解釈を一連の反復的な循環の中に重ね合わせる。この生物学的な類似（枝，茎，実，葉）で構成された主要素を抽象的なダイアグラムから建築術的デザインへと転換する。

アブダビの文化地区の中央軸線は、シェイク・ザイード国立美術館から海へ延びる歩行者回廊である。この中央軸線は、海辺の遊歩道と互いに交流して、分岐するいくつもの幾何学形態を生み出す。そ

れらは建物内部にアイランドを形成し、分離されて、センターの主要な空間を収める個別の"ボディ"へと転化する。

互いに交流する通路がつくりだすこのダイアグラムは建物の主要な組織システムとなり、このデザインに欠かせない特色となっている建物全体を貫く人々の動きをつくりだす。

舞台芸術センターの彫刻的形態は、このリニアな動きから生まれ、連続する枝のネットワークが徐々に芽生え、成長する有機的な組織へ発展して行く。それは敷地を曲がりくねって進み、建築は複雑さを増し、高く、奥行き深く立ち上がり、舞台空間を収めた"ボディ"のなかに集合的な頂点をつくりあげる。それは葡萄の木に実る果実のように、構造体から芽生え、海の方、西に顔を向ける。

62mの高さに達する建物は、島の南端に計画されている海洋博物館（設計：安藤忠雄）から、北端に予定されているアブダビ現代美術館（設計：フランク・ゲーリー）に至る、傾斜する形態を持つ建築群の一部となる。

海辺に接する側にそのマッスの中心を置いた舞台芸術センターは、そのヴォリュームの焦点を敷地の中央軸線沿いに合わせる。この配置は、海とアブダビのスカイラインの眺めに向けて開きながら、中央軸線でブロック・マトリックスを遮る。

〈空間構成〉

コンサートホールは低層に位置する4つの劇場の上にあり、内部に昼光を引き入れ、舞台背後にある巨大な窓からは海と都市のスカイラインの壮麗な眺めが望める。各劇場のロビーは海に向き、それぞれの劇場への観客は常に周囲の風景を目にすることができる。

建物北側では、レストランが広い、日除けの付いたルーフテラスを提供し、ここへは叙事詩のような趣きを持つ劇場の上にある、隣接する会議センターを抜けてアクセスできる。

舞台芸術アカデミーは南側の実験劇場の上にある。彫刻的な建物の東側端部には店舗エリアがあり、舞台芸術センターを中央歩行者ゾーンと結ぶブリッジが歩行者の流れを誘い込む。

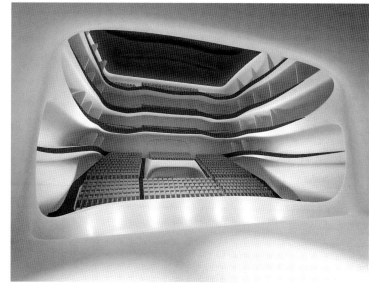

Concert hall

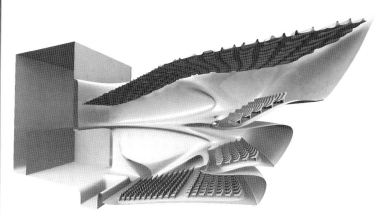

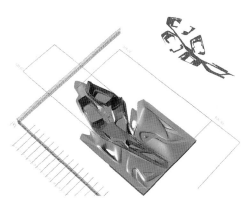

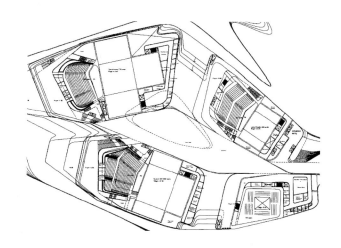

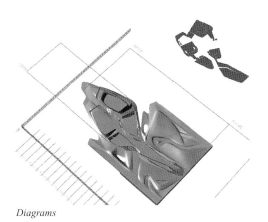

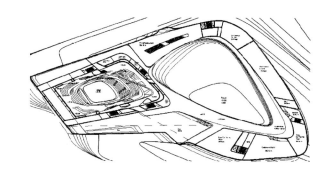

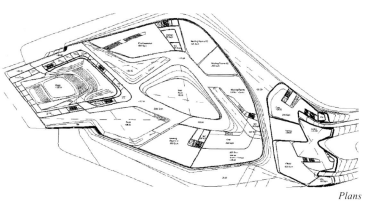

Diagrams

Plans

ATELIER NOTIFY

Paris, France
Design: 2007–   Construction: –2008

At the heart of the Parisian fashion district, the unique character of this concept brief produces an interesting mix of retail and industry, taking the customer through every step of the process of creating a garment, showcasing the brand's dexterity and craft with denim fabric.

Like an installation, the space is constructed with an elegant sculpture like gesture, organizing the interior and creating differentiated spaces. Its surface cuts through the facade and slabs, to allow natural light to flow down to the basement. It also contains the main stairs bringing guests to the heart of the atelier, establishing an effective connectivity between ground and basement levels.

The interior walls are thickened and embedded with storage and display units. They contain the services infrastructure necessary for the operation of the industrial machinery. Secondary back of house access is also concealed allowing staff to work around the shop in a seamless way.

By consolidating natural light with key circulation, the centre piece becomes fundamental in structuring the legibility of the shop, anchoring the shop's entrance at Rue Saint-Hyacinthe it creates a dynamic flow that is sequenced through the different components of the program. reception on the ground floor, bar and lounge in the basement, followed by tailoring and fitting, colouring, washing and drying. The ground floor on the Rue de la Sourdière side is connected only through the basement creating a space of opportunity, that can be flexibly operated as part of the atelier or as an independent gallery/event space/shop.

The facade creates a fluid transition between exterior and interior, using different levels of transparency and expressing lightness. It brings to the street a playful interaction between the sculptural contemporary interior and the historic street that can be emphasised by the selection of materials and the lighting design.

The atelier is therefore a hybrid, neither shop, nor production line, it conveys an insider's fashion experience that is polarized through a seamless architectural design, creating a niche destination that appeals to the five senses.

パリのファッション地区の中心に、小売店と産業の興味深い混合をつくりだす、特異な性格を持つコンセプトである。顧客は、婦人服をつくる一つ一つのプロセスを見ながら進み、デニム布地を使った細やかな職人技を目にすることになる。インスタレーションのように、優雅な彫刻に似たジェスチャーで空間を構築し、インテリアを組み立て、それぞれ性格の違うスペースをつくりだす。彫刻のような面は、自然光が地階に流れ落ちるように、ファサードやスラブを切り進み、主階段を取り囲み、客をアトリエの中心に導き、1階と地階の間を効果的に結ぶ。

内壁は厚く、収納と展示ユニットが嵌め込まれ、機械を動かすのに必要なサービス・インフラが設置される。業務用の2つ目の通路は、スタッフが店内のあちらこちらを回って働けるように、継ぎ目を見せない方法で隠される。自然光を集めることで、中心的存在である主動線は、空間を判読しやすくする基点となり、店の入り口をサン・ジャンサントゥ通りにしっかりと留め、1階のレセプション、地階のバーとラウンジ、そして仕立て、仮縫い、染め、洗い、乾燥と続く、プログラムの異なる構成要素を次々に通り抜けるダイナミックな流れをつくりだす。1階のスゥルディエール通りに面した側は地階を通してのみ連結され、アトリエの一部としても、独立したギャラリー／イベント・スペース／ショップとしてもフレキシブルに使える空間を構成する。ファサードは、透明度を何段階にも変え、軽さを表現することで内と外との滑らかな移行をつくりだし、彫刻的でコンテンポラリーな内部と古い歴史を持つ街路の間に、遊び心に富んだ交流を運び込む。それは材料の選択や照明デザインでさらに強調されるだろう。

従って、アトリエはハイブリッドな存在であり、ショップでも生産ラインでもなく、シームレスな建築デザインによって特化された、内部のファッション体験を伝え、五感に訴えるニッチな目的地をつくりだす。

Architects: Zaha Hadid Architects—
Zaha Hadid with Patrik Schumacher, design;
Ana M. Cajiao, project leader; Muthahar Khan,
Hooman Talebi, Maria Araya, design team
Client: Crystal Denim SAS
Consultant: AKT, structural; FirstQ ltd., mechanical,
electrical and plumbing
Program: atelier concept
Total area: 500 m²

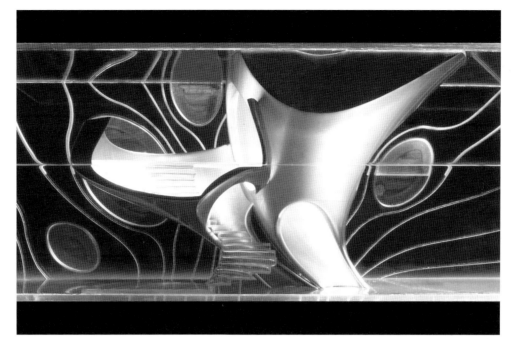

CENTRO URVASCO OFFICES

Vitoria, Spain
Design: 2007–

View from north

Aerial view

Architects: Zaha Hadid Architects—
Zaha Hadid with Patrik Schumacher, design;
Tiago Correia, project architect;
Aurora Santana, Alejandro Diaz, Victor Orive,
Jessica Knobloch, Maria Araya, Hooman Talebi, project
team
Clients: Centro Urvasco
Program: office and expo centers
Total floor area: 10,000 m²

View from west

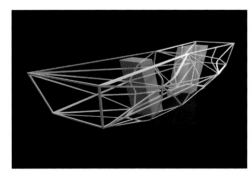

Diagram

View from east

The new corporate headquarters for Centro Urvasco is located in one of Vitoria's most prominent arteries, C/ Portal de Foronda, a generous boulevard with a large central lane park.

The proposed building works as a gateway to the city centre when arriving from other major cities, creating an important landmark of the entrepreneurial character of the Basque country.

The building mass and scale are skilfully knit into the new Lakua district, working as a transition element between the dominantly residential neighbourhood and the major thoroughfare.

The design criteria were to create a very slender, horizontal building with dynamic form which appears to hover over the park landscape. The reflective quality of the envelope grants the building an elegant lightness.

The buildings articulated volume will be dominantly glazed, allowing for excellent working conditions of natural light and ventilation, enhancing the building's sustainable performance.

The elongated floor plan is combined with the strategic position of the inclined cores to improve the vertical circulation, allowing for a flexible use of the office space.

The internal circulation strategy includes social spaces adjacent to the feature stairs, creating social pockets—reception, waiting and lounge spaces—for each floor, enabling different distributions and stimulating synergies between the different departments.

The building's four stories are supported by the two cores and the two perimeter trusses, using a triangulated geometry to optimize the primary structure.

The trusses create large cantilevers at the two ends of the building, releasing the ground to create a green landscape that brings the park into the surrounding fabric.

The architectural design concept lends a solid symbol for the Centro Urvasco companies and the building's establishment as a regional icon.

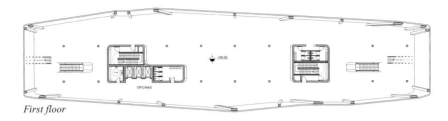
First floor

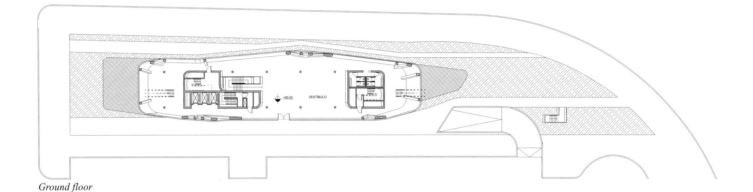
Ground floor

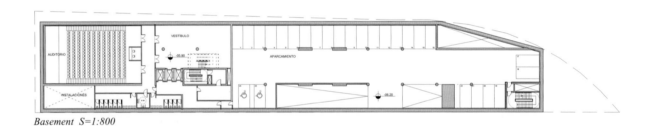
Basement S=1:800

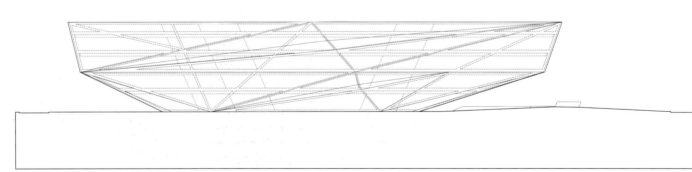
Southwest elevation

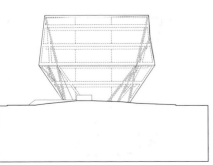
Southeast elevation S=1:800

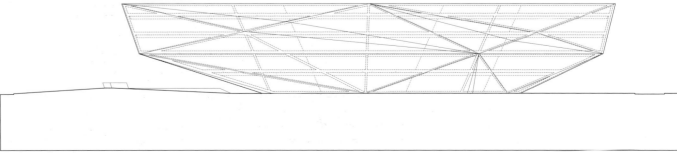
Northeast elevation

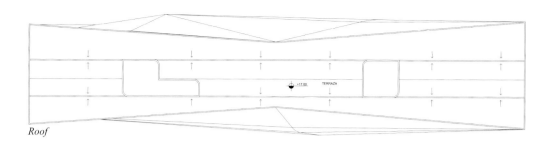

Roof

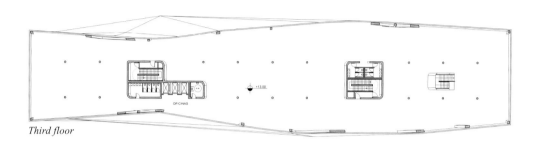

Third floor

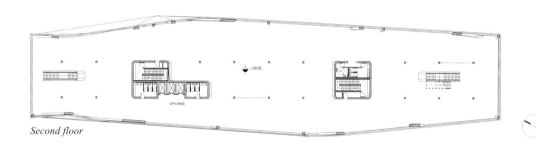

Second floor

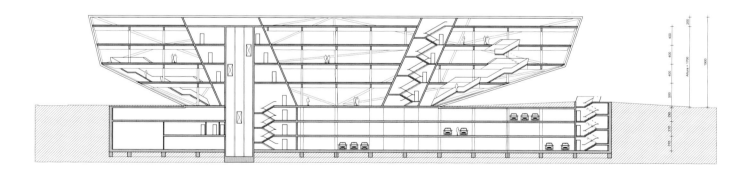

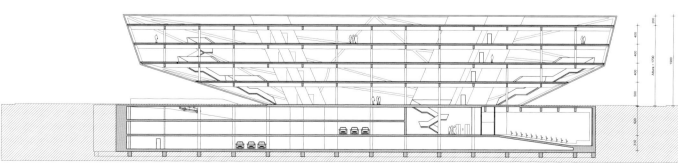

Longitudinal sections S=1:800

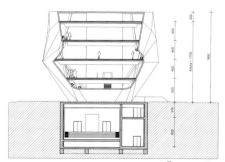

Cross section

セントロ・ウルバスコの新しい本社屋は，ビトリアの最も有名な幹線道路の一つ，中央レーンが広い緑地帯となっている大通り，C ／ポルタル・デ・フォロンダにある。

計画した建物は，他の主要都市から到着した時，市の中心へ向かう玄関口を示し，バスク国自治州の起業家精神を表現する重要なランドマークとなる。

建物の量塊とスケールは新ラクア地区に巧みに編み合わされ，大半が住宅地となっている周辺地域と幹線道路の間をつなぐ移行部としての役割を果たす。

デザイン上のクライテリアは，緑の多い風景の上を舞うように現れ，ダイナミックな形態を持つ，細身の，水平に広がる建物とすることであった。反射性のある外被は，建物に優雅で軽快な感じを与える。建物の分節されたヴォリュームは，大半がガラスで包まれ，自然光と自然通気のなかに快適な仕事環境を提供し，建物のサステイナビリティの度合いを高める。

長く延びた平面構成は，垂直動線を補うために傾斜をつけたコアの意図的な配置と組み合わされて，オフィス空間のフレキシブルな使用を可能にする。

内部の動線計画には，各階にソシアル・ポケット（レセプション，待合室，ラウンジ）をつくりだす，階段に隣接したソシアル・スペースが含まれ，異なる部局の間に個別の交流ルートが生まれ，共力作用を促す。

4 層の建物は 2 本のコアと，周縁部の 2 本のトラスで支持され，基本構造を最大活用するために三角形を単位としたジオメトリーを用いる。

トラスは建物の両端に大きな片持ちの張り出しを構成し，地上を解放して，緑に包まれたランドスケープをつくり，周囲の街並みのなかに公園を運び込む。

建築的なデザイン・コンセプトは，セントロ・ウルバスコ社のための堅固なシンボル，地方的なアイコンとしての建物の確立に力を貸す。

NILE TOWER

Cairo, Egypt
Design: 2007–

The new Nile Tower is designed as a gracious volume that elegantly borders the Nile River in the heart of Cairo.

The main structural elements of this 70 storey hotel and apartment tower are concrete fin walls that rotate gently over the full height of the tower. The gradual rotation of the fin walls generates a wide selection of orientations for the hotel rooms and apartments. These fin walls are reflected on the external facade, giving the tower its dynamic appearance.

On the west side—overlooking the river—the tower bulges out at the upper floors to maximize the views from hotel rooms and apartments. On the east side the tower is pulled out as a triangle on the lower floors to offer maximum stability. These opposite extensions make the overall tower seemingly lean over towards the Nile.

While enhancing the perspective when looking up from the foot of the tower this geometry also makes the tower seem in motion. This seeming rotation is further enhanced by emphasizing the diagonals running along the north and south facades.

The facade geometry on the west facade culminates at the lower levels in a volume overhanging the road towards the river, housing the common program of the tower.

At the foot of the tower, the facade drapes down over the large column free space next to the tower footprint where it forms a continuous glass plaza.

A high quality contribution to the east bank of the Nile, The Nile Tower also forms a valuable addition to the skyline of Cairo.

ナイル・タワーは，カイロの中心部に，ナイル川を優美に縁取る洗練されたヴォリュームとしてデザインされている。

ホテルと住戸の入る70階建てのタワーの中心的な構造要素は，タワーの高さ全体をだんだんに回って行くコンクリートのフィン状の壁である。徐々に回されたフィン・ウォールはホテルの部屋と住戸の方位に大幅な選択肢をつくりだす。これらのフィンは，外壁に光を反射させ，タワーにダイナミックな外観を与える。川を見晴らす西側で，タワーの上層は外側に膨らみ，ホテルの部屋や住戸からの眺めを大きく広げる。東側は安定性を高めるために，下層が引き伸されて三角形をかたちづくる。この逆方向への延長によって，タワー全体がナイル川に向かって傾いているように見える。

こうした幾何学的構成は，足下から見上げたときの遠近感を強める一方で，タワーが動いているような感じを与える。この見せかけの回転は，北と南のファサードに沿って通る対角線によって強められる。

西側ファサードの構成は，共有スペースの置かれた低層階の，川に向かう道の上に張り出したヴォリュームで頂点に達する。

タワーの足下で，ガラス張りの広場をかたちづくる1階に隣接して広がる無柱空間の上に，ファサードは優美なひだになって降りてくる。

Architects: Zaha Hadid Architects—
Zaha Hadid with Patrik Schumacher, design;
Joris Pauwels, project architect; Feng Xu,
Paulo Flores, Sharifah Alshalfan, Tariq Khayyat, project team
Program: hotel and apartment tower

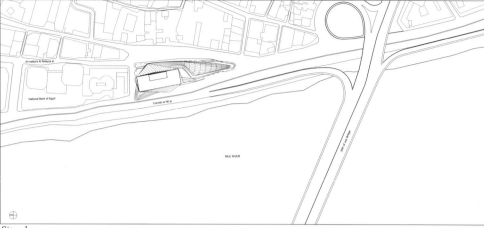

Site plan

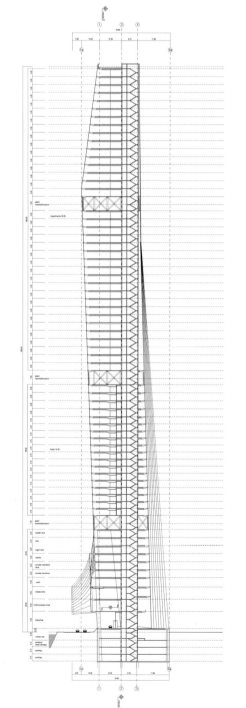
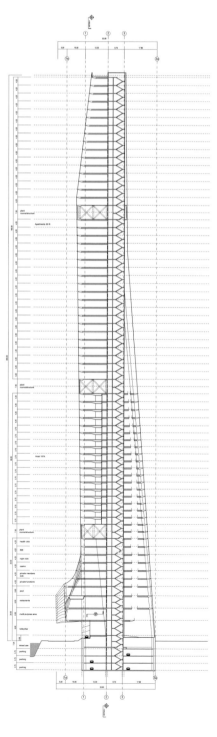

Sections

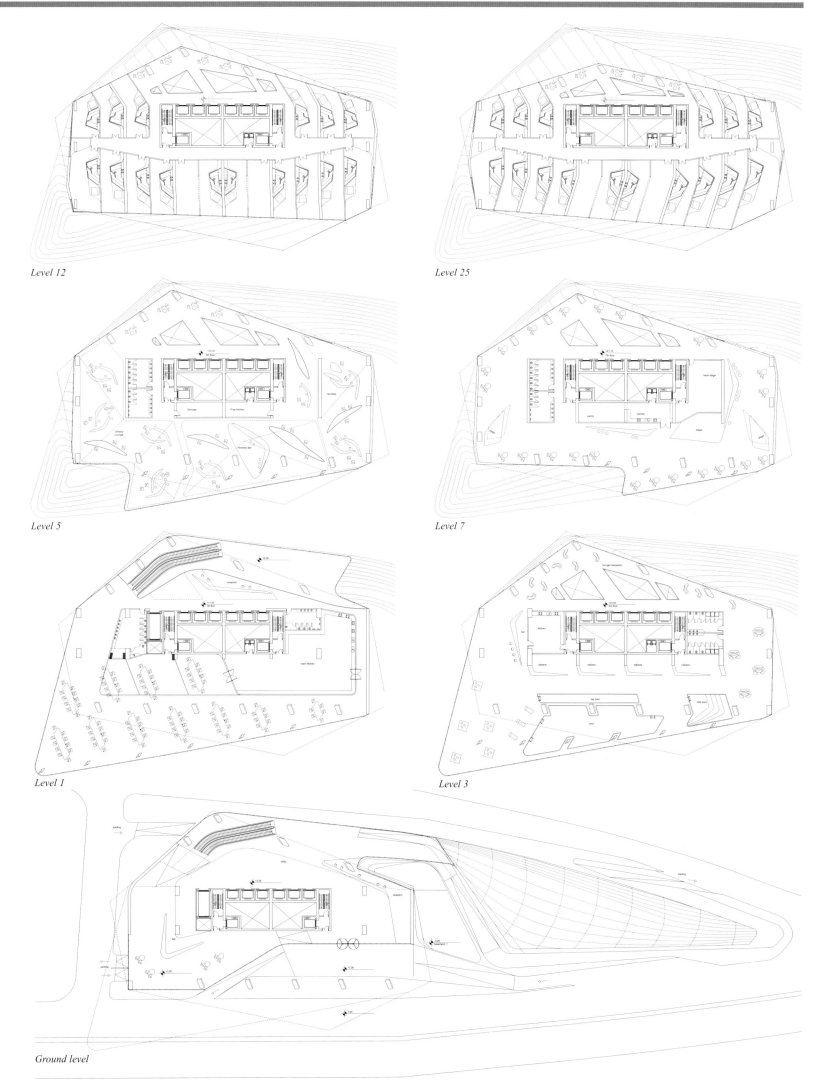

Level 12

Level 25

Level 5

Level 7

Level 1

Level 3

Ground level

FRANKFURT WESELER WERFT EXHIBITION SPACE

Frankfurt am Main, Germany
Design: 2007–

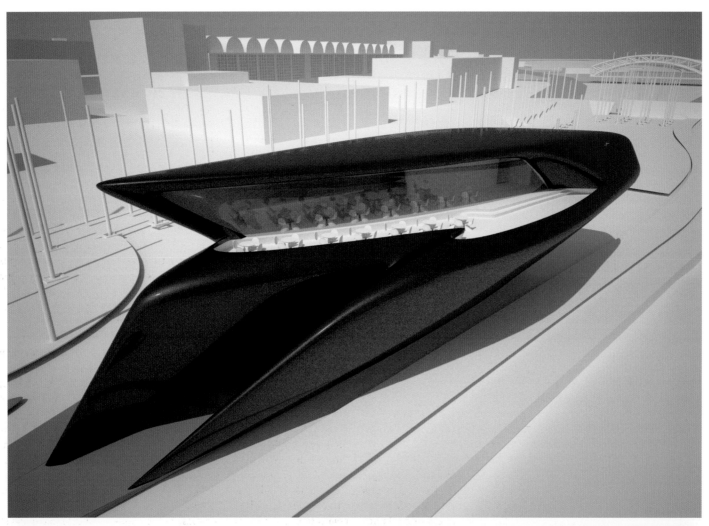

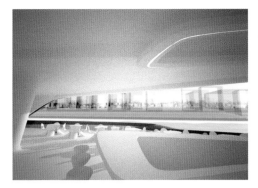 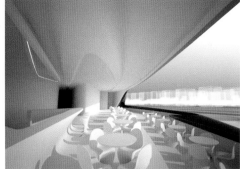  

Deustche Bank's art collection will require a temporary home over the renovation period.

One of the main reasons to build a public exhibition space in Frankfurt is Deustche Bank's long standing commitment to provide access for Frankfurt's citizens to the exquisite works of art on display inside the towers.

Frankfurt is Germany's fifth largest city with within the greater Frankfurt Rhine Main Area with over 5 million inhabitants.

Frankfurt as one of Germany's main cultural centres is well represented by its numerous museums and galleries located along the south shore of the Main River (e.g. Städelsches Kunstinstitut und Städtische Galerie) and museums like the Schirn Kunsthalle located the old city next to the Dom (Frankfurt Cathedral). Frankfurt's thriving and living culture's most recent additions is i.e. the Porticus, a small museum on a river-insula south of the city's centre.

Frankfurt is also an important location for the internet. Frankfurt is home to Germany's largest internet exchange point, DE-CIX, and is where domain names are registered for the top-level-domain .de.

The proposed site is located directly at the north bank; the newly reinstituted river promenade on the former Weseler Werft. Within the context of central Frankfurt it lays within 1 km distance east of the historic city centre between the districts Bornheim, the Osthafen and Sachsenhausen on the south bank of the river Main.

The site is part of an area that currently has been undergoing a dramatic change. The former industrial landscape—represented by its docks and large trade and storage plants is beginning to be converted into a contemporary mix of residential and cultural facilities. At its core is the introduction of the conversion of the former central meat market's building into the Headquarters of the European Central Bank. The construction site is directly adjacent to the proposed site and due for completion by 2011.

The new building is to house a single exhibition space that enables the host to hold approximately four exhibitions per year; allowing to show Frankfurt's citizens a good portion of the tower's art works in this new and dramatic setting. Part of the brief is the re-introduction of a river-shuttle—similar during a project of the artist Ayse Erkmen in 2001. The shuttle boat is intended to connect various cultural locations at the river and also providing additional transport and access to the temporary exhibition space at the Weseler Werft.

Schematic Design Proposal

As the main purpose of the building is to house exhibitions of art pieces it was our first aim to establish a spatial connection between the two sites: the client's own property and the new, temporary site at the Weseler Werft. The axis and orientation of the site towards Frankfurt's 'downtown' area and the two towers is therefore imbedded into the design of the pavilion. The Building is formed by a series of elements established through the brief. The outer shape is that of an agglomeration of interlocking bodies which have been eroded by the flow and modified by the interference of its program and the building's context.

The site's exclusive location within the city and its accessibility alongside and from the river is a further key to our design approach. Being at the center of a drastically developing part of Frankfurt and directly positioned next to the EZB site, the building will be part of a new landscape and addition to the Visitors and Citizens of Frankfurt. Our proposed design has a clear connection to its site, the river and should indicate its dynamic, temporal nature.

The Program and Circulation

The proposed building is located directly adjacent to the river bank. It is raised by 2.5 meters above the ground level in order to provide safety against flooding. The main access to the building is via a generous staircase which is directed towards the city center; leading visitors up to the second floor. The internal vertical distribution is offered by a vertical core, a staircase and elevator, by which the visitors have access to the first floor's gallery space and means of escape onto the ground level.

Disabled access from the ground level into the building is provided by using the centrally controlled elevator that serves barrier free access to both internal levels.

All secondary functions either share the same vertical circulation or have key operated access to non-public areas branching of the main core and circulation.

The Upper Floor

Arriving at the top of the staircase the visitor enters the building on the upper level. A central lobby provides access to the ticketing, the small gallery shop, the wardrobe and the general washroom facilities. From this point the visitors can continue via the stair core into the gallery on the first floor level. Visitors for the restaurant on the second floor are also distributed from the central lobby. The restaurant is located around the central core and at the fully glazed front part of the space. Entering the restaurant the visitors find a bar for refreshments and general seating along the front facade which also extends onto the large terrace overlooking the Main River. The internal floor level is raised in proportion to the terrace in order to provide an unrestricted view for the seated person.

The restaurant's kitchen and secondary functions are located at the eastern end of the upper level. Access and supply to these spaces are currently considered to share the key operated elevator. Additional cold storage and bin storage space are located in the base level on the ground.

The Gallery and Administration Space

The gallery space is organized in such way as to provide a maximum amount of flexibility for the curation of the various exhibition layouts. Nevertheless, the general access route is programmed to allow for a separate access and exit into and from the space in order to avoid collision. The visitors flow therefore circulates around the building's core from which both sides they enter and exit the gallery. A discreet connection to the external staircase at the opposite end of the space acts as secondary means of escape and also provides access for larger art works and equipment onto this floor.

The gallery's administration is also located on the lower level and is accessed discreetly from the key operated access from the elevator. The administration is comparatively small but is autonomous. The small office has a tea kitchen and a staff washroom. The small office space enjoys views over the eastern section of the Main River and is sized to house desk work of the residing administrator and small meetings.

Services

All services of the building are located on the roof above the secondary areas on the second level. The reduction of ceiling levels allows for an incorporation of the plant space invisible under the outer skin of the building. The main supply of air into the gallery is then run via vertical shaft routes and in-between the interior cladding to the supply positions in the gallery and into floor supply points at the restaurant.

Construction

As the proposed building is a temporary pavilion with a projected usage of 4 years we propose a composite construction with a steel frame as its main structure. This type of construction allows for a quick installation given the short timeframe of the project. The later added proposed outer cladding (as a cold facade) and the interior cladding will allow the building to be sealed as soon as possible, so that the continuation of the fit-out and the remaining external works can be run in parallel.

The main structure and most of the cladding could be fabricated to allow for a re-assembly should the pavilion be re-erected after its first period of usage.

Facade

We envisage the materiality and the appearance of the building to be that of a smooth shell. The material we are proposing is a metal cladding; treated to have the least amount of visible joints in order to eliminate any notion of scale. Several proposals for a texture treatment of this shell cladding show the range in which we want to locate a consensus between glossiness and an up-close texture which we think will also enhance the sculpture-like quality of the building. The glazed facade elements are seen as inlays into the outer shell and should therefore be treated as smooth transitions of the general curvature. We consider these glazing to be slightly mirrored or tinted in order to complete the outer shape and appearance of the building.

Site plan

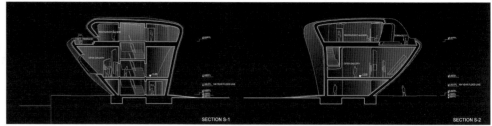

Cross sections

Architects: Zaha Hadid Architects—
Zaha Hadid with Patrik Schumacher, design;
Helmut Kinzler, project leader;
Daniel Fiser, project designer;
Jan Huebner, Cornelius Schlotthauer,
Lourdes Sanchez, Brian Dale, Shiqi Li,
Nantapon Juungurn, Susanne Lettau, project team
Program: temporary exhibition space

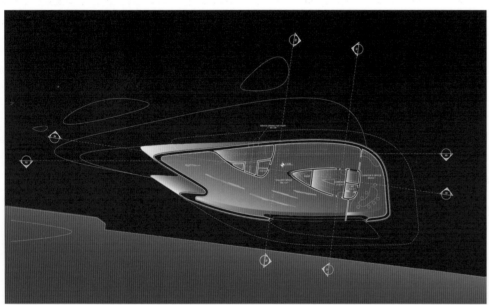

Second floor

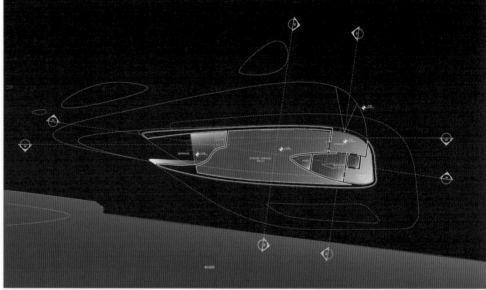

Third floor

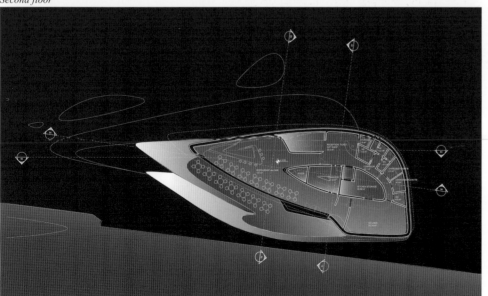

First floor

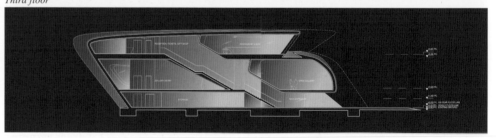

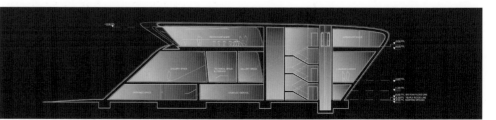

Longitudinal sections

ドイツ銀行のアートコレクションは，改修が終わるまで一時的な収蔵場所を必要とすることになるだろう。

フランクフルトに公的な展示スペースを建設しようという主な理由の一つには，フランクフルト市民に高層ビルのなかに飾られた，素晴らしい芸術作品に触れてもらうことにドイツ銀行が長く関わってきたことがある。

フランクフルトはドイツで5番目の大都市であり，グレーター・フランクフルト・ライン・マイン地域には500万人を越える住民がいる。ドイツに於ける文化の中心の一つとしてのフランクフルトは，マイン川の南河岸に沿って並ぶ数多い美術館やギャラリー（例えばシュテーデル美術館と市立美術館），そして旧市街のドーム（フランクフルト大聖堂）の隣にあるシルン美術館などによく示されている。フランクフルトの繁栄し，活気のある文化状況のなかへごく最近加わったのが，都心の南にある川の中の島に建つ小さな美術館，ポルティクスである。

フランクフルトはまた，インターネットの重要拠点として，ドイツ最大のインターネットエクスチェンジDE-CIX（ドイツ商用インターネットエクスチェンジ）の本部があり，ドメインネームはトップレベルドメインの.deが登録されている。

敷地は，マイン川北岸の堤に直接位置している。ここは以前のヴェーゼラー・ヴェルフトに再整備された新しい川沿いの遊歩道である。フランクフルトの中心部のコンテクストのなか，ボルンハイム地区と，マイン川の南河岸に面し，オスタフェンとザクセンハウゼンの間に広がる旧市街から東に1kmの場所に横たわっている。

敷地は最近急激に変貌を続ける地域に属している。ドックや大規模な取引場，貯蔵プラントに代表される，以前の産業地としての風景は，住宅や文化施設のコンテンポラリーな混合施設に変わりはじめ，その中心となるのが，以前の中央食肉市場の欧州中央銀行本店への転換である。2011年に完成が予定されているその建設地は，このプロジェクトの敷地に隣接している。

新しい建物は，年に4回ほどの展覧会を開催できる単一の展示空間を持ち，フランクフルト市民に，高層ビル内にある芸術作品のなかの優品をこの新しい，ドラマチックな背景のなかで鑑賞してもらうことができる。設計概要には，2001年のアイシャ・エルクメン展の開催期間中に行われたと同様に，リバーシャトルを再び導入することが含まれている。シャトルボートは川沿いの様々な文化施設を結ぶと共に，ヴェーゼラー・ヴェルフトに設置される仮設の展示場への輸送手段とアクセスを加えるだろう。

〈計画案の概要〉
建物の主要な目的は芸術作品の展覧会を開催することなので，2つの敷地，クライアント自身が所有するタワーとヴェーゼラー・ヴェルフトの新しい，仮設のサイトとの間の空間的な連結を確立することを第一に目指した。従ってフランクフルトのダウンタウン地区と2本のタワーに向かう，敷地の軸線と方位は，パヴィリオンのデザインのなかに埋め込まれている。建物は概要を通して設定された一連のエレメントによって形成されている。外形は，噛み合された岩のような塊が，流れに浸食され，プログラムと建物のコンテクストの干渉によって，いくぶん形を変えた，そんな姿に見える。

敷地の，都市の中の独占的な位置と，横手と川からのアクセスの容易さは，デザインを進める上でのさらなる鍵となった。フランクフルトの，徹底的な開発が進行する地区の中心，また欧州中央銀行の敷地の隣という場所にあって，建物は新しいランドスケープとなり，フランクフルトへの訪問者と市民にとって新しい顔になるだろう。提示案は，敷地と川に対する明快な結びつきを持ち，そのダイナミックで仮設的な性格を示唆するだろう。

〈プログラムと動線〉
建物は，川の堤に直接配置され，洪水に対する安全を確保するために地表から2.5mほど高く持ち上げられる。メイン・アクセスは都心方向に向いた広い階段を経て，来館者を3階まで導く。内部の垂直動線は，階段とエレベータが収まった垂直のコアで，来館者はここを経由して2階のギャラリーへ出られる。これは1階を飛ばして進む方法ともなる。

1階から建物へ入る身体が不自由な人のアクセスは，2つの階へのバリアフリーアクセスとしての機能を持つ中央制御されたエレベータからである。すべての二次的な機能スペースは，同じ垂直動線を共有するか，メイン・コアと動線の分岐する非公共的なエリアへ，鍵で駆動するエレベータを利用する。

〈上階〉
階段の最上部に着くと，来館者は建物の上階に出る。中央ロビーが切符売り場，小さなギャラリー・ショップ，クローク，一般洗面所へのアクセスを提供する。この地点から，階段コアを経て，2階のギャラリーへ進むことができる。3階のレストランへ行くにもまた中央ロビーから進む。レストランは中央コアの周りと，この空間の全面ガラスになった正面部分にある。レストランに入ると，軽食用のバーとマイン川を見晴らす広いテラスへも延びている正面ファサードに沿って一般席が並んでいる。レストラン内の床は，座っている人にも眺めがよく見えるように，テラスに合わせて高さを上げている。

レストランの厨房と二次的な機能は上階の東端に置かれる。これらのスペースへのアクセスと補給は現在，鍵で駆動するエレベータを共有することを考えている。追加の冷蔵室と瓶の収蔵場所は1階の基部に置かれる。

〈ギャラリーと管理事務スペース〉
ギャラリー・スペースは，多様な展示構成に最大限のフレキシビリティを与えるように構成されている。とはいえ一般のルートは衝突を避けるために，このスペースへの出口と入口を分けている。このため，来館者の流れは，片側にギャラリーの入り口，片側に出口のあるコアの周りを循環することになる。スペースの反対側の端にある外階段への控えめな接続部は，二次的な避難路の役割も果たし，またこの階への大きな芸術作品や設備の搬入口となる。

ギャラリーの管理部門もまた下の階に位置し，鍵で駆動するエレベータから目立たずに出入りできる。管理部門のスペースは比較的小さいが，自立している。小さなオフィスにはティー・キッチンやスタッフ用の洗面所が付き，マイン川の東側部分を見晴らす眺めを楽しめ，在勤する事務管理者のデスクワークと少人数の会合に対応できる広さがある。

〈サービス〉
建物のすべてのサービスは，3階の二次的なエリアの屋根の上に配置されている，天井の高さを抑えることで，建物の外被の下に，見えないようにプラント・スペースを合体できる。このためギャラリーへの主な給気は垂直のシャフトや内部の被覆の間を通ってギャラリーの給気口に，そしてレストランの床の給気口へ流れる。

〈建設〉
建物は，4年間の使用を予定した仮設のパヴィリオンなので，鉄骨枠組を用いた混構造を提案した。この建設方式によれば，プロジェクトに与えられた時間枠の中で，迅速な据え付けができる。後から付加される，外側の被覆（コールド・ファサード）と内部の被覆が可能な限り素早く建物を密封し，備品の取り付けの継続と残りの外側の作業を平行して行えるだろう。主構造と被覆の大半は，組み立て直せるように製作され，パヴィリオンの最初の使用期間の後に再び組み上げることができるだろう。

〈ファサード〉
建物の材質感と外観は，滑らかなシェルのようになると予想している。提案した材料は，メタル被覆である。スケールのどのような概念をも消去するために，目に見えるジョイントは最小限にするように処理する。このシェル被覆に対するテクスチャーの扱いについてのいくつかの提案は，建物の彫刻的な質を強めることにもなる，光沢ときめの細かいテクスチャーが調和する次元を探した範囲を示している。ガラスのファサードは，外側のシェルに嵌め込まれたものとみなし，全体的な湾曲のなめらかな移行として扱われる。これらのガラス面は，建物の外形と外観を完全なものにするために，軽い鏡面仕上げにするか薄い色をつけることを考えている。

HEYDAR ALIYEV MERKEZI CULTURAL CENTER

Baku, Azerbaijan
Design: 2007–

Auditorium

Auditorium

Introduction

Haydar Aliyev Cultural Centre will give the city of Baku, Azerbaijan a major new venue and a landmark building for the city. Dedicated to the former president of Azerbaijan, the Cultural Centre will house a conference hall with 3 auditoriums, a library and a museum.

Site Strategies

This ambitious project will play an integral role in the intellectual life of the city. Located close to the city centre, the site will play a pivotal role in the redevelopment of Baku. The site neighbouring the Haydar Aliyev Cultural Centre is designated for residential, offices, a hotel and commercial centre, whilst the land between the Cultural Centre and the city's main thoroughfare will become the Cultural Plaza—an outdoor piazza for the Cultural Centre as well as a welcoming space for the visitors.

Design

The proposal for the Haydar Aliyev Cultural Centre envisions a fluid form which emerges by the folding of the landscape's natural topography and by the wrapping of individual functions of the Centre. All functions of the Centre, together with entrances, are represented by folds in a single continuous surface. This fluid form gives an opportunity to connect the various cultural spaces whilst, at the same time, providing each element of the Centre with its own identity and privacy. As it folds inside, the skin erodes away to become an element of the interior landscape of the Cultural Centre.

The museum faces out into the landscape—participating in the urban fabric of the city developing around the site. Its glass facade is slightly interrupted with the sculptural interplay between the outer skin and the ground. The interior is an extension of the natural topology of the site with the glass facade flooding the museum in natural light. The ground surface of the museum begins to fold and merges to the outer skin which allows the new extension to become part of the topography of the site, whilst ramps connect the ground floor with the mezzanine levels above.

The library faces north for controlled daylight and has its own entrance on this elevation. The reading and the archive floors are stacked on top of each other, and wrapped within the folds of the outer envelope. The floors fall to each other with ramps connecting them, creating a continuous path of circulation. The library and the museum are also connected by a ramp that leads through the ground floor of the library to the first floor of the museum. Additionally, the library is connected to the conference hall via a bridge that 'flies' through the library's entrance foyer.

The conference hall accommodates 3 auditoriums of different sizes. Its form leans into the Cultural Plaza to create the necessary inclination for the seating. All three auditoriums and their associated facilities have a direct access to the plaza. The main entrance is located in the void created by the outer skin being 'stretched' between volume of the museum and the library tower. A secondary entrance is situated on the north side of the building.

Landscape

The landscape emerges from the ground to merge with the building. This rippling, manifest as earth mounds, fades as it moves away from the main building to radiate like waves. The building itself is also merges into the landscape to become the Cultural Plaza—further blurring the boundary between the building and the ground. These landscape formations also direct the circulation of visitors through the building and Cultural Plaza, where outdoor activities and performances take place.

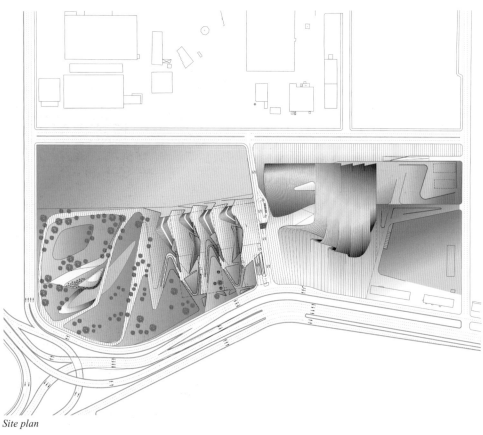

Site plan

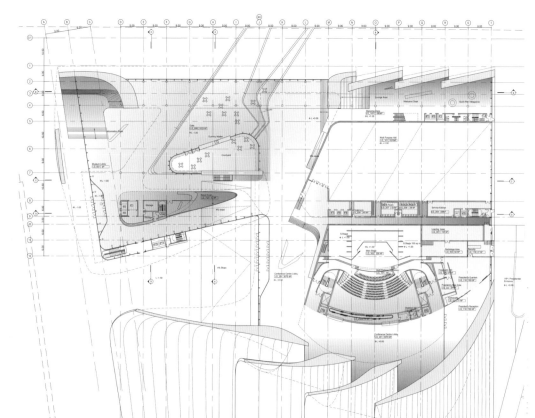

Ground level

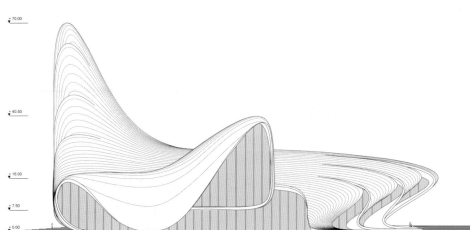

Southwest elevation

Southeast elevation

ハイダル・アリエフ文化センターは, アゼルバイジャンのバクー市に, 新しい活動が発生する場とランドマークを提供するだろう。アゼルバイジャンの前の大統領に献じられた文化センターは3つのホールを持つ会議場, 図書館, 美術館で構成される。

〈敷地〉
この野心的なプロジェクトは, 都市の知的生活のなかで不可欠な役割を演じるだろう。都心に近い敷地は, バクーの再開発の中枢を占めることになる。ハイダル・アリエフ文化センターの周辺は, 住宅, オフィス, ホテル, コマーシャルセンターに指定され, 一方, 文化センターと街の幹線道路の間の土地は文化センターの屋外広場であり, 訪れる人を迎える文化広場となる。

〈デザイン〉
ハイダル・アリエフ文化センターの計画案では, 風景をかたちづくる自然の地形を折りたたみ, センターの個別の機能を包み込むことから生まれる流れるような形態が構想されている。すべての機能空間はエントランスと共に, 一つの連続する面が構成する折りたたまれたひだの重なりで表現される。この流体のような形態は, 様々なスペースを連結する格好の状況をつくりだす一方で, センターの各要素に独自の性格とプライバシーを与える。内側を包み込みながら, 外被は浸食され, 文化センター内部のランドスケープの一要素となる。

美術館は, 敷地周囲に発展を続ける都市構成に加わるランドスケープに面している。そのガラスのファサードは, 外被と地表の間の彫刻的な相互作用によってわずかに遮られる。内部は敷地の自然な地形の延長であり, ガラスのファサードが美術館を自然光で満たす。美術館の1階の床は折りたたまれ, 外被と合体して新たな延長部を形成して敷地の地形の一部となり, 一方, スロープが1階と上のメザニン階を結ぶ。

図書館は昼光を制御するために北に面し, この立面に専用のエントランスがある。閲覧室とアーカイブ階は, 上下に積み重ねられ, 外被の折りたたまれたひだに包まれる。2つの階は両者をつなぐスロープで互いに流入し, 連続する動線通路をつくりだす。図書館と美術館はまた, 図書館の1階を通って美術館の2階に至るスロープでも結ばれる。さらに, 図書館は, そのエントランス・ホワイエ全体を"飛ぶ"ように架け渡されたブリッジで会議場と連結される。

会議場には大きさの違う3つのホールがある。建物は文化広場の方に傾きをもたせて構成され, 座席に必要な傾斜をつくりだす。3つのホールとその付属施設からはすべて広場へ直接出られる。メイン・エントランスは美術館と図書館タワーの間に"引き伸された"外被がつくりだすヴォイドのなかにある。二次的なエントランスは建物の北側にある。

〈ランドスケープ〉
ランドスケープは地表から立ち上がり, 建物と合体する。このさざ波のような起伏は, 地球の小さな丘のように現れ, 主屋から波のように放射状に広がって進みながら消えて行く。建物そのものもまた, ランドスケープと合体して文化広場となり, 建物と地表との境界をさらに曖昧にする。これらのランドスケープ構成はまた, 建物を通り抜け文化広場へと, 来館者の動線を方向付ける。広場では戸外での活動やパフォーマンスが行われる。

Architects: Zaha Hadid Architects—
Zaha Hadid with Patrik Schumacher, design;
Saffet Kaya Bekiroglu, project architect;
Jaime Bartolome, Marc Boles, Simone Fuchs,
Fadi Mansour, Liat Muller, Shiqi Li, Lillie Liu,
Deepti Zachariah, project team

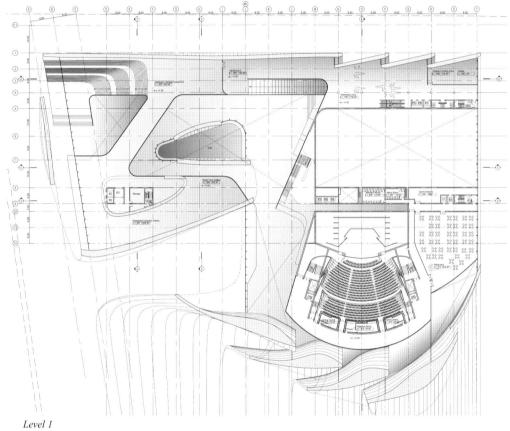

Level 1

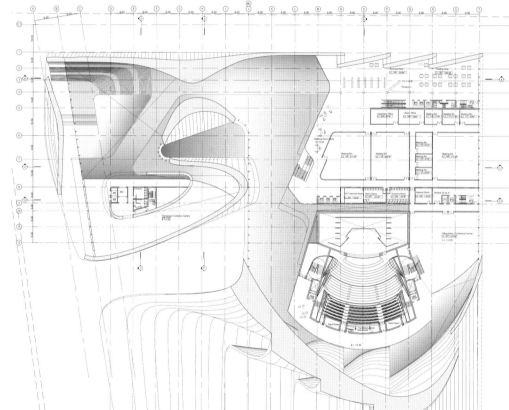

Level 2

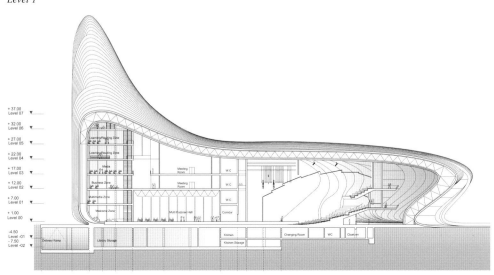

◁*Section A-A*

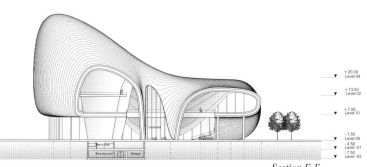

Section E-E

SAL ADAMS RESORTS

Munandhua Island, Maldives
Design: 2007–

This study for a high-end luxury resort, developed in conjunction with Sal Adams Resorts is targeted at the pinnacle of the exclusive travel market. The resort's reception lobby, restaurants and spas are located in the heart of the island, whilst each private residential villa for guests extends beyond the shoreline creating an autonomous resort for the twenty visiting parties.

The unique guest villas consist of both on-shore and offshore components. The onshore units of each villa contain private spa and sauna areas and are connected via a pier to the 500 m² residential villas. The master bedroom and guest bedroom are housed in separate wings of each villa, centred on a multi-levelled living space, courtyard and pool area. This central space is all housed beneath a retractable glass roof. A spectacular underwater living room has been situated beneath the swimming pool, allowing the guest to explore the underwater world of the reef.

This study explores the latest construction technologies to create a unique spatial experience. Minimum-footprint foundations on the sea bed increase to their maximum diameter at the surface to support each villa. The entire superstructure and all of the building's surfaces are finished in glass of different levels of opacity. This radical approach to surfaces combined with purist aesthetics and distinctive spatial features create a unique experience for each guest at the resort.

サル・アダムス・リゾートとの共同で開発された最高級の贅沢なリゾートのためのスタディは，特権的旅行マーケットの頂点を目指したものである。リゾートのレセプション・ロビー，レストラン，スパは島の中心にあり，客が個別に占有できるヴィラは海岸線を越えて広がり，20組のグループのための独立したリゾートをつくりだす。

宿泊客用の独特なヴィラは，海岸と浅瀬の中，両方に配置された2つの部分で構成されている。各ヴィラの浜辺の上にあるユニットには専用のスパとサウナがあり，500平米の住宅ヴィラへ桟橋でつながる。各ヴィラには，多層のリビングスペース，コートヤード，プールを中心にして，主寝室とゲスト寝室が両翼に分かれて配置され，この中央空間はすべて，伸縮自在のガラス屋根の下に収まっている。ドラマチックな水中の居間が水泳プールの下にあり，浅瀬が広がる水中の世界を探検できる。

スタディでは，特別な空間体験ができるように最先端の建設技術の可能性についていろいろ検討してみた。海底で最小限に面積を抑えた基礎は，海面ではその直径を最大限に広げ，各ヴィラを支える。上部構造全体と建物のすべての表面は，様々な度合いの不透明性を持つガラスで仕上げられる。この表面構成に対する徹底的な方法は，ピュリストの美学，特徴のある空間と組み合わされて，一人ひとりの客がユニークな体験をすることのできる環境をつくりだす。

Architects: Zaha Hadid Architects—
Zaha Hadid with Patrik Schumacher, design;
Nils-Peter Fischer, project director;
Britta Knobel, project leader;
Daniel Widrig, Melike Altinisik, design team
Client: Sal Adams Group/Sal Adams Resorts
Consultants: Prof. Matthias Schuler, Transsolar Energietechnik GmbH, environmental, mechanical and electrical
Program: high end luxury resort on Munandhua Island, the Maldives; residence prototype

WINTER FESTIVAL HALL ERL

Erl, Austria
Design: 2007–

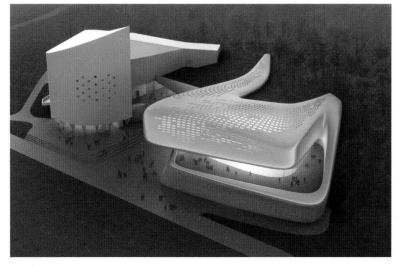

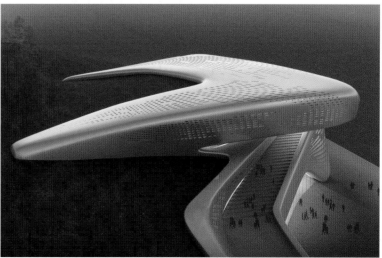

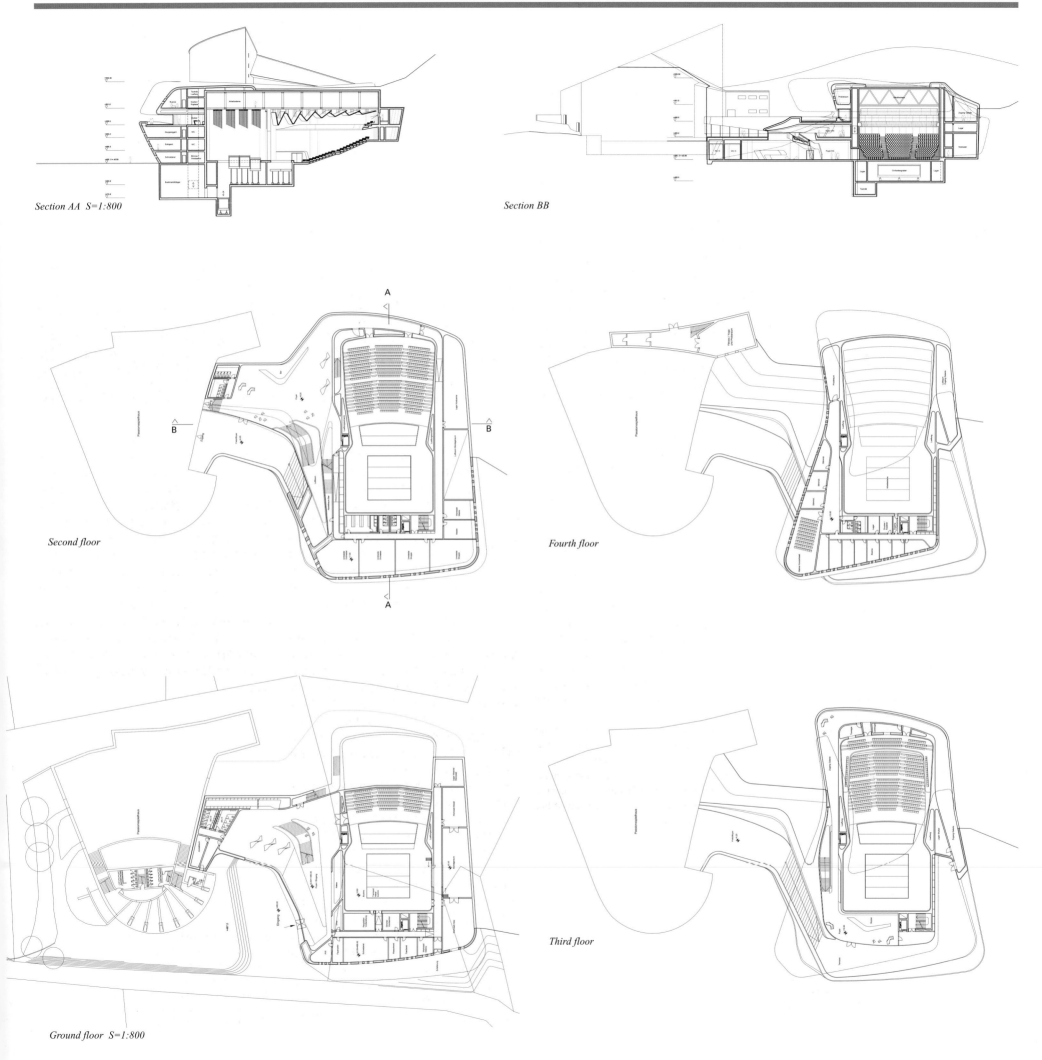

Section AA S=1:800

Section BB

Second floor

Fourth floor

Ground floor S=1:800

Third floor

Auditorium

Entrance hall

The brief called for an extension of the existing Festival Hall in Erl, Austria. The existing building, an un-insulated listed building can not be heated during the winter period and is subsequently in use only during the summer. The proposed extension will house the Winter and additional Summer programmes and bring year round use to festival hall. The design for the new building comprises a concert hall for an audience of 750, lobby areas, bars, dressing rooms, offices, and workshops (rehearsal studios). Areas such as lobbies, offices, workshops and rehearsal studios serve both the extension building as well as the existing Festival Hall.

The nearby woods form the inspiration for the architectural concept, specifically the root systems of the trees. The new building merges with the landscape in a similar way to the complex intersection of root systems in the ground. The building can be also understood as a continuous loop which on one side gently touches the existing Festival Hall and on the other side merges with the landscape. Furthermore, the geometry of the new building relates to the contour lines of the hill. In this way the new building can also be understood as an extension of the natural landscape.

The design intention was not to over-shadow the existing building but to respect its original design and create one new ensemble, one coherent entirety. This is achieved through the creation of a new architectural language that is a contemporary interpretation of the existing hall.

The new building is separated in two areas— the public areas (lobbies, bar, terrace and auditorium) and the staff and backstage areas (stage, workshops, offices, changing rooms and staff rooms). The entrance/lobby area of the new building can be utilised by both the audiences of

the existing Festival Hall and those of the new extension. The new entrance is also a focal point both framed and well defined by the two complementing buildings.

The non-public areas are located in the south and west adjacent to the auditorium. The workshops are designed to be on the ground floor level and to be accessible from stage. The auditorium and the stage are acoustically detached from the workshop areas via an additional corridor which is also used as an emergency exit. The storage for the scenery is located on level 2 which can be accessed with the stage lift system. A core which is located westwards of the stage includes the vertical circulation, sanitary facilities and storage rooms. The offices are located on the 4th floor. This level cantilevers up to 20 m and covers the below terrace and foyer areas.

Three foyer areas guide the audiences to the circles. Openings in the floor slabs connect the lobbies vertically, form one continuous space and enable views through the entire lobby area. The bar area is located adjacent to the terrace and can be utilised by both the spectators of the new and old Festival Hall.

設計概要は，オーストリア，エルルにある祝祭ホールの拡張を求めている。既存の建物は，断熱されていない，文化財指定の建物で，冬季に暖房は出来ないことから，夏の間だけ使われている。提案した増築では，冬季と新たに加わる夏のプログラムが開催でき，祝祭ホールは年間を通して使えるようになる。新しい建物のデザインは，750席のコンサートホール，ロビー・エリア，バー，洗面所，オフィス，ワークショップ（リハーサル・スタジオ）で構成される。ロビー，オフィス，ワークショップ，リハーサル・スタジオのようなエリアは，増築棟と既存の祝祭ホールの両方で使われる。

近くの森からは，特に，木々の根のシステムから建築コンセプトのヒントを得た。新しい建物は，地中にある根の複雑な交差と同じような方法で風景に融合する。建物はまた，片側が既存の祝祭ホールに緩やかに触れ，もう一方の側が風景に合体する連続するループとして理解することも出来る。さらに，新しい建物のジオメトリーは丘の等高線と結びついている。この点から言えば，建物は自然風景の延長として理解することも出来る。

デザインの意図は，既存の建物の影を薄くするのではなく，その固有のデザインをリスペクトし，新しい調和，完全なまとまりをつくりだすことである。これは既存ホールのコンテンポラリーな解釈である新しい建築言語の創造によって達成される。

新しい建物は次の2つのエリアに分かれている。パブリック・エリア（ロビー，バー，テラス，オーディトリアム）とスタッフ／バックステージ・エリア（舞台，ワークショップ，オフィス，更衣室，スタッフルーム）。新しい建物のエントランス／ロビー・エリアは，既存の祝祭ホールと増築棟，その両方の観客が利用できる。新しいエントランスはまた，2つの補完し合う建物によって枠取られ，明快に輪郭を定められた焦点を構成する。

非公共的なエリアは，オーディトリアムに隣接し

て南と西に配置されている。ワークショップは1階に配置され，舞台からアクセス出来るようにデザインされている。オーディトリアムと舞台は，ワークショップ・エリアから，緊急時の出口にもなる補足的な廊下によって音響的に引き離されている。舞台装置の収納場所はレベル2にあり，舞台のリフト・システムを使って出入りする。舞台の西に向かって位置するコアには垂直動線，洗面所，収納が含まれる。オフィスは5階にある。このレベルは片持ちで20m張り出し，下のテラスとホワイエ・エリアを覆っている。3つのホワイエが聴衆を桟敷席に導く。ロビーを垂直に結ぶ，床スラブにとられた開口は，連続する一室空間をかたちづくり，ロビー・エリア全体が見通せる。バー・エリアはテラスの隣に置かれ，新旧の祝祭ホールの両方の観客によって利用される。

Architects: Zaha Hadid Architects—
Zaha Hadid with Patrik Schumacher, design;
Markus Planteu, project leader;
Eirini Fountoulaki, Thomas Mathoy,
Theodora Ntatsopoulou, Markus Planteu, design team
Consultants: Bollinger und Grohmann, structural; Alp-
solar, mechanical and electrical

OPUS, OFFICE TOWER DUBAI

Dubai, United Arab Emirates
Design: 2007–   Construction: –2010

Design Philosophy

We see the masterplan concept and realization as a monumental attempt to in the modification and evolution of the existing urban fabric of Dubai. The masterplan clearly proposes a series of unique buildings connected by a series of low rise podia and streets that together with the canal create a unified new whole, that is the Dubai business bay.

It is clear that from its inception, the masterplan seeks interconnectedness and uniqueness. We sought to apply these two qualities within our design repertoire in our research for providing unique, variable and fluid spaces within a project that is outward looking and relating to a series of landmark projects in this new development.

Masterplan Context

The site for the development of the Omniyat flagship office/retail tower is located in a prominent location in the Business Bay masterplan. The two plots that are interlinked by a continuous low level podium structure which essentially unites the project and provides the unique possibility to interpret the project as one mass.

Location on Site

The building volume extends to the corners of the overlap area that is between the podium and the building envelope. The covered walkway is given on all four sides of the building, directly located where envisaged by the masterplan guidelines, in order to provide continuity in the pedestrian access, while the building mass is set back, allowing the continuity of the facade.

The Cube

The two buildings are conceived as a united mass taking the form of a cube hovering off the ground. The cube is carved or eroded by a free-form void—what is essentially the setback space between the two tower envelopes. The cube is structured by a conventional system of slabs stacked vertically serviced by central cores, allowing for the areas near the facade to be occupied.

The Void

The void, which is treated as a volume in its own right, being the space inside the build-mass, is free form and fluid and cuts through the edges of the cube, appearing as if it extends beyond the immediate boundaries of the cube. The interior is clad in polished metal, which is perforated to allow for views into the void. The external plateaus within the void will be accessible to provide areas for recreation and rest.

Ground Level

The ground floor space is developed as a trans-parent open field with multiple interlays of the different pathways, which are drawn into the interior of the plan areas within the two separate lobbies. Each lobby opens out to the four sides of the plot, maximizing the accessibility of the building from the ground level. A traffic artery is diverted under the building to provide full car access and easy drop-off areas.

The ground level retail areas are organized in two zones, and although the configuration can be altered, they form an outer ring which is accessible from the outside, while internal retail areas would be accessible from the lobbies.

Facade

Reflective fritting patterns in the form of pixe-lated striations are applied on to the glass facade to provide a degree of reflectivity and material-ity to the cube while assisting the reduction of the solar gains inside the building.

Light and Lighting

The interchange of perception of the tower at night time is an important factor to this proposal. While the cube appears full in day time and the void as empty, the night time perception would be one of opposites, where the cube appears dark and dematerialized, while the void could be activated with light, visible form a great distance.

The Cores/Internal Circulation

Each one of the towers starting from the lobby has its own core. The western block is served by one concentrated core which corresponds to its consolidated office and retail areas.

The eastern core on the other hand has a split core ie. two interdependent cores of smaller size which are interconnected.

The volume of the eastern block being split, the two mini-cores, can function both together in terms of services distribution and independently in terms of circulation. Additionally, vertical mini-atriums are carved out between the edges of the slab and the facade, to provide vertical local continuity between floors, for companies and organizations that may wish to occupy floor area vertically rather than horizontally. The vertical atria can also serve as passive-ventilation airways, for cooling the building.

Rentable Area Configurations

The rentable area configurations are based on the conventional system, while the form of the building allows for the floors to be subdivided easily into a variety of configurations, without the excessive use of partitioning systems.

The rentable areas are at 90.3% of the GFA.

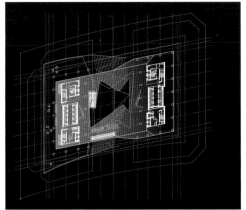

Upper ground floor

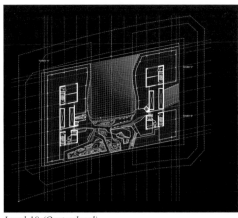

Level 18 (Oyster level)

Architects: Zaha Hadid Architects—Zaha Hadid, design; Christos Passas, project architect; Vincent Nowak, team manager; Daniel Baerlecken, Gemma Douglas, Alvin Huang, Paul Peyrer-Heimstaett, Saleem Jalil, competition team; Wenyuan Peng, Javier Ernesto Lebie, Chiara Ferrari, Thomas Frings, Paul Peyrer-Heimstaett, Phivos Skroumbelos, Marilena Sophocleous, Dimitris Akritopoulous, project team
Local architect: Arex Consultans
Client: Omniyat Properties—Graham Hallett, client representative
Consultants: gleeds, project management; whitbybird, structural, mechanical, electrical and facade engineering
Program: retail and lobby, 16,101m² (ground floor, upper ground floor, level P1 and P2); offices, 68,091m² (levels 01 to 17)
Oyster level,1,446m² (The Oyster Concept provides non work activities so that occupies need not leave the office for relaxation, executive dining, keep fit activities and re-charge activities (nap shells) located in the bridge. The bridge level is 4 stories, 3 dedicated for offices, 1 for the Oyster
Built area: 14,055 m²
Total floor area: 85,641 m²
Height: 93 m

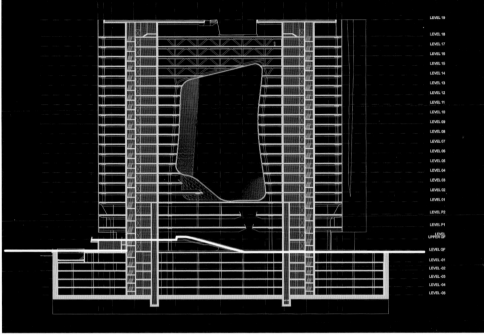

Section

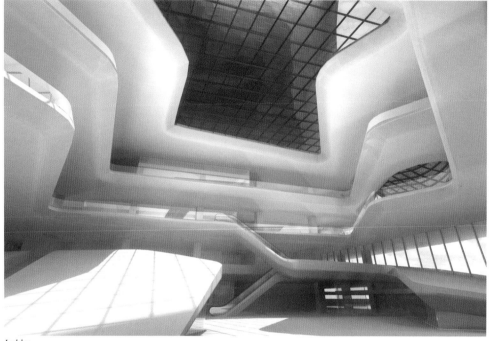

Lobby

〈デザイン方針〉
全体計画のコンセプトとその具体化は，ドバイの既存の都市構成を修正し，発展させるための，モニュメンタルな試みであると私たちは考えている。全体計画は，低い基壇と道路で連結された一連のユニークな建物が，運河と一つになって統合された新しい地区，つまりドバイ・ビジネス・ベイをつくりだすという明快な構想を提案している。当初から，全体計画が相互の連結性と独創性を探し求めていることは明白であった。この2つの特色を，ビジネス・ベイに計画されている一連のランドマーク・プロジェクトと関わることになる，この，外向的な顔を持つプロジェクトに付加する方法を，ユニークで，変化に富み，流れるようなスペースを提供するために私たちが研究してきたすべてのデザイン手法のなかに探した。

〈全体計画のコンテクスト〉
オムニヤット社旗艦オフィス／店舗タワー計画の敷地は，ビジネス・ベイ全体計画のなかの目立つ場所にある。2つの敷地は連続する低い基壇で相互につながれる。基壇はこのプロジェクトを本質的に統合し，一つのマッスとして解釈するためのユニークな可能性を提供する。

〈敷地上の配置〉
建物のヴォリュームは，基壇と建物の外殻の間に生まれる重なり合う領域の各コーナーに延びて行く。屋根の付いた通路が，建物の4つの側面のすべてに付与される。歩行者のアクセスに連続性を与えるために，全体計画のガイドラインによって想定されたそのままの場所に位置する建物が，一方ではセットバックしてファサードの連続性を保つ。

〈キューブ〉
2つの建物は，地上を離れて舞い上がるキューブの形をとった，一体化されたマッスとして考えられている。キューブは自由な形をしたヴォイド，本質的には2つのタワーの外殻の間のセットバック・スペースによって切り分けられ，あるいは浸食される。キューブは，中央コアからサービスされる，垂直に積み重ねられたスラブという伝統的なシステムで構築され，ファサードの近くにスペースを残す。

〈ヴォイド〉
他に依存しないヴォリューム，建ち上げられたマッスの内側に存在するスペースとして扱われているヴォイドは，自由な，流れるような形で，キューブの端部を切り込み，あたかもキューブに隣接する境界を越えて延びて行くように現れる。内部は磨かれたメタルで被覆され，ヴォイドのなかを覗き込めるように孔があけられる。ヴォイド内に広がる屋外の"台地"は気晴らしや休息のエリアとして，簡単にアクセスできる。

〈地上階〉
地上階は，様々な通路が多種多様に差し込まれた透明性なオープン・フィールドとして展開され，2つに分かれたロビーのなか，計画エリアの内部に引き込まれる。それぞれのロビーは，敷地の4つの側面に開かれ，地上階からの建物へのアクセスを容易にする。幹線道路は建物の下で，全車両のアクセスと降車エリアを提供するために方向転換する。地上階の店舗エリアは，2つのゾーンで構成され，配置を変えることが出来るが，外からアクセスできる外側の環を形成する一方，内側の店舗エリアはロビーから入れる。

〈ファサード〉
細分化された細い溝がかたちづくる，反射し，溶解するパターンがガラスのファサードに付加され，キューブにかなりの反射性と物質性を与え，建物内部の熱取得の減少を助ける。

〈光と照明〉
夜間に於けるタワーの知覚の入れ替わりは，この提示案の重要な要素である。キューブは昼間は全体を現し，ヴォイドは空白として現れる。夜になると見え方は正反対になる。キューブは黒く，物質性を失い，ヴォイドは光で生き生きとなり，遥か遠くからも見えるだろう。

〈コア／内部の動線〉
ロビーを起点とする各タワーにはそれぞれ専用のコアがある。西棟は，オフィスと店舗が統合されているのに対応して，集中したコアによってサービスされる。一方，東棟はスプリット・コア，つまり相互に連結された，依存し合う2つの小さなコアである。東棟のヴォリュームは縦に裂かれているので，2つのミニ・コアはサービスの配分の点では両者が一緒になって機能し，動線の点では個別に機能する。加えて，スラブとファサードの端部の間にミニ・アトリウムが刻み出され，水平方向より垂直方向にフロアを占めたいと望む会社や組織のために，各階の間に局部的な垂直の連続性を提供する。垂直のアトリウムはまた，自然な通気の場所としても働き，建物を涼しくする。

〈賃貸エリアの構成〉
賃貸エリアの構成は，伝統的な方式に基づいているが，建物の形態によって，各フロアの平面構成は，間仕切りシステムを過剰に使うことなく，多様な編成へと簡単に細分化できる。賃貸エリアは延床面積の90.3％を占めている。

CHANEL TRAVELLING EXHIBITION PAVILION

7 Locations Worldwide
Design: 2007– Construction: –2008

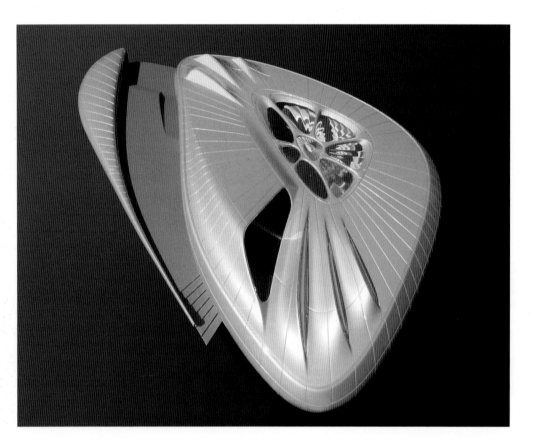

The form of the Chanel Pavilion is a celebration of the iconic work of Chanel, unmistakable for its smooth layering of exquisite details that together create an elegant, cohesive whole.

The resulting structure is very much tied to that original inspiration—elegant, functional, and versatile both in its overall structure and detail. The architectural structure of the Pavilion is a series of continuous arch-shaped elements, with a courtyard in its central space.

The glass ceiling adjusts to allow for control of the interior temperature in response to the particular climate conditions of each venue city. Natural light descending from three elements on the ceiling meets artificial light pushed up from gap between the walls and raised floor to emphasize the "arched" structure, and assist in the creation of a new artificial landscape for art installations. In addition to the lighting and colour effects of the interior space, the spatial rhythm created by the seams of each segment gives strong perspective views throughout the interior.

The size of the pavilion will be 29 m x 45 m, a total of 700 sqm. Included in this space is a 95 sqm lounge and sales area, 20 sqm reception area, and 25 sqm cloak-room. The overall height is 6 m, with the floor raised 1.00 m above the existing ground surface. In light of the extensive ship-ping between cities, each structural segment will be a maximum of 2.25 m wide.

The interior and exterior construction materials currently under consideration are FRP (fibreglass reinforced plastics), EPS (expanded polystyrene) and architectural membrane. Reflective materials allow the exterior skin to be illuminated with varying colours which can be tailored to the differing programmes of special events in each city.

The dichotomy between the powerful sculptural mass of the Chanel Pavilion's structure and the lightness of its envelope create a bold and enigmatic element. The Pavilion's exterior develops into a rich variety of interior spaces that maximize the potential to reuse and rethink space due to the innate flexibility of its plan.

洗練されたディテールのなめらかな層が一つになって、全体を優美にまとめあげているシャネル・パヴィリオンの形態は、間違いなく、シャネルのイコンのような作品に対する賛美である。

建物は、全体構造とディテールの両方が、優雅で、機能的で、万能な、シャネル本来のインスピレーションに堅く結ばれている。パヴィリオンの建築構造は、連続するアーチ形のエレメントで、その中央空間のなかにコートヤードがある。ガラスの天井は、開催地となる各都市に固有の気候条件に応じて内部の気温を調節できる。天井の3つのエレメントから降り注ぐ自然光は、壁と"アーチ"になった構造を強調するために持ち上げられた床とのあいだの隙間から上に広がる照明と合流し、アート・インスタレーションのための新しい人工のランドスケープの創造を助ける。内部空間の照明と色彩効果に加え、各区分の継ぎ目がつくりだす空間的なリズムが内部全体に強い遠近感のある眺めを与える。

パヴィリオンの大きさは29m×45mで、総面積は700平米になるだろう。ここには、95平米のラウンジとセールス・エリア、20平米のレセプション・エリア、25平米のクロークルームが含まれる。全体の高さは6mで、床は実際の地盤面から1.00m高く上げられる。各都市のあいだを長距離輸送することを考え、一つ一つの構造部分は最大で2.25mの幅に抑えられるだろう。

内部と外部の建設材料は目下、FRP（繊維強化プラスチック）、EPS（発泡プラスチック系断熱材）、膜構造を検討している。反射する材料は、それぞれの都市が計画する独自のプログラムに合わせて、パヴィリオンの外被を、様々に変化する色彩で照明することができる。シャネル・パヴィリオンの構造体の力強い彫刻的なマッスと、その被膜の軽さとの二項対立は大胆で、不思議なエレメントをつくりだす。パヴィリオンの外観は、そのプランに本来的に備わっているフレキシビリティによって、再利用、空間の再考への可能性を最大限に活用する、内部空間の豊かな変化のなかへ展開して行く。

Architects (internal scenography): Zaha Hadid Architects—Zaha Hadid with Patrik Schumacher, design; Thomas Vietzke, Jens Borstelmann, project architects; Helen Lee, Claudia Wulf, Erhan Patat, Tetsuya Yamasaki, Daniel Fiser, project team
Client: Chanel
Program: travelling exhibition pavilion designed for chanel; 7 locations worldwide (Hong Kong, Tokyo, Los Angeles, New York, Moscow, London, Paris)

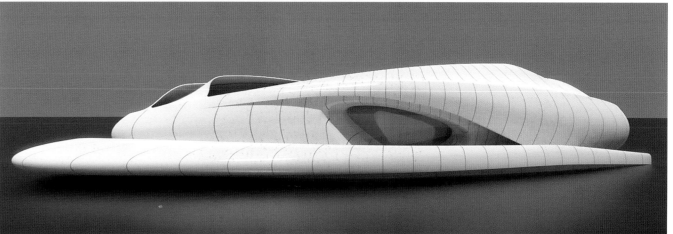

Front elevation

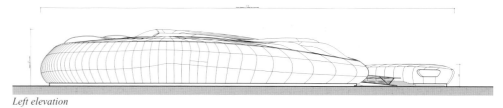

Left elevation

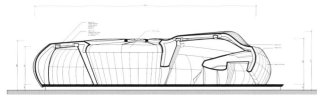

Cross sections AA S=1:450

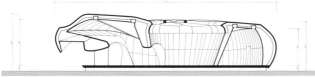

Longitudinal sections BB

Tea & Coffee Piazza, 2003

This is a table sculpture that splits into 4 elements: tea pot, coffee pot, milk jar and sugar pot. Like a three-dimensional puzzle, the pieces fit together to form a whole. They sit within a tray that guides the user through the multiple configurations, the form changing according to whether or not the set is in use.

The "representative mode", when the set is unused, is a compact structure that is easily carried around. Formally speaking, the sculpture exploits the idea of contrasting and combining extremely vertical with extremely horizontal objects. The teapot is a wide, flat organic shape, whilst the coffee pot rises from this landscape like a tower.

In the "functional mode" the objects are flipped and turned, facilitated by the template of the tray. Each shape has a cut/ section that enables the piece to slide onto a different axis, exposing openings for pouring, and producing a completely different composition.

"Tea-time" takes on a whole new significance: it becomes a sculptural riddle. The user manipulates the sliding, flipping and revolving parts, and finds the answers contained in the tea tray.

Max Protetch Bench, 2003

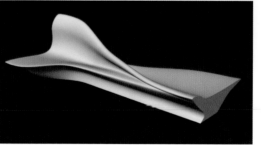

Table sculpture composed of 4 elements, tea pot, coffee pot, milk jar and sugar pot.
Architect: Zaha Hadid Architects—Zaha Hadid with Patrik Schumacher, design; Woody K.T.Yao and Thomas Vietzke, design team
Client: Alessi Spa

Bench
Architect: Zaha Hadid Architects—Zaha Hadid with Patrik Schumacher, design; Thomas Vietzke, project designer
Client: Max Protetch
Material: aluminium
Size: 141.8 x 37.75 x 31.6 inches
Photo: coutesy of Max Protech Gallery

Vortexx Chandelier, 2005

The design language explored in the Vortexx is in line with a series of furniture pieces realized in collaboration with Sawaya & Moroni. Fluidity and seamlessness are conceptual terms that best describe the appearance of this 1.8 m wide and 0.8 m high chandelier. Its complex curvilinearity follows a double helix connecting its beginning to its end and therefore forming an endless ribbon of light. In plan the object resembles a star with its protrusions pointing outwards from the center, emphasizing an imaginary centrifugal force.

Two transparent acrylic light spirals are inscribed in the chandelier's otherwise opaque surface. A recessed LED light strip provides ani-mated and programmable light sensations. Direct as well as indirect light can optionally be emitted to the environment. Consequently different lighting atmospheres may be created by the user in order to match the specific space in which the chandelier is installed. This new interior design language is fuelled by advanced digital design possibilities and manufacturing methods such as CNC-milling and 3D printing. The user is invited to creatively explore its interactive qualities and respond to its unfamiliar aesthetics.

Aqua Table, 2005

Table
Architect: Zaha Hadid Architects—Zaha Hadid with Patrik Schumacher, design; Saffet Kaya Bekiroglu, project designer; Tarek Shamma, design team
Client: Established & Sons
Size: 420 x 145.8 x 72 cm
Photo: ©Toben Smith

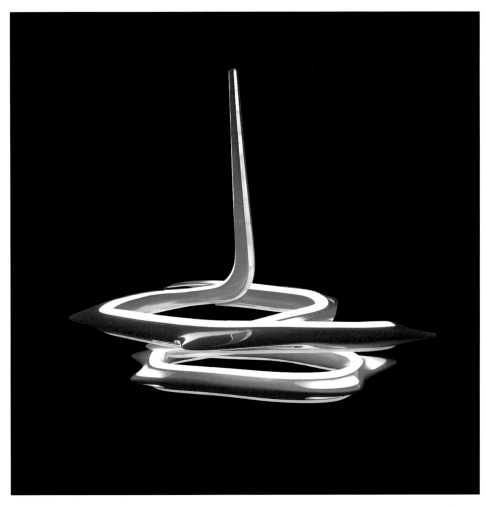

The enigmatic, liquid form of the Aqua table awakens one's curiosity. The user is invited to explore the forces of motion that created such a form. The form is blurring the relationship between horizontal top and vertical legs. The three blisters bulging out to form legs below the table surface register as indentations at the top surface.

The Aqua table is an organic body flowing within space. Rather than being static, it implies motion by adopting the dynamic gestures of liquid to form a continuous surface. The table's asymmetrical, irregular tabletop and varying edges create an ergonomic solid that offers endless relationship possibilities with its user and its environment.

Through surface mutations at three local points, the table's legs emerge to form a singular, unbroken surface, elevating the tabletop and stabilizing from beneath. These mutations are inflected in the tabletop surface to enhance the singular monolithic form of the Aqua table. The translucent silicon gel of the tabletop surface has a smooth top with 3 deformities on its lower side. Gradual alterations in the colour of the tabletop reflect these deformities, creating a surreal visual effect that draws us explore the difference between the actual/perceived depth of the pad by touching the surface to reveal its true nature.

The table consists of two material elements:
1. A lower structural body made from polyester that allows its geometry and enables weight reduction.
2. The top silicon gel with a tactile non-slip surface that brings stability to the uneven tabletop.

The design and manufacture of the Aqua table has only been made possible through the latest advances in technology. Its form was generated on complex geometry software (using nurb surface modeller). This design was then sculpted by CNC (Computer Numerical Control) milling to enable manufacture.

Chandelier
Architect: Zaha Hadid Architects—Zaha Hadid with Patrik Schumacher, design; Thomas Vietzke, design team
Client: Sawaya & Moroni
Size: 1.8 m in diameter
Material: fiberglass, car paint, acrylic, LED

Ordrupgaard Bench, 2005

Belu Bench, 2005

Belu is conceived as an autonomous single-celled body that allows for multi-functional use; as a table, counter, chair, container, or simply as a surface to lean on, rest on... With the dynamic complex geometry of a fluid volume, Belu is able to generate varying adjacency conditions in its direct relationship with the human body. Belu is not just an object for display, but a dynamic gesture that spatially defines its surroundings whilst serving a variety of functions.

In a re-visitation of the original concept, these unique geometries of Belu have been maintained yet scaled down in all three dimensions. This series affords Belu further possibilities of direct inter-vention within the domestic environment.

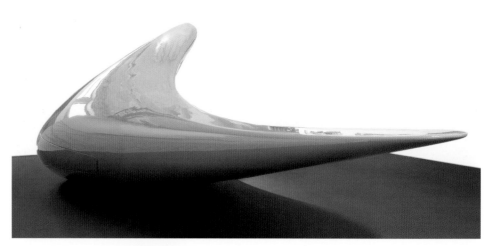

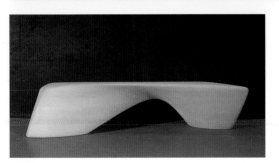

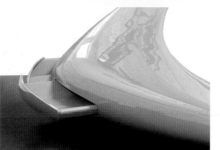

Bench designed for Ordrup-
gaard Museum Extension
Architect: Zaha Hadid Archi-
tects—Zaha Hadid with
Patrik Schumacher, design;
Ken Bostock, project de-
signer
Manufacturer: PP Møbler,
Denmark
Material: solid ash
*Highly organic shapes were
cut by CNC machine

Seating area
Architect: Zaha Hadid Archi-
tects—Zaha Hadid with
Patrik Schumacher, design;
Saffet Kaya Bekiroglu, pro-
ject designer; Maha Kutay,
Tarek Shamma,
Melissa Woolford, project
team
Client: Kenneth Schachter

Swarm Chandelier, 2006

Louis Vuitton Icone Bag, 2006

The opportunities of reinterpretation of the iconic LV Bucket bag lead us to reflect on its condition as a generic container.

The combination of a series of formal operations (extrusion, distortion, peeling and slicing) and the selection of materials, created a family of differentiated bags, hybrid crossings between traditional bag typologies, i.e. pochette and clutch, and the bucket.

Clustering the bags generated a series of possible relations between the different buckets, the containers and the contained, which allowed for its parts to be interchangeable under one coherent composition.

The possibility of different combinations of containers, buckets, triggers a playful and interactive relationship with the user, allowing for a customization of the bucket's form and program to each occasion.

Chandelier
Architect: Zaha Hadid Architects, design;
Saffet Kaya Berkiroglu, project architect
Client: Established & Sons
Material: crystal

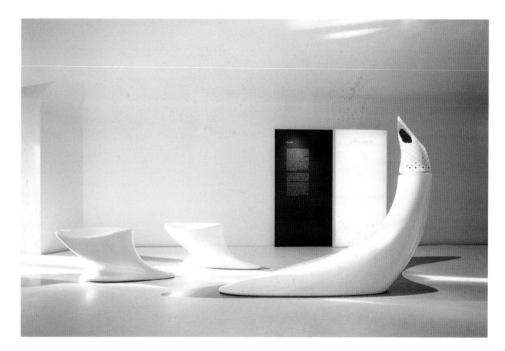

The Swarm Chandelier by Zaha Hadid Architects for Established & Sons expresses the continued sense of motion that is characterized in the architecture of Zaha Hadid. Like a controlled explosion, it is a composition of black crystal volumes in forms that are dynamic rather than static and that slash through space, creating movement through actual and perceived time.

The intricately layered spatial formation of the chandelier presents itself as a unified whole, only revealing the forces that created its varied modulations and sub-articulations upon closer examination. It does not presuppose any proportional system, nor does it privilege symmetry. Instead integration is achieved via various modes and spatial relationships created from the dynamic forces of this controlled explosion. The parts—the petals of the chandelier—are brought together to form a larger organic whole. They do not remain pure and indifferent to each other, but are mutually adapting to each other and to the forces of the generating explosion.

The swarm of drifting volumes of the Swarm Chandelier is a spatial composition with the highest degrees of complexity that define the forces generated by an explosion of the original mass.

The ability to produce such intricately moulded forms is continuously enhanced by the utilization of ever more sophisticated digital modelling tools, including animation software to illustrate the force-fields of the creation explosion.

Product design
Architect: Zaha Hadid Architects—Zaha Hadid with Patrik Schumacher, design;
Ana M. Cajiao, project designer; Muthahar Khan, design team
Client: Louis Vuitton Malletier
Photos: ©Werner Huthmacher

Seamless Collection, 2006

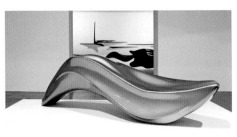

*

The 'Seamless' furniture collection for Established & Sons represents the result of Zaha Hadid Architects' exploration into a world of seamless fluidity. It is a built manifesto towards the potential for a new language of design and architecture, which is driven by the latest in digital design processes and the most cutting edge manufacturing techniques.

With the overall conception of the designs ultimately driven by the new possibilities created by significant technological advancements in three dimensional design software, as well as our inherent desire to test and engage with the very latest manufacturing capabilities, the resulting collection of furniture is a dialogue of complex curvilinear geometries and detailed ergonomic research that provides the opportunity for us to reinvent the balance between furniture and space. To this end, the forthcoming exhibition of the Seamless Collection at Phillips de Pury will feature a number of pieces significant not only as stand alone objects, but for their ability to collectively project a different, sensual universe that draws the audience into its ambit.

These unique pieces are an obvious evolution of the architectural language explored by the practice: soft meets sharp, the combination of convex and concave, and a sculptural sensibility that impact on our self-conception as bodies. The rhythm of folds, niches, recesses and protrusions follows a coherent formal logic. With the formal dynamic of a fluid mass, we are able to emphasize the continuous nature of the design and the smooth evolution between otherwise disparate elements. The evolutionary lineage of the pieces is easily discernable through re-visitation of past projects such as Z-Scape (2000), Ice Storm (2003), Aqua Table (2005), the Hotel Puerta America interiors (2005) and Elastika (2006). Seamless represents the culmination of this morphological series and a new beginning in terms adding new surface sensations.

Seamless Collection is the special edition for the the exhibition held by the auction house, Phillips de Pury & Company with the furniture manufacturer, Established & Sons.

All the pieces in the show are manufactured out of polyester resin. Five of the pieces are painted in a 'bespoke' polyester color and finally finished to the highest of standards in a polyurethane lacquer.

Alongside Established & Sons, the paint colors have been specially created by Zaha Hadid for the 'Seamless' collection and will only be used on those edition pieces.

First complete line of furniture by Zaha Hadid Architects
Architects: Zaha Hadid Architects— Zaha Hadid with Patrik Schumacher, design; Saffet Kaya, Melodie Leung, Helen Lee, Alvin Huang, Hannes Schafelner, design team
Material: polyester resin
Exhibition "Seamless ": November 27 to December 15, 2006, Phillips de Pury & Company, New York
*Photo: ©Jack Coble

"CREVASSE" Vase, 2006

The two vases are cut from a single block, and scored along two diagonal lines, creating a warped, inverted surface. They can be assembled together in alternative configurations, creating solid forms, or they can stand alone as distinct objects. The playful nature of the set means that the configurations can be altered to make a variety of different shapes, and the user can build a family of objects, like an endlessly mutating jigsaw puzzle.

Flower vase in 18/10 stainless steel
Architect: Zaha Hadid Architects—Zaha Hadid with Patrik Schumacher, design
Woody Yao and Thomas Vietzke, design team
Manufacturer/client: Alessi Spa

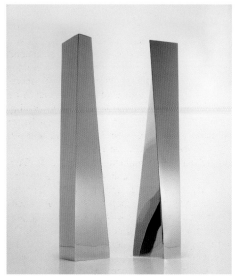
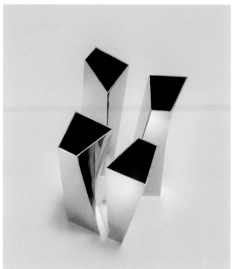

Z.Island with DuPont Corian, 2006

Z.Car, 2006

The Z.CAR is a two-seater city car with a three-wheel base. Using Hydrogen as a source of energy it is a very quiet zero-emission vehicle. The inclination of the passenger pod is speed adjusted. At low speeds it is in the upper position and gives the driver a better street vision. A shortened wheelbase then also requires less parking-space. At higher speeds the pod lowers on the hinged rear suspension, moving the car's center of gravity closer to the road for safer handling and improved aerodynamics. Reflecting the organic language of the office, the shape of the car is streamlined in order to generate a fluid design with minimum wind friction. The body consists of lightweight carbon-fibre composite with a large asymmetric door hatch giving the passengers a panoramic vision.

The interior design is based on ergonomics embracing both driver and passenger that sit side by side. The steering wheel connects with "drive-by-wire" technology to motors that operate the steering mechanism and it holds controls that manage other functions.

2 Free-standing kitchen islands, 1 Modular wall panel system, 1 Shelving system Architect: Zaha Hadid Architects—Zaha Hadid with Patrik Schumacher, design; Thomas Vietzke, project architect; Georgios Maillies, Maurice Martel, Katharina Neuhaus, Ariane Stracke, design team Client: DuPont, Ernestomeda Manufacturer: Hasenkopf Size: 4.5 (l) x 0.8 (w) x 1.8 m (h), main island; 1.2 x 1.6 x 0.9 m, 2nd Island; 100 pieces @ 0.6 x 0.6 m, wall panels Photo: coutesy of DuPont™ Corian®, ©Leo Torri

The Z.Island is in line with a series of formal studies that have been performed in ZH's Studio emphasizing the conceptual term of "fluidity". Previously the "Ice-Series" had its formal trigger in the observation of natural phenomena such as the melting of ice or the flow of glaciers and their moraines. The Z.Islands can be perceived as variations of that theme. Due to the application of advanced 3D software from the field of ship design the office is enabled to explore complex surfaces (NURBS_Surfaces) and their productivity for domestic environments. A major benefit of this design language is that it will not only appear continuos but it also blends in seamlessly into the ergonomic needs of a kitchen island.

The overall composition contains the main cooking island, the secondary island as well as a background of wall panels. The main Island is an elongated cantilevering shape (450 cm x 70 cm), which evolves from a horizontal cooking and eating surface continuously into a vertical digital surface. In contrast to this stretched figure the secondary Island resembles a point/drop. It contains the sink the dishwasher as well as a shelving unit. The background is an elevation of a wavy morphological puzzle consisting of modular 60 cm x 60 cm thermoformed corian elements that are rotated and reassembled in various ways creating complex patterns on the interior walls.

Both Islands are free standing. They are conceived as centre points within a larger loft like environment. On the main island's top surface all cooking functions are inscribed plus a series of electronic features creating a futuristic outlook on what a kitchen might be in the 21st century. The table integrates nearly 2000 LEDs which are programmable by the user showing e.g. the cooking timer or the seating order. 3 aromatic scent dispensers are responsive to the users wishes to create certain scents in the flat. An especially developed heating membrane is invisibly integrated in the corian surface and allows for keeping the food warm over an extended period of time. The food is prepared on an induction cooking hob that is flush with the neighbouring surface. Via a main user friendly touch control panel all functions will be steered from a central point. In the main island's vertical surface we integrated a flat LCD screen enabling the user to surf the internet or to watch the news in the morning while having breakfast. A mini mac is integrated underneath the LCD screen in order to allow for listening to iTunes etc. As an extension of the Island serves a wall paneling system which integrate animated light sources as well as acoustic devices that will fill the atmosphere with changing light and sound according to the specific occasion. In certain areas these panels become more than a decorative speaker and light system. They serve as shelving unit doors and hide additional storing areas. The overall environment is responsive to the users needs and might be adjusted addressing all senses in various ways.

All cladding is manufactured from Corian Glacier White. Thermoformable properties as well as translucency and endurance are key factors for choosing this solid surface material. The vacuum forming techniques allow for manufacturing geometrically demanding surfaces and also build them with very low tolerances. The material's solid nature strengthens its endurance in a highly functional and hygienic context.

London Motor Show

Concept car
Architect: Zaha Hadid Architects—Zaha Hadid with Patrik Schumacher, design; Jens Borstelmann, project designer
Client: Kenny Schachter
Size: 3.80 (l) x 1.80 (w) x 1.70 m (h)

MOON System, 2007

MOON redefines the idea of modular seating systems by making each element a module in its own right: the system reconfigures itself by rotating, interlocking, and hiding its individual elements to allow an integration of formal disparate pieces within an overall ensemble.

Ergonomics and beauty are blended in a continuous shape. MOON liquifies the traditional sofa typology to accommodate a variety of users in a flexible and comfortable design.

The complex double-curvature geometries introduced by Zaha Hadid allow the smooth transition between the surrounding space and pieces themselves. MOON is able to constantly reconfigure the equilibrium between solid and void, positive and negative, object and space.

Zaha Hadid Bowl 60-70 & Metacrylic, 2007

A fluid form of curvilinear geometry, this silver bowl is a continuation of the morphological design language Zaha Hadid has explored and developed over the past three decades.

The elegant sculptural mass of the bowl is slightly concave in its centre and responds to the diffusion of energies that are generated at its perimeter, inviting an exploration of natural forces and affording a unique contextual relationship within any environment.

Whilst at first appearing unscripted and spontaneous, the total fluidity of the bowl's volume follows the overriding formal logic of Hadid's research into systems of continuous transformations and smooth transitions. The silver bowl further develops this dialogue, allowing the architect to capture the ephemeral qualities and diffused forms of clouds, solidifying them in sterling silver.

Zaha Hadid has generated an additional dimensional relationship beyond the reflection of light from the bowl's surface. By encouraging an exploration into the dichotomy between the powerful solidity of sterling silver and the organic fluidity of its form, Hadid has created an exquisite and sensual piece that continues her thirty-year repertoire of morphological conception.

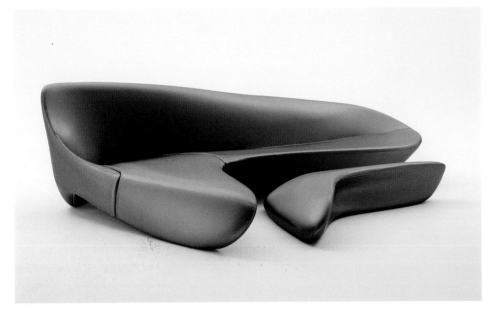

Seating
Architect: Zaha Hadid Architects—Zaha Hadid with Patrik Schumacher, design; Viviana Muscettola, design leader; Michele Pasca di Magliano, design team
Client: B & B Italia
Photos: ©Fabrizio Bergamo

A bowl available in sterling silver (2 separate sizes) and metacrylic
Architect: Zaha Hadid Architects—Zaha Hadid with Patrik Schumacher, design; Saffet Bekiroglu, design leader; Maha Kutay, Melissa Woolford, Tarek Shamma, design team
Client: Sawaya & Moroni
Size
Bowl 70, Bowl metacrylic: 700 mm (w), 325 mm (d), 130 mm (h)
Bowl 60: 600 mm (w), 275 mm (d), 130 mm (h)
Photos: ©Fabrizio Bergamo

FLOW, 2007

FLOW has been designed by Zaha Hadid and Patrik Schumacher as an experiment in coupling advanced 3d modelling techniques and the technology of rotational moulding.

FLOW defines a new typology in product design, vase and sculpture, a sinuous object through which Cartesian geometries are blended in a continuous three-dimensional surface.

Vase and Sculpture
Architect: Zaha Hadid Architects—Zaha Hadid with Patrik Schumacher, design; Michele Pasca di Magliano & Viviana Muscettola, design leader
Client: Serralunga
Size: ø146 cm x 200 cm (h), ø117 cm x 120 cm (h)

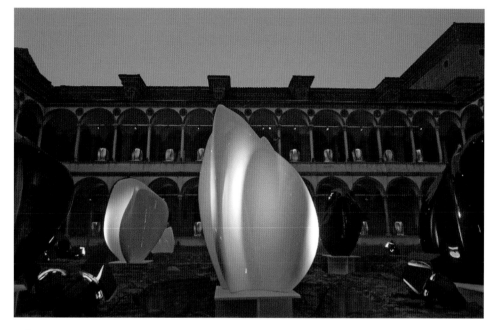

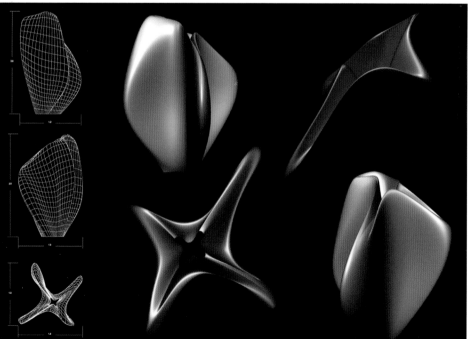

MESA, 2007

Table
Architect: Zaha Hadid Architects—Zaha Hadid with Patrik Schumacher, design; Saffet Kaya Bekiroglu, project designer, Chikara Inamura, Melike Altinisik, project team
Client: Vitra
Photo: ©Barbara Sorg

Zaha Hadid's architecture sees form and space pulled around, out of shape and into breathtaking, fluid spatial progressions. Hugely theatrical and enticingly urbane her buildings have begun to transform notions of what can be achieved in concrete and steel, blending the revolutionary aesthetics of constructivism with the liquid organicism of expressionism. The progression in Zaha's buildings from the jagged, suprematist forms of the Vitra Fire Station (1993) to the awesome, flowing urban spaces of the Phaeno Science Centre, Wolfsburg (2005) show a consistent desire to question the traditional orthogonal plan, form always pulling towards an invisible mass, space and time warped and woven around structure. These are buildings which emerge from the city as sculpture yet which are also capable of knitting disparate blocks together, always surprising but also constantly making connections.

The Mesa table evolved from an architectural experiment which was similarly to do with creating connections. Elastika was an installation created in the Moore Building in 2005 for the Miami Art Fair. The brief had been a sculptural structure to revivify the 1921 building's atrium. Zaha's proposal was an organic set of tentacles which linked spaces and floors across the atrium, defying changing levels and criss-crossing each other in mid-air. The effect was like a huge, sticky chewing gum pulled out of shape across the interior. It is a sci-fi alien piece which transforms the heart of the building, reaching across space. It looks as if the structure was attempting to re-solve itself back into a single solid.

The Mesa table takes as its starting point a similar situation. Stripping the formal idea back to its constituent parts; ground; structure; surface, the design creates a world in between the two horizontal planes, a world which becomes structure but in which the voids express the form as much as the solids. Those voids do not appear merely as holes but go on to define the surface. Zaha compares it to water lilies sitting on a pond, flat mats supported by an unseen, complex and organic structure beneath. This highly unusual attenuation of surface from structure gives form to four organically-shaped sections which constitute defined divisions on the surface, described as 'place-mats'. As one end is attracted by an invisible gravitational force, it skews the symmetry, an attenuated prow dragging the other forms along with it while the structure below stretches elastically to accommodate the distortions.

The Mesa table becomes a microcosmic extrusion of the spatial ideas inherent in Zaha's architecture. Form doesn't follow only function but instead is drawn along by the narrative of the plan and flow of space. It becomes something plastic and elastic, more Einsteinian than Cartesian, an evocation of a world shaped by unseen forces and dark matter, a fluid, flowing, four-dimensional world in which a table can distort the space within it and around it. It transforms any space into a Zaha room.
Edwin Heathcote

CRATER, 2007

Table
Architect: Zaha Hadid Architects—Zaha Hadid with Patrik Schumacher, design; Saffet Kaya Bekiroglu, project designer; Chikara Inamura, Chrysostomos Tsimourdagkas, design team
Client: David Gill Galleries

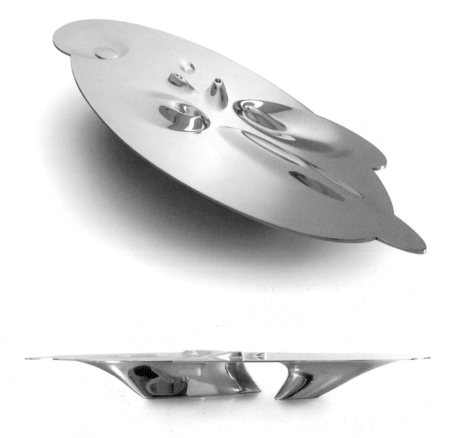

Crater represents the latest manifestation of Zaha Hadid's 30-year exploration and research that continues to challenge our preconceptions of design. With Crater, Hadid's experimentation leads to an entirely unique line of questioning that explores the relationship between the table and disparate objects placed upon its surface.

Hadid has reduced the substance of the table and these objects on its surface into the purest of forms—an absolute expression of function that liberates our expectations and allows us to reconsider this relationship. She then reconnects each function with a sensual fluidity generated by her dialogue of smooth transitions between elements.

We witness objects emerging from the Crater's surface that appear definite, yet when examined from an alternative perspective, these bowls or candleholders have no independent solidity—they are simply integral elements within continuous topology of the table's surface. Hadid's overriding logic of morphological conception enables us to embrace such connections The field conditions that define the table's surface (creating the ob-

jects we had previously assumed as separate entities) are applied to three singularities beneath this same surface to form the table's signature. Three craters are molded by invisible forces into the complex curvilinear geometry mastered by Hadid—a design language that incorporates the radical aesthetics of the Russian Avant-Garde together with a fluidity reminiscent of Expressionism.

Two of these craters extend reassuringly to the floor. The third crater is suspended in space, and clearly a bowl. With this truncation, we are, once again, provoked to question the separation between table and object.

An aspect of Hadid's vision is her interest in the rigorous interface between cutting-edge design and current material technologies. Such a process often results in unexpected and dynamic forms. Using the latest developments in three dimensional design software, Zaha Hadid's experimentations into the unique properties of aluminium have created the fluid and enigmatic forms of Crater.

GREAT UTOPIAS

*Solomon R. Guggenheim Museum, New York, U.S.A.
1992*

In the Russian avant-garde exhibition at the Guggenheim, all the paintings were suspended so you saw them all in one go. We had only two months to do the whole show, so we spent day and night at the Guggenheim. I got to know it much better as I nearly lived there. I'm amazed that we managed to do it, but we wet the floors and slid PVC to make these very large shapes. It was an unbelievable event, putting water and soap on the floor in the Guggenheim and gliding the plastic on—then you had to push the water out to make it stick perfectly with no bubbles. All these tricks.

There was almost a religious moment when they opened up Malevich's Black Square (1913). Every curator in the Russian world was there to witness it, despite the fact that we had thought they didn't like Malevich. We had to open the box at two in the morning and hang the black square. It was an interesting moment in terms of the history of the Guggenheim. It was just after Russia and the Soviet republics had opened up, but it was also a shop window of works that had been borrowed from institutions under one umbrella. If you did the show again you'd have to borrow works from I don't know how many countries. We wanted to use the spiral to make a story, and the idea of moving seamlessly began to emerge, as if walking on a slope. We wanted to see how you could interrupt it with obstacles. We used the screens in the museum to show posters, which pushed you to the edge of the ramp. That's why I like the Guggenheim—because of the ability to see different perspectives all at the same time.
Zaha Hadid, Frieze Talks, 21 October 2005

グッゲンハイム美術館で開かれたロシア前衛美術展においては，全ての絵画が吊り下げられて空中に浮遊し，それら全てを行く手に見通すことが出来るようになっていた。この展覧会全体の準備には2ヶ月しかなく，昼夜を問わず私たちはグッゲンハイムで作業を続け，ほとんどそこに住んでいるかのような状況の中で，私はこの美術館についてより深く知ることができた。

今となってはよくあのようなことが出来たと驚くばかりだが，私たちは床を濡らしてPVCを滑らせ，非常に大きな形状のものをいくつも作り上げた。水と石鹸をグッゲンハイムの床に流し，プラスチックの部材を滑らせることで水分を押し出して，泡を作

らないように床に完全に張り付かせる。こうしたトリックの数々。信じられないようなイベントだった。

マレビッチの "Black Square (1913)" を展示のために開けた時は，ほとんど宗教的な瞬間となった。「マレビッチを彼らは好きではないのではないか」という私たちの予想を裏切って，全ロシアの全てのキュレーターがこの瞬間を目にしようとそこにいた。"Black Square" の箱を開封し吊り下げ作業を行うのは午前の2時になってしまったが，グッゲンハイム美術館の歴史を考える上では興味深い瞬間だったであろう。当時はちょうどロシアとソビエト連邦が解放された頃で，まだ一つ屋根の下にある各機関らから作品群をまとめて借り出して一同に会すことができたが，再びこのような展覧会を開いたならばいくつの国から作品を借りなければならないか，わかったものではない。

私たちはグッゲンハイムの螺旋を利用して物語を作り出したいと考え，そこからまるで丘の上を歩いているかのような継ぎ目のない移動というアイディアが浮かんできた。またそこに置かれた障害物となるものが歩いてくる人をどのように中断させるかを知りたかった。そこで私たちはポスターを展示する

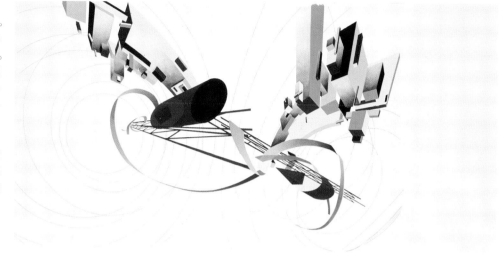

ためのスクリーンを用いて，見る人をグッゲンハイムの傾斜路の端へと押しやるような仕掛けを作った。私がグッゲンハイムを好きな理由は，なぜならその空間が異なった物の見方を全て，同時に見せてくれる力を持っているからである。

（ザハ・ハディド，2005年10月21日）

Architects: Zaha Hadid Architects
Program: exhibition design for "The Great Utopias": The Russian and Soviet Avant-Garde, 1915-1932

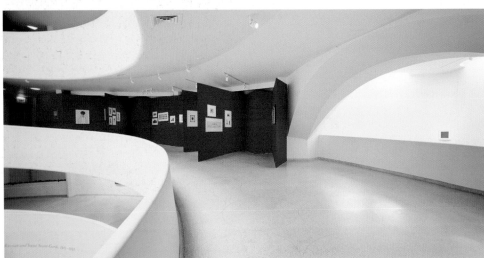
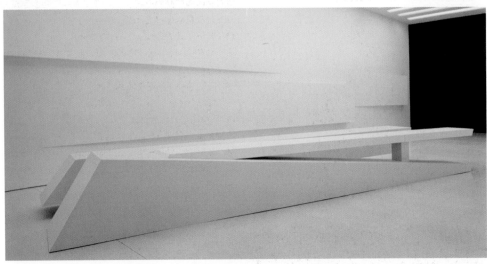

SERPENTINE GALLERY PAVILION

Kensington Gardens, London, U.K.
2000

Situated in Kensington Gardens, The Serpentine Gallery commissioned a specially designed pavilion by Zaha Hadid for its 30th anniversary Gala event. Situated on the front lawn outside the Gallery, the brief was to accommodate an external enclosure for 400 seated guests.

The design was to create a tent typology, which via a triangulated roof seeks to play with the traditional notion of a tensile fabric construction. Whilst it maintains their sense of ephemerality, its folding form of angular flat planes subverts the lightness of the fabric by giving it an illusion of solidity. The roof creates a clear span internal space of 600 m² using a steel primary structure, which is clad with an external and internal fabric panel.

The nature of the folding planes engages with the site by extending itself to the ground at points whilst at the same time undulating to create a variety of internal spaces. These undulations are further exploited by the positioning of lighting between the two roof fabrics, which incurs gradual changes over time by shifting contrast through the roof planes. The internal ground plane is occupied by a field of specially designed tables which create a movement through the space where their colour graduates from white to black reinforcing a sense of movement dissipating through the tent.

Although originally erected for only five days, it was extended by demand till September, where it has served as an outside cafe for the Gallery.

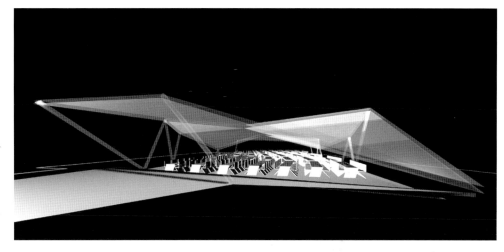

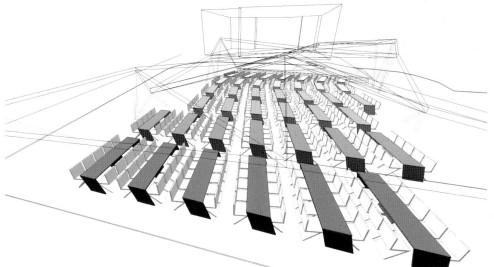

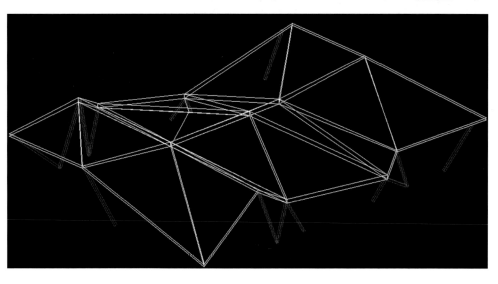

ケンジントン・ガーデンの中にあるサーペンタインギャラリーは，開館30周年を記念するイベントに向け，特別デザインのパヴィリオンの設計をザハ・ハディドに依頼した。これはギャラリー外部の前面芝生に建てられ，400人のゲストを収容できる外殻である。

デザインに関しては，テントの類型を創り出すことを主眼とし，三角形の屋根を用いながら伝統的な布地の伸張力による構造と戯れている。そのはかなげな雰囲気は保ちつつも，角張った平面の折り曲げられた形状はソリッドであるかのような錯覚を与えることで，軽い布地の印象を覆す。布製パネルで外部と内部を覆われた鉄の屋根構造は，そのスパンにより内部に600平方メートルの空間を生み出す。

折り曲げられた平面の本質は，それが延長されることで場所によっては地面と接し，同時にうねりながら内側に多様な内部空間を創り出すことで敷地と結びついてゆく。こうしたうねりの様相は二つの屋根布材の間に照明を配置する際にさらに追求されており，時間の推移とともに屋根平面のコントラストが移り行くことによって次第に変化を受けてゆく。内部のグランド・レベルは，空間内に動きを生み出す，色が白から黒にグラデーションをもって変化していく特別にデザインされたテーブルによって占められており，テントの内部に拡散していく感覚を強めている。

元々は5日間のみ建てられている予定であったが，強い要望により9月まで延長され，ギャラリー外部のカフェとして機能している。

Architects: Zaha Hadid Architects—Zaha Hadid with Jim Heverin, design;
Eric Gabriel, project manager
Clients: The Serpentine Gallery
Consultants: Howard Associates, quantity surveyor; Maurice Brill Lighting Design, lighting; CETEC Consultant, structural
Contractor: Gap Sails and Structures
Program: pavilion design, Serpentine Gallery 30th Anniversary Gala Structure

©Hélène Binet△▽

MIND ZONE, MILLENNIUM DOME

London, U.K.
2000

The "Mind Zone" is one of fourteen individual exhibition spaces within the Millennium Dome. Comprising a unique undertaking, ZHA designed both the curatorial aspects and the architectural scheme.

The design engages the complex subject matter of the Mind, in a structure of three overlapping sections, unfolding to create a continuous surface that can be floor wall or soffit and that allows for a fluid journey through the space.

The content of the exhibit and the exhibit structure, are presented and experienced as a single idea; the exhibit structure of folding continuous surfaces is seen as a host, the physical presence on which and within which the content can be located.

As a narrative strategy, the three elements complement the primary mental functions; 'input', 'process', and 'output' represented variously through perspectival and visual distortion, explanatory exhibits, sculpture, computers, audiovisual installations and interactive elements.

The design strategy avoids being overtly pedagogical and is rather interactive and thought provoking. It was because of this underlying premise that artists were proposed as the main exhibitors. Structurally the exhibit integrates the content with the usage of evolutionary materials. Its materiality is focused on the synthetic, the mind made materials of the present.

The brief to create a continuous floor/wall/soffit has produced a unique lightweight transparent panel made from glass fibre skins with an aluminium honeycomb structure. Similarly the base steel structure is layered with translucent materials, which seek to create an ephemeral temporal quality befitting an exhibition with a design life of one year.

'マインド・ゾーン' はミレニアム・ドーム内の14の個別の展示空間の一つである。このユニークな仕事を成立させるために，ザハは展示責任者的な要素と建築的な計画の両方をデザインした。

このデザインは「心」という複雑な主題に関わっていくものであり，3つの重なり合う構造が広がっていくことで床，壁，底板等と位置づけることの出来る連続した表面を創り出し，空間における流れるような移動を可能にする。

展示の内容と展示自体の構造は一つのアイディアとして提示され，経験される——展示の構造となっている折り畳まれ連続した面は，展示内容がその内部空間もしくは面そのものの上に現れる身体的な存在として，案内者的な存在となる。

説明の方向として，3つの要素が基礎となる精神の機能を補足する——「入力」「プロセス」そして「出力」といった要素が遠近法的，視覚的な歪曲，説明的な展示，彫刻，コンピュータ，そしてインタラクティブな要素などを通じて様々な形に提示される。

デザインの方針においては，アーティストが主な展示出品者であるという前提から，明らかに教育的すぎるものは避け，よりインタラクティブで思考を促すものとした。構造的にも展示は新しく開発された素材と展示内容が一体化され，素材は人工的な，人の手で生み出された最新の素材を用いることに留意した。

連続した床，壁，底板を創り出そうとした結果，グラスファイバーの表皮を持つ透明で軽量なアルミのハニカム構造パネルを制作した。同じように，基礎となるスティールによる構造は，1年という短い展示期間にふさわしい短命で一時的な性格の半透明の素材が重ねられている。

Architects: Zaha Hadid Architects—Zaha Hadid, design; Jim Heverin, project architect;
Patrik Schumacher, Graham Modlen, Barbara Kuit, Ana Sotrel, project team
Client: The New Millennium Experience Co Limited
Program: exhibition pavilion
Consultants: Ove Arup & Partners, structural, services; Hollands Licht, lighting; B consultants ltd., cladding; Davis Langdon & Everest, costing
Program: pavilion design
Area: 2,500 m²

Photos: Y. Futagawa

PET SHOP BOYS, WORLD TOUR 1999-2000

1999-2000

Architecture and the performing arts are not necessarily easily put together as they are each subject to very different sets of rules.

In the case of the project for Pet Shop Boys this proved to be a challenging and inspiring process, which led to a hybridisation of both disciplines. Rather than composing spatial sequences

Zaha Hadid Architects unfold a white canvas that contains and directs the dynamics of the pop concert. A single continuous surface is thrown into a relief as it bends and splits to create background, structure and floor. Other parts of this surface become detachable mobile elements that act as choreographic tools on a three-dimensional luminous landscape of projection and sound. The set becomes neither background nor foreground but dynamic and visually versatile space.

建築と舞台美術は，それぞれまったく異なるルールがあるため，一つのものとして構成するのは必ずしも容易ではない。

ペットショップボーイズの舞台セットは，これがやりがいのある，そして強烈に印象的なプロセスであることを示した。それは二つのルールのハイブリッドな融合をもたらした。空間のシークエンスを創作するという以上に，である。

ザハ・ハディドは，ポップ・コンサートのエネルギーを内に包み演出する，白いキャンバスを展開させた。ひとつながりの表面が，背景や構造体，床を構成するように，曲げられたり引き裂かれたりして立体となる。キャンバスの他の部分は取り外し可能な可動エレメントとなり，映写や音響のための３次元的な発光するランドスケープの上で，振り付けのツールとして使われる。セットは背景でも前景でもなく，ダイナミックで視覚的に多様なスペースとなる。

Architects: Zaha Hadid Architects
Program: stage set for the Pet Shop Boys' World Tour

LATENT UTOPIAS

Graz Festival of Culture 2003, Graz, Austria
2003

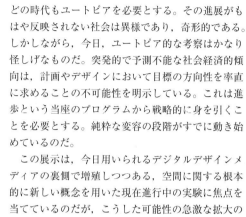

Every time needs its utopia(s). A society that does no longer reflect its development is uncanny, a monstrosity. However, utopian speculation is rather dubious today. The unpredictability of emergent socio-economic patterns spells the impossibility of straightforward goal orientation in planning and design. This necessitates a strategic retreat from the immediate program of progress. A phase of pure mutation is launched. The exhibition focuses on current experiments with radically new concepts of space that are proliferating on the back of the new digital design media available today. This explosion of possibilities requires the profession to "play" and experiment. In this respect the mode of production of the architect is assimilated to artistic processes. The final purpose, meaning and fulfillment of these artistic experiments lies beyond the scope of the architect/artist and requires the creative appropriation through its audiences. We believe that this kind of proto-architecture requires engaging exhibitions as testing ground.

Architect: Zaha Hadid Architects—
Zaha Hadid with Patrik Schumacher, design
Program: exhibition design for the part the Graz Festival of Culture 2003

どの時代もユートピアを必要とする。その進展がもはや反映されない社会は異様であり，奇形的である。しかしながら，今日，ユートピア的な考察はかなり怪しげなものだ。突発的で予測不能な社会経済的傾向は，計画やデザインにおいて目標の方向性を率直に求めることの不可能性を明示している。これは進歩という当座のプログラムから戦略的に身を引くことを必要とする。純粋な変容の段階がすでに動き始めているのだ。

この展示は，今日用いられるデジタルデザインメディアの裏側で増殖しつつある，空間に関する根本的に新しい概念を用いた現在進行中の実験に焦点を当てているのだが，こうした可能性の急激な拡大の最中においては，試行と実験を遂行していく専門職性も必要とされる。その意味で建築家の創造の様態は美術的なプロセスと類似したものだと言えるだろうが，こうした美的な実験の最終的な目的，意味合い，またその成就は建築家やアーティストの領域を超えた所に存在し，また聴衆を通した独創的な流用化を必要とする。我々は，こうした建築の原型を訴求する場面に於いて，人を惹き付けるこうした実験場としての展示と提示が必要であると信じて疑わない。

Photos: ©Hélène Binet

ZAHA HADID ARCHITECTURE, MAK

MAK, Vienna, Austria
2003

Ice-Storm

Ice-Storm is an installation that was conceived and created for the MAK, Vienna. It is a built manifesto towards the potential for a new domestic language of architecture, driven by the new digital design and manufacturing capabilities. The installation is suggestive of new types of living/lounging environments. In this respect it is a latent rather than manifest environment. Neither familiar typologies nor any codes of conduct are yet associated with its morphology.

The installation collects and fuses a series of previously designed furniture elements and installations: Glacier, Moraine, Stalactite, Stalagmite, Iceberg, Z-Play and Domestic Wave including Ice-Flow. These divers elements are drawn into a dynamic vortex. In addition two new hard sofas have been designed to be integrated into the installation.

The semi-abstract, molded surface might be read as an apartment that has been carved from a single continuous mass. The rhythm of folds, niches, recesses and protrusions follows a willful formal logic. This formal dynamic has been triggered by a series of semi-functional insertions, which hint towards the potential for sofas, day-bed, desk, tables etc.

The design language explored here emphasizes complex curvelinearity, seamlessness and the smooth transition between otherwise disparate elements. This formal integration of divers forms has been achieved by the technique of "morphing". Via this morphing operation the preexisting furniture pieces are embedded within the overall fluid mass of the ensemble and become integrated organs of the overall organism. Those elements, which are not contiguous with the overall, figure—the Z-Play pieces—are nevertheless morphologically affiliated and appear like loose fragments that drift around the scene at random.

The installation asks the visitors to occupy the structure and to explore for themselves this new open aesthetic, which invites us to reinvent ourselves in terms of posture, demeanor and life-style.

Architect: Zaha Hadid Architects—
Zaha Hadid with Patrik Schumacher, design;
Woody Yao, Rocio Paz, Thomas Vietzke, design team
Program: installation for the Zaha Hadid retrospective
Client: MAK

Photo: ©Hélène Binet

〈アイス・ストーム〉

「アイス・ストーム」はウィーンのMAKのために着想され生み出されたインスタレーションである。これは、最新のデジタル・デザインとマニュファクチャリングの可能性によって後押しされた建築という分野における、新たな言語の可能性を探るための顕在化されたマニフェストだ。インスタレーションは新たな居住と憩いの環境の様態を示唆しているが、その点ではこれはマニフェストされた環境と言うよりは潜在的なものを暗示している。その形態は見慣れたタイポロジーやどんな体系の方向性とも関連づけられるものではない。

このインスタレーションでは過去にデザインした様々な家具の要素とインスタレーションの数々が纏められ融合している。「氷河」「氷堆石」「鍾乳石」「石筍」「氷山」「Zプレイ」また「アイス・フロー」を含む「ドメスティック・ウェーブ」等から成るのだがこれらの多様な要素がダイナミックな渦に引き込まれている。加えて新たに２つの硬いソファがデザインされインスタレーションに組み込まれている。

半抽象的に成型された曲面は、一つの連続する量塊から削り出された居住空間と読みとることも出来る。襞のリズム、空隙、くぼみと隆起は、意図的な形態の論理に従うが、こうした形態における動的な様は、ソファや寝椅子机やテーブル等半ば機能的な要素と成り得る可能性を暗示する、一連の挿入要素によって引き起こされている。

ここで追求したデザイン言語は、複雑な曲線継ぎ目のなさ、そしてつながりのない要素間での滑らかな変容に重点を置いている。多様な形状の形態における一体化は"モルフィング"の技法によって実現されている。

このモルフィングの操作を通じて既存の家具達は、流動的な量塊のアンサンブル全体に組み込まれ、有機的な総体における器官として一体化される。この全体に対し直接包含されていない要素──「Zプレイ」部分──はそれでも形態論的には関連づけられ、この場面において無作為に漂う断片を図表している。

このインスタレーションは、来場者自身が構造物に陣取って、この新しく自由な美的感覚を探求するよう求めている。それは、所作や振る舞い、生活の様態を自身で再定義することを誘引する。

SNOW SHOW

Lapland, Finland
2004

Ice and snow landscapes are exciting nature made entities, striking for their fluid shapes and coherent formations. We aim to create an artificial 'man made' landscape that intensifies the experience of the space provoking similar joy and inviting the visitors to explore it. It expresses the essence of the transformation from one condition to the next.

The sculpture is formed out of two mirrored landscape formations, one of it made out of snow the other out of ice. The landscape transforms into a piece of furniture, a public living room, where an 'ice bar' might find it's way.

The artist Cai Guo-Qiang is doing his intervention in the snow formation, creating a surreal landscape of blue flames, that come down the structure covering it with blue streams, pools and terraces. Thus, reshaping the structure and transforming the piece into an (artificially) melted space, creating another layer of intervention.

The other one, made out of ice, is left to the metamorphosis generated by natural conditions. Ice is taken here as a medium to be sculpted and carved. Vaulting floating spaces and canyons form a space that envelopes the visitor in a glowing ever changing glacier. Walls are curving into ceiling and into floating structures challenging gravity.

They give the visitor the perception of being in a frozen but a fluid space.Light informs the space as 'veins' of lights are created of different intensities and qualities and interwoven into the structure.

In the melting process, in state of constant change, the installation will open up other hitherto unknown realities, volumes and spaces within.

氷と雪のランドスケープは，流動的な形態と整合性を保ったその形態形成が非常に印象的な，自然が生み出した刺激的な存在である。我々の目的は，それと同じような喜びや来場者が探索したくなる気持ちを誘い出す，空間経験を強めるような「人の手による」人工的なランドスケープを作り出すことにあった。これはある状態から次の状態へと変容することの本質を表現している。

この彫刻作品は一方は雪による，もう一方は氷による鏡像化された2つのランドスケープの形態により形成されている。ランドスケープは，一つの家具，パブリックな居住空間へと変容しつつ「アイスバー」はそれ自体独立して存在するだろう。

アーティストである蔡國強は雪による形成部分に，彼独自の介入製作を行っている。構造物を青い炎が流れ落ち，青い小川，プール，テラスで覆って青い炎による超現実的なランドスケープを生み出している。このようにして構造体を作り直し，作品を（人工的に）融解しつつある空間へと変容させ，別の階層における介入を造り出す。

もう一方の氷による作品は，概ね自然の状況によって引き起こされる変容に任せている。ここでは氷は彫りこまれ，刻みつけられるメディアの一つとして用いられ，アーチ状の丸屋根を持つ浮遊空間と深い狭間が，常に変化しつつ成長する氷河のような空間を形成して来場者を包み込む。壁は天井と重力に拮抗して，浮遊する構造体に向かって曲線を描いてゆく。

来場者は凍り付いているが，また同時に流動的な空間に入りこんだという感覚を受けるだろう。異なる強さと質の様々な光が構造物に編み込まれ，光の「編目」として空間を満たしている。

氷の融解過程によって絶え間なく変化し続けるインスタレーションは，これまで知り得なかった本質的なもの，空間のヴォリューム，そして空間そのものの姿を内に垣間見せてくれるだろう。

Architect: Zaha Hadid Architects—
Zaha Hadid with Patrik Schumacher, design;
Rocio Paz, Woody K. T. Yao, project architect;
Yael Brosilovski, Thomas Vietzke, Helmut Kinzler, project team
Client: The Snow Show
Consultant: Adams Kara Taylor, structural;
Zumtobel Staff in conjunction with the HFG,
Scenography Class—Prof M. Simon, lighting
Program: ice and snow installation in collaboration with the artist Cai Guo-Qiang

Photos: ©Hélène Binet

25 YEARS COLLECTION DEUTSCHE BANK

Deutsche Guggenheim, Berlin, Germany
2005

The Deutsche Bank Collection celebrated its 25th anniversary by holding an exhibition at the Deutsche Guggenheim. The collection was initiated in the 1970's and has become the world's largest corporate art collection with over 50,000 pieces of art.

Concept
Curated by the Deutsche Bank, the exhibition was based on a selection of twenty five people from within the Deutsche Bank. These 'godfathers' or 'godmothers' were ask to choose their favourites pieces from the whole collection to represent the development of the collection over its 25 years of existence. A criterion for choice was a personal relationship with the selected work.

Design
The exhibition is housed in two areas of contrasting spatial qualities, an exhibition hall and a large, tall glass roofed atrium. The intervention designed for the exhibition hall of the Berlin Guggenheim Museum is a carved-out solid. As a result the visitor is walking through a series of carved ellipsoid voids reflecting the curational concept and forming niches containing aspects of the individual 'collections' of the godfathers/godmothers. The spatial interrelation of the ellipsoids was developed using the size and amount of selected works. In the progression of the visitors route through the exhibition the ellipsoids becoming more dynamic and turn into solids as they enter the atrium hall. In the atrium hall the ellipsoids are dramatic shell-like horizontal and vertical structures that rise up to the glass.

ドイツ銀行コレクションはその25周年を記念してドイツ・グッゲンハイム・ミュージアムで展覧会を開催した。コレクションは1970年代に創始されたもので、50,000点余りもの作品を擁し、企業が保有するアートコレクションとしては世界でも最大のものとなった。

〈コンセプト〉
ドイツ銀行の企画による展覧会は、ドイツ銀行に属する25人が選んだ作品をベースとしている。これらの‘ゴッドファーザー’と‘ゴッドマザー’は、全コレクションの中から、25年にわたって拡張してきたそのコレクションを代表するようなものでかつ自分の好きなものを選ぶよう依頼された。選択の基準は、その作品との個人的な関連性を示すものであった。

〈デザイン〉
展覧会は、展示ホールと大きな背の高いガラス屋根のアトリウムという、空間として対照的な二つのエリアで行われた。ベルリン・グッゲンハイム・ミュージアムの展示ホールになされたのは、立体から彫り出すという操作である。結果として、来場者は連続する彫り抜かれた楕円体のヴォイドのなかを歩く。これは企画意図を反映し、ゴッドファーザー／ゴッドマザーの‘コレクション’を別々に収めるくぼみを生み出す。楕円体の相互関係は、選ばれた作品のサイズと量で検討された。展覧会の見学ルートを進むにつれて、楕円体はよりダイナミックになり、アトリウム・ホールに入る頃には立体になってゆく。アトリウム・ホールでは、楕円体は水平にも垂直方向にも伸びるドラマティックなシェル状の構造体となって、ガラス壁に向かって立ち上がる。

Architect: Zaha Hadid Architects—
Zaha hadid with Patrik Schumacher, design;
Helmut Kinzler, design leader;
Tetsuya Yamazaki, Yael Brosilovski, Saleem A Jalil, Joris Pauwels, Manuela Gatto, Fabian Hecker, Gernot Finselbach, Judith Reitz, Daniel Baerlecken, Setsuko Nakamura, design team
Client: Deutsche Bank
Program: travelling exhibition design for 25 years Deutsche Bank Collection, April 30 ti June 27, 2005

Photos: M. Schormann, ©Deutsche Guggenheim, Berlin

Tokyo Blossoms: Deutsche Bank Collection, Tokyo
Hara Museum of Contemporary Art, March 25 to May 21, 2006

All the Best, Deutsche Bank Collection, Singapore
Singapore Art Museum, September 1 to November 20, 2006

Photo: ©Hirotaka Yonekura

Photos: ©Katrin Paul

ELASTIKA

Moore Building, Miami, U.S.A.
2005

The aim was to do something site specific; a design which complements and at the same time contradicts and questions the Moore Building built in 1921.

The existing Moore Building has two major (implied) architectural moves; horizontal circulation on layered mezzanines and four stories vertical columns that stretch upwards to embrace the central atrium.

Pushing the envelope of current spacial concepts, we have instilled a dynamic tension within this existing Cartesian layout. Oblique 'stretches' span the space like chewing gum, establishing an elastic/plastic connection between different floors: creating a new understanding in architectural order, geometry, materiality and structural systems.

The design and manufacture of the installation has only been made possible through the latest advances in technology. Its form was generated on complex geometry software (using nurb surface modeller). This design was then sculpted by CNC (Computer Numerical Control) milling to enable manufacture.

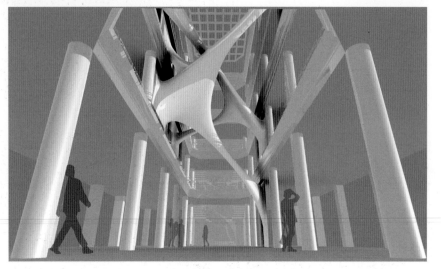

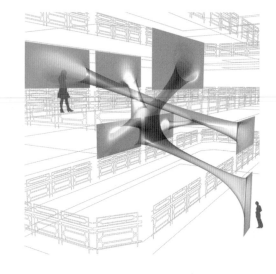

我々はかねがね，その敷地に対して何か特定のことをしたいと考えていた。1921年に建てられたムーア・ビルディングに対して，それを賞賛しつつも同時に抗論し，疑問を投げかけるようなデザインである。

既存のムーア・ビルディングは二つの重要な建築的な動きを含んで（暗示して）いる。階層化された各メザニンレベルにおける水平方向の動線と，中央のアトリウム空間を取り囲む垂直方向に伸びた4階分の柱によるものだ。

この現在の空間コンセプトの枠を超えるために，我々はこの既存のカルテジアン的な構成にダイナミックな緊張感を持ち込んだ。斜め方向にまるでチューインガムのように伸縮したかのような形態が橋渡しされ，異なるフロア間を伸縮性と可塑性を持ってつなぎあわせている。これは，様式，幾何学的構成，物質性，また構造システムといった建築のおける新しい解釈を提案するものである。

このインスタレーションのデザインと製作は，最新の進化した技術によってのみ可能になったものだ。その形態は複雑な幾何学ソフトウェア（NURB=Non Uniform Rational B-Spline サーフェス・モデラー）によって生成されている。こうしてできたデザインは，CNC（Computer Numerical Control）と呼ばれるフライス加工機械によって彫り出され，ようやく製作が可能になっている。

Architect: Zaha Hadid Architects—
Zaha Hadid with Patrik Schumacher, design;
Saffet Bekiroglu, project designer
Melodie Leung, Ceyhun Baskin and Markus Planteu, design team
Client: design.05 Miami
Program: installation for the Moore building, December 1 to December 5

EXHIBITION 'ZAHA HADID'

Solomon R. Guggenheim Museum, New York, U.S.A.
2006

Program: a retrospective exhibition of Zaha Hadid's
works, over the past 30 years
June 3 to October 25, 2006

Architects: Zaha Hadid Architects—
Zaha Hadid with Patrik Schumacher, design;
Woody Yao, project architect;
Melodie Leung, Ana Cajiao, Thomas Vietzke,
Helmut Kinzler, Tiago Correia, Ken Bostock, design team
Muthahar Khan, Miya Ushida, Jevin Dornic,
Andrea B. Caste, Josefina del Rio, support team;
Antonio de Campos, artist consultant
Guggenheim team: Germano Celant, senior curator,
contemporary art; Monica Ramirez-Montagut, assis-
tant curator, architecture & design
Client: Solomon R. Guggenheim Museum, 1071 Fifth
Avenue (at 89th Street), New York City

Photo: David M. Heald, ©SRGF, New York

◁△Photos: ©Werner Huthmacher

IDEAL HOUSE

IMM Cologne, Cologne, Germany
2007

Zaha Hadid Architects is very interested in bringing new typologies of living space to the forefront by creating an interpretation or manifestation of an ideal house. Ideal House Cologne is an excellent opportunity for the practice to experiment on a smaller, more temporal scale. To test out ideas in a non-permanent environment and find out what works, and what needs fine-tuning. Our design for Ideal House '07 is indicative of what we might wish future living to be—a built manifesto that suggests an entirely new type of living environment. It is a re-invention of space, a latent environment whose morphology is not yet associated with familiar typologies or codes of conduct. We see a shift in thought process regarding the idea of the home, whereby people are beginning to see the importance of the environments they live in, in terms of the possibilities of how to make a space really work for them, both in the functional sense, but also the more intangible benefits of being grounded in a space that is aesthetically pleasing. The complete marriage of form and function is crucial—one should never be sacrificed for the other.

Architects: Zaha Hadid Architects—
Zaha Hadid with Patrik Schumacher, design;
Woody Yao, project architect;
Melodie Leung, Eddie Can, Daniel Baerlecken, Muthahar Khan, design team;
Client: 2007 Cologne Furniture Fair German Design Council
Size/specification
Volume: 400 m³ (polystyrol)
Structure: 6 tons (steel)
Base: 200 m² (wood)
Production time: 5 weeks
Assembly: 10

ザハ・ハディドは，理想の家に対する解釈，あるいはそれを表明し形にすることによって，住空間の新しいタイポロジーをもたらすことに興味がある。ケルン・イデアル・ハウスは，期間限定の小さなものでそれを体験するスタディとして，素晴らしい機会となった。期間が限られた環境でそのアイディアを試し，何が有効か，どんな調整が必要かをチェックするのである。2007年のケルン・イデアル・ハウスのためのデザインは，未来の住空間に何を望むか──まったく新しい住環境に対するマニフェスト──を提示するものである。これは，空間の再発見であり，一般的なタイポロジーや規範と形態がまだつながっていない潜在的な環境である。自分が住んでいる環境の重要性，つまり，機能的な意味でも，また美しく心地よい空間に身を置いたときの形にならない効果という意味でも，どうやって本当に役に立つ空間をつくれるか，人々がそれを考え始めているという点で，住まいに対する考え方の思考過程に変化を見る。形態と機能の完璧な融合が極めて重要だということである。それはお互いがお互いを犠牲にするものあっては決してならない。

Photos: ©Constantine Myer

DUNE FORMATIONS

Scuola dei Mercanti, Venice, Italy
2007

Dune Formations emerge as a series of distinct elements, all generated by a common series of topological rules and differentiated by unique design features. The elements nest into each other to form a dynamic three-dimensional ensemble, where each object affects its neighbours and at the same time has the ability to live on its own as a piece.

Dune Formations for Scuola dei Mercanti in Venice is an organic ensemble of unique furniture elements ranging from wall shelving units, tables, benches and an artificial tree. Every piece of the installation challenges traditional Cartesian geometries by blending vertical and horizontal into continuous three-dimensional surfaces. Advanced 3d modeling techniques are combined with processes of digital production and innovative materials. Metal and resins are melted into sinuous shapes finished with a bespoke golden orange colour.

Domestic objects are redefined into abstractions that lead to a unique interpretation of an interior landscape. Each element suggests a multiplicity of possible uses, introducing a creative combination of horizontal surfaces, display areas and seating elements.

Architects: Zaha Hadid Architects—
Zaha Hadid with Patrik Schumacher, design;
Michele Pasca di Magliano and Viviana Muscettola, design team
Client: David Gill Galleries
Material: aluminum & resin
Size: 24 x 13 m
Dune Formation for David Gill Galleries was showcased at Suola dei Mercanti in during the Venice Bennale, 2007

Photo: ©ORCH

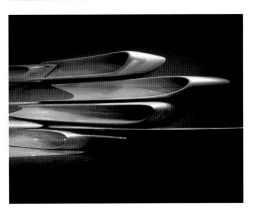

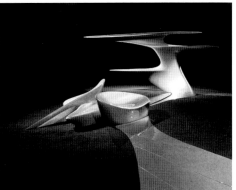

◁△Photos: ©Hélène Binet

砂丘の形体は、全てに渡って共通したトポロジカルな規則により生み出されながらも、おのおの独自の形態的特徴によって識別され得る一連の個別要素の集まりとして現れる。これら要素はお互いに組み入れられ編み込まれて、近接するもの同士がそれ自身として生き延びる能力を持ちつつも相手に影響を与えるような、ダイナミックな3次元的アンサンブルを形成している。

ヴェニスのスクオラ・デイ・メルカンティのための「砂丘形成」インスタレーションは、壁のシェルフ・ユニットやテーブル、ベンチ、そして人工的な木といった、ユニークな家具要素の有機的なアンサンブルによるものだ。インスタレーションのすべての要素は、垂直方向性や水平方向性を混交することで連続した3次元曲面へと変容させ、従来のカルテジアン的幾何学様相に対し挑戦している。最新の3次元モデリング技術と、画期的な素材を用いたデジタル製作のプロセスが組み合わされた。金属と樹脂が溶け合わされて曲がりくねった形を生成し、特別に調合した黄金オレンジ色で仕上げられている。

家庭に置かれる見慣れた物が抽象的なオブジェに再定義され、インテリア空間のランドスケープといったユニークな再解釈へと導かれて行く。個々の要素は多様な利用形態を示唆し、水平の表面、ディスプレイの場所、座席の要素といったものの創造的な組み合わせを提案する。

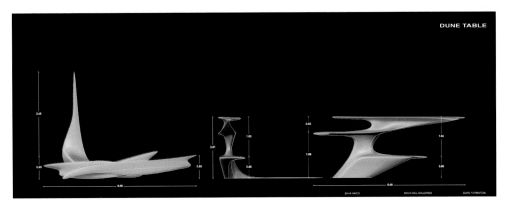

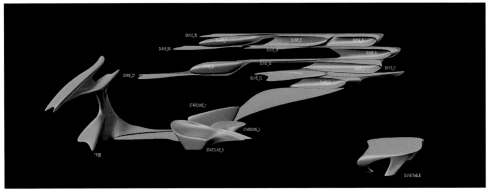

TOTAL FLUIDITY AT ALL SCALES

Lisbon Triennale, Lisbon, Portugal
2007

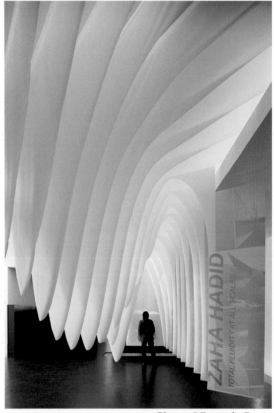

Photos: ©Fernando Guerra

Total Fluidity at all Scales is a continuation of the morphological design language Zaha Hadid has explored and developed over the past three decades. The formal dynamic of the installation has been conceived as an inverted landscape using complex curvilinear geometry, seamlessness, and smooth transitions—integrating the diverse forms of Hadid's unique brand of urbanism to connect disparate cityscapes. Whereas the total fluidity evident in her work demonstrates such morphological research, this installation deconstructs these organic forms into a series of suspended vertical elements that capture moments of time throughout the continuous transformation of the piece. As in time-lapse photography, the ephemeral qualities and diffused form have been frozen at irregular intervals in frames that illustrate Hadid's repertoire.

"あらゆるスケールにおける完全なる流動性"は, ザハ・ハディドが30年に渡り追求し展開してきた形態学的なデザイン言語の延長にあるものだ。このインスタレーションにおける形状のダイナミクスは, 複雑な幾何学曲線や継ぎ目のない形状, またハディドのトレードマークとして確立されている, 様々に異なる都市景観をつないでゆく都市論に根ざした多様な形状が, 次々とスムーズに変容していく様より着想されている。彼女の作品に明らかな "完全なる流動性" は, 時間の中の瞬間々を捉えながら, 一つひとつの形状が連続して変容していく様を一連の浮遊した垂直な要素へと有機的に解体し, 形態学研究の一環として明示されている。写真に於ける時の経過に見られるように, エフェメラルな性質を持ち拡散していくかのような形体は, ハディドのレパートリーを描き出すかのようなフレームの中に, 不規則な間隔で焼き付けられている。

Architects: Zaha Hadid Architects—
Zaha Hadid with Patrik Schumacher, design;
Tiago Correia, project architect
Program: Zaha Hadid retrospective at Lisbon Triennale

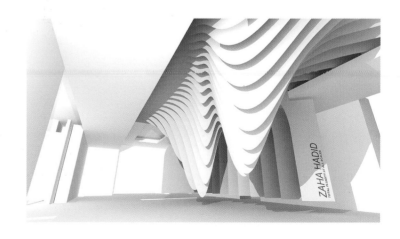

LILAS

Serpentine Gallery's Summer Party, Kensington Gardens, London, U.K.
2007

The Serpentine Summer Party Installation is designed as an open air space raising 5.5m that consists of three identical tensile fabric structures or parasols arrayed around a central point. Each parasol develops sculpturally from a small articulated base to a large cantilevered diamond shape. Taking inspiration from complex natural geometries such as flower petals and leaves the three parasols overlap to create the pavilion's main conceptual feature: complex symmetry, interweaving all-the-while without touching, allowing air, light and sound to travel through narrow gaps in a state that is both open and likewise tending toward closure.

Raised on a low platform located within an open field flanked by a row of trees just South of the Serpentine Gallery, the Serpentine Summer Party Pavilion is free standing and accessible from all sides. Accommodating movement throughout the site, the Pavilion is enigmatic. In the day it provides shading, while at night the pavilion undergoes an energetic transformation into a source of illumination. From continuous lighting around each base, light is thrown up the fabric surfaces along very thin seams that radiate about the parasols that act like corseting or the veining of flowers revealing the geometric intricacy of the pavilion and highlighting the overall architectural form in calligraphic arcs.

Photos: ©Luke Hayes

サーペンタイン・サマーパーティ・インスタレーションは，3つの同じ張り布式構造もしくは中心点の廻りに配置されたパラソルによって5.5m持ち上げられた屋外スペースである。個々のパラソルは，小さくまとめられたベースから大きく片持ちに張出したダイアモンド形状によって彫刻的な形状を生みだしている。花の花弁や葉といった複雑な自然の幾何学形状から着想を得て，3つの重ねられたパラソルがパヴィリオンのコンセプトの骨子を作り出している──風や光，音などが通り抜けられる狭い隙間が開いていたり，閉じようとしていたりというように，どちらの状態にもあり，おのおのは互いに触れることなく編み上げられた複雑な対称性を持つもの。

サーペンタイン・ギャラリーの南側にある，木立の並びに挟まれながら開けた場所の中に置かれた，低い踏み台に隆起したかのようなサーペンタイン・サマーパーティ・インスタレーションは自立しており，またどの側からもアクセスできるようになっている。これは敷地内における移動をすべて受け入れている，謎めいたパヴィリオンである。日中は日陰を提供し，夜間はエネルギッシュな変容を遂げて辺りを照らし出す照明となる。各基礎部分の周りに連続する形で配された照明は，布地による表面の非常に細い継ぎ目から光を投げかけ，広がろうとするパラソルをコルセットのように締め付けながら，書によって描かれた弧のような形状が，全体の建築形体を際立たせる花の葉脈のようにパヴィリオンの幾何学的な複雑さを浮き彫りにする。

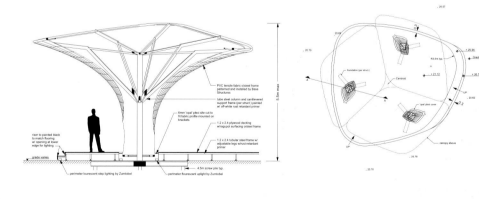

Sections and plans

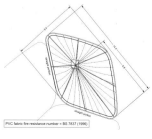

Architects: Zaha Hadid Architects—
Zaha Hadid with Patrik Schumacher, design;
Kevin McClellan, Charles Walker, project leaders
Client: Serpentine Gallery
Consultant: ARUP, structural; Sheetfabs Ltd., steel fabrication; Base Structures Ltd., membrane fabrication; Zumbotel, lighting
Furniture provided by Established & Sons, Kenny Schachter, Sawaya & Moroni, Serralunga, Max Protetch, Swarovski
Program: temporary tensile fabric Installation consisting of 3 parasols for the Serpentine Gallery's Summer Party located in Kensington Gardens.
Size: 5.5 m, height; 22.5 m, width; 22.5 m, length; 310 m², total floor area

ARCHITECTURE AND DESIGN

Design Museum, London, UK
2007

Architects: Zaha Hadid Architects—
Zaha Hadid with Patrik Schumacher, Woody Yao,
Melodie Leung, Marcela Spadaro, design
Design Museum team: Deyan Sudjic, director;
Nicole Bellamy, Sophie McKinlay, curators;
Annabel Moir, assitant curator
Client: Design Museum
Program: Zaha Hadid retrospective, featuring paint-
ings, architectural models, and furniture
June 29 to November 25, 2007

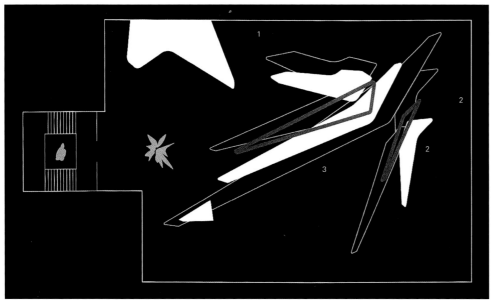

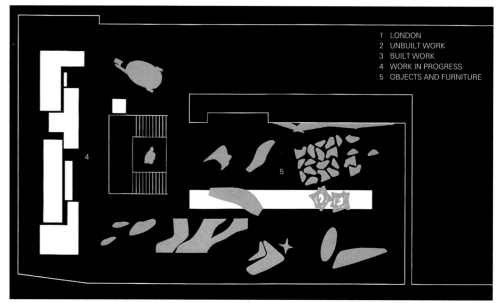

1 LONDON
2 UNBUILT WORK
3 BUILT WORK
4 WORK IN PROGRESS
5 OBJECTS AND FURNITURE

First floor

Second floor

The exhibition open with an introduction to Hadid's most significant completed projects: the Rosenthal Centre for Contemporary Art, Cincinnati; the Phaeno Science Centre, Wolfsburg, recently shortlisted for the RIBA Stirling Prize; and the BMW plant, Leipzig, Germany. A series of models, plans and renderings will establish her achievement as an architect building today, and will demonstrate her ability in pioneering a new vocabulary for architecture. Process will be examined with an in-depth analysis of the Maxxi Centre for Contemporary Art in Rome. The exhibition will demonstrate the importance of London for Hadid, from her formative experiences at the Architectural Association, the influence of the people she met there including Rem Koolhaas and Bernard Tschumi, and the first steps to building a practice, to her future plans for the 2012 Olympics Aquatic Centre. A special section of the exhibition will be dedicated to the many products that Hadid has designed including her limited edition projects for Established & Sons, such as the Seamless Collection, the Aqua Table and Swarm chandelier.

Closing with a look at future plans with a city of models of Hadid's buildings, Zaha Hadid – Architecture and Design will leave visitors with an insight into the huge breadth and power of the Hadid office, and a very different world from the conventional architectural circuit.

この展示会はハディドの実現されたプロジェクトの中でも最も特筆すべき作品のイントロダクションとともに幕を開けた——シンシナティのローゼンタール現代美術センター，また最近RIBAスターリング賞の候補に選ばれたウォルフスブルグのファエノ科学センター，そしてドイツはライプツィヒのBMW工場—中央棟などである。数々の模型や平面図，レンダリング・イメージなどは，今日，建物を実現している建築家の成果として彼女の地位を確固としたものとするだろう。ローマの中央現代美術館の踏み込んだ検討により，彼女の設計プロセスは詳しく考察されると思われる。展覧会は，ザハにとってロンドンという場所がいかに重要な意味を持っているかを明らかにするだろうが，それらは形体に関する彼女自身の経験から，AAスクールで出会ったレム・コールハースやベルナール・チュミらによる影響，実務を立ち上げる際の最初の歩み，そして2012年オリンピックに於ける水上センターのための将来計画などにわたるものとなる。展覧会の特別な一区画は，ハディドがデザインしたEstablished & Sonsのためのシームレス・コレクション，アクア・テーブル，スワーム・シャンデリアなどの限定プロジェクト等に当てられている。

ハディドの建物による未来都市の将来モデルを見ながら展示会は幕を閉じ，ザハ・ハディドの建築とデザインは，訪れた人々にハディド事務所の大きな息吹と力を見出させ，既存の建築回路とは非常に異なった世界をかいま見せてくれるだろう。

Photos: Y. Futagawa

Global Architecture

GA

English and Japanese texts
Size: 364 × 257 mm
48 total pages, 8～20 in color

An Encyclopedia of Modern Architecture

Apart from those seminal works of architecture which imply new directions, those columns also introduce some of the classic work by such masters of modern architecture. They will become an encyclopedia of modern architecture.

現代建築の名作をじっくり見ていただくために企画された大型サイズのシリーズ。現代建築の歴史に残る名作を，1軒ないし2軒，総48頁で構成。回を重ねるごとに現代の名建築の百科事典となるでしょう。

GA6 ¥2,400
Eero Saarinen *Bell Telephone Corporation Research Laboratorys, Deere & Company*

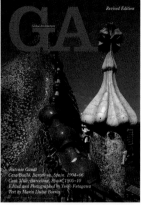

GA17 (Revised Edition) ¥2,800
Antonio Gaudí *Casa Batlló, Casa Milà*

GA45 ¥2,400
Carlo Aymonino/ Aldo Rossi *Housing Complex at the Gallaratese Quarter*

GA48 (Revised Edition) ¥2,800
Luis Barragán *Barragán House, Los Clubes, San Cristobal*

GA61 ¥2,400
Jørn Utzon *Church at Bagsvaerd*

GA64 ¥2,400
Manteola, S. Gomez, Santos, Solsona/ Viñoly *Banco de la Ciudad de Buenos Aires*

GA65 ¥2,400
Sepra & Clorindo Testa *Banco de Londresy América del Sud*

GA67 ¥2,400
Alvar Aalto *Villa Mairea*

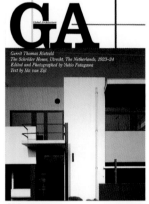

GA68 ¥2,806
Gerrit Thomas Rietveld *The Schröder House*

GA69 ¥2,806
Arata Isozaki & Associates *Tsukuba Center Building*

GA70 ¥2,806
Walter Gropius *Bauhaus, Fagus Factory*

GA72 ¥2,806
Louis I. Kahn *National Capital of Bangladesh*

GA73 ¥2,806
J. A. Brinkman & L. C. van der Vlugt *Van Nelle Factory*

GA74 ¥2,806
Giuseppe Terragni *Casa del Fascio, Asilo Infantile Antonio Sant'Elia*

GA77 ¥2,800
Rudolph M. Schindler *R.M. Schindler House & James E. How House*

GA DETAIL

GA Detail is a series of publications introducing masterpieces of modern/contemporary architecture by detail drawings in large format. GA Detail is to be continued to pick up masterpieces of architecture, our age's as well.

克明なワーキング・ディテールにより現代建築の名作を解析する図面集。第1巻は1976年初版の，大好評を得たディテール集の改訂版，ミース・ファン・デル・ローエの名作，ファンズワース邸。このシリーズは再び現代建築の名作をピックアップして順次出版いたします。

Japanese and Enaglish texts, Size: 364 × 257 mm

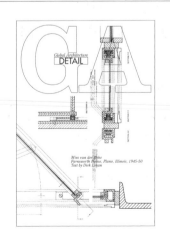

1
Mies van der Rohe Farnsworth House

Plano, Illinois, 1945-50
Text by Dirk Lohan

ミース・ファン・デル・ローエ
ファンズワース邸

文：ダーク・ローハン／製図：北村修一

64 total pages
¥2,476

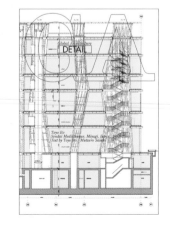

2
Toyo Ito Sendai Mediatheque

Miyagi, Japan, 1995-2000
Text by Toyo Ito/Mutsuro Sasaki

伊東豊雄
せんだいメディアテーク

文：伊東豊雄／佐々木睦朗

64 total pages
¥2,476

表記価格に消費税は含まれておりません。

LIGHT & SPACE
MODERN ARCHITECTURE

光の空間

Edited and Photographed by Yukio Futagawa
Introduction by Paolo Portoghesi Text by Riichi Miyake

企画・撮影＝二川幸夫
序文＝パオロ・ポルトゲージ
文＝三宅理一

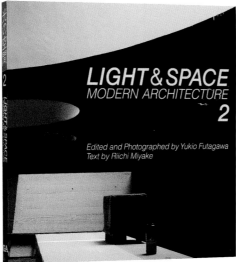

Light is a fundamental element of architecture.
Through the finest examples
from the beginning of Modernism to the present,
this compendium examines
the way natural light is captured,
altered, and shaped in
architectural space.

空間を構成する根源的な要素である光。
あふれる自然の光をとらえ，
絞り込み，屈折させ，
形を与えて内部に導き入れる。
近代建築の黎明期から現代にいたる，
光と影を主役として織りなされてきた
建築空間の集大成。

Japanese and Enaglish texts, Size: 364×257 mm

Vol. 1

216 pages, 30 in color ￥5,806

Vol. 2

216 pages, 24 in color ￥5,806

COMBINED ISSUE 合本
（*HARD COVER* 上製）
426 pages, 54 in color ￥14,369

La Maison de Verre

Pierre Chareau EDITED & PHOTOGRAPHED by **Yukio Futagawa** TEXT & DRAWINGS by **Bernard Bauchet** TEXT by **Marc Vellay**

ガラスの家：
ダルザス邸

企画・撮影＝二川幸夫   文・図面＝ベルナール・ボシェ／翻訳：三宅理一

Built in the center of Paris, La Maison de Verre is neither a work which can be overlooked for it avant-garde qualities, nor as a landmark in the history of Modern Architecture. This volume attempts to give an overall picture of this major work with photographs and survey drawings.

1932年，パリのサンジェルマン大通りに近い，古いアパートの1，2階に嵌め込まれた＜ガラスの家＞は，スチールとガラスブロックの大胆な構成で，近代建築史上，その前衛性からも注目すべき建築である。光の浸透というテーマがどのような構成の原理と空間構成のテクニックのうえに成立しているのか。特別撮影の写真と実測図面により解明する。

English/Japanese texts
Size: 300×307 mm／180 total pages, 42 in color／￥5,806

GA Global Architecture HOUSES

GA HOUSES documents outstanding new residential architecture from all over the world. Included in each issue also are retrospective looks at residential works of the past which are now considered epoch-making. This magazine is essential not only for architects and architectural students but for those who wish to master the art of living.

世界各国の住宅を現地取材により次々と紹介してゆくシリーズ。最近の作品はもちろん、近代住宅の古典の再検討、現代建築家の方法論、集合住宅のリポートなど、住宅に関わる問題点を広い範囲にわたってとりあげてゆきます。

Vols. 1–16, 18–24, 28, 31, 34, 52, 55, 74, 80 are out of print.
1–16, 18–24, 28, 31, 34, 52, 55, 74, 80号は絶版。
(17, 25, 26, 30, 37, 47, 48, 49, 53, 56, 59, 60, 63, 68, 70, 72, 73号は在庫僅少)
Size: 300×228 mm

85
連載：〈家具デザイナー〉⑤吉岡徳仁／〈世界の村と街VIII〉イタリア、プーリア州オストゥニ
作品：S・ホール／T・ウィリアムズ・B・ツィン／高砂正弘／スミス＝ミラー＋ホーキンソン／塩田能也／インターデザインアソシエイツ／布施茂／田辺芳生／山下保博
Furniture Designers: ⑤ Tokujin Yoshioka; **Villages and Towns VIII:** Ostuni, Aplia, Italy
Works: S. Holl; T. Williams B. Tsien; M. Takasago; Smith-Miller + Hawkinson; Y. Shioda/Interdesign Assoc. Architects; S. Fuse; Y. Tanabe; Y. Yamashita
160 pages, 88 in color　　¥2,848

86
特集号：プロジェクト2005
国内外の建築家70組による現在進行中の住宅プロジェクト74点を収録
Special Issue: Project 2005
70 Architects' 74 Works in Progress
196 pages, 112 in color　　¥2,848

87
連載：〈家具デザイナー〉⑥ハイス・バッカー
作品：W・ブルダー／D・ノタ／高砂正弘／プー＋スカルパ／岡田哲史／藤本壮介／遠藤政樹＋池田昌弘／有馬裕之／S・サイトウィッツ／BGPアルキテクトゥーラ
Furniture Designers: ⑥ Gijs Bakker
Works: W. Bruder; D. Nota; M. Takasago; Pugh + Scarpa; S. Okada; S. Fujimoto; M. Endoh + M. Ikeda; H. Arima; S. Saitowitz; BGP Arquitectura
160 pages, 96 in color　　¥2,848

88
ミラノサローネ・レポート2005　連載：〈家具デザイナー〉⑦ミケーレ・デ・ルッキ
作品：A・カラチ／J・ポーソン／安藤忠雄／城戸崎博孝／八木敦司／田辺芳生、池田昌弘／安部良／アトリエ・ワン／遠藤秀平／岸和郎
Milano Salone Report 2005　Furniture Designers: ⑦ Michele De Lucchi
Works: A. Kalach; J. Pawson; T. Ando; H. Kidosaki; A. Yagi; Y. Tanabe, M. Ikeda; R. Abe; Atelier Bow-Wow; S. Endo; W. Kishi
160 pages, 92 in color　　¥2,848

89
連載：〈インテリア／ランドスケープ・デザイナー〉ペトラ・ブレーゼ／〈巨匠の住宅〉A・アアルト、アアルト自邸　特集：ホテル・プエルタ・アメリカ　作品：隈研吾／A・フォガロン／三分一博志／C・ローズ／藤森照信＋大嶋信道／S・アーリック／T・フジモリ＋N・オオシマ／A・C・バエサ／山下保博／駒田剛司＋駒田由香
Interior/Landscape Designer: Petra Blaisse; **Residential Masterpieces:** A. Aalto, Aalto House, Finland; **Report on Hotel Puerta America, Madirid　Works:** K. Kuma; A. Fougeron; H. Sambuichi; T. Fujimori + N. Ohshima; A. C. Baeza; Y. Yamashita; T. Komada + Y. Komada
160 pages, 112 in color　　¥2,848

90
連載：〈世界の村と街IX〉イタリア、プーリア州アルベロベッロ
作品：S・ホール／W・ブルダー／西沢立衛／古市徹雄／コリンズ＆ターナー／ドーソン・ブラウン・アーキテクチャー／ダーバック・ブロック・アーキテクツ／高砂正弘／岸和郎／菅正太郎
Villages and Towns IX: Alberobello, Aplia, Italy
Works: S. Holl; W. Bruder; R. Nishizawa; T. Furuichi, Collins and Turner; Dawson Brown Architecture; Durbach Block Architects; M. Takasago; W. Kishi; S. Suga
160 pages, 96 in color　　¥2,848

91
作品：A・カラチ／R・ジョイ／eer／古谷誠章／長田直之／W・ルウィン＆G・マーカット／駒田剛司＋駒田由香／ジョンストーン・マークリー／布施茂／P・エブナー＋F・ウルマン／高砂正弘／テン・アルキテクトス、BGPアルキテクトゥーラ／BGPアルキテクトゥーラ
Works: Alberto Kalach; Rick Joy; eer; Nobuaki Furuya; Naoyuki Nagata; Wendy Lewin and Glenn Murcutt; Takeshi Komada + Yuka Komada; Johnston Marklee; Shigeru Fuse; Peter Ebner + Franziska Ullmann; Masahiro Takasago; TEN Aruquitectos/BGP Arquitectura
160 pages, 96in color　　¥2,848

表記価格には消費税は含まれておりません。

92
特集号：プロジェクト2006
国内外の建築家58組による現在進行中の住宅プロジェクト64点を収録
Special Issue: Project 2006
58 Architects' 64 Works in Progress
184 pages, 100 in color　　¥2,848

93
ミラノサローネ・レポート2006　作品：ドリューズ＋ストレンジ／ボレス＋ウィルソン／カーン・アーキテクテン／L・ビンスト／米田明、池田昌弘／宮本佳明／福島加津也／都留理子／アイスベルグ・アーキテクチャー・スタジオ／中山英之／アトリエ・ダルシテクチュール・マルク・グロンダル
Milano Salone Report 2006　Works: Drewes + Strenge; Bolles + Wilson; Caan Architecten; L. Binst; A. Yoneda, M. Ikeda; K. Miyamoto; K. Fukushima; R. Turu; iceBERG Architecture Studio; H. Nakayama; Atelier d'Architecture Marc Grondal
160 pages, 104 in color　　¥2,848

94
作品：レゴレッタ＋レゴレッタ／P・スタッチベリー／トゥレーヌ＋リッチモンド・アーキテクツ／安藤忠雄／S・ゴッドセル／岡田哲史／隈研吾／永山祐子／デントン・コーカー・マーシャル／原田真宏＋麻魚／P・フランソワ／B5アーキテクテン
Works: Legorreta + Legorreta; P. Stutchbury; Touraine + Richmond Architects; T. Ando; S. Godsell; S. Okada; K. Kuma; Y. Nagayama; Denton Corker Marshall; M. Harada + Mao; P. François; B5 Architecten
160 pages, 88 in color　　¥2,848

95
連載：〈巨匠の住宅〉アルヴァ・アアルト、ヴィラ・マイレア
作品：鈴木了二／城戸崎博孝／ドリューズ＋ストレンジ／米田明、池田昌弘／ブランク・スタジオ／北川原温／今永和利／布施茂／五十嵐淳
Residential Masterpieces: Alvar Aalto, Villa Mairea, Finland
Works: Ryoji Suzuki; Hirotaka Kidosaki; Drewes+Strenge; Akira Yoneda, Masahiro Ikeda; Blank Studio; Atsushi Kitagawara; Kazutoshi Imanaga; Shigeru Fuse; Jun Igarashi
160 pages, 104 in color　　¥2,848

96
作品：スティーヴン・ホール／坂茂／宮本佳明／中村拓志／塚田修大／駒田剛司＋駒田由香／筒井康二／ローカン・オハーリヒー／プー＋スカルパ／デイヴィッド・ハーツ／スティーヴン・アーリック
Works: Steven Holl; Shigeru Ban; Katsuhiro Miyamoto; Hiroshi Nakamura; Nobuhiro Tsukada; Takeshi Komada + Yuka Komada; Koji Tsutsui; Lorcan O'Herlihy; Pugh + Scarpa; David Hertz; Steven Ehrlich
160 pages, 80 in color　　¥2,848

97
作品：西沢立衛／ピーター・スタッチベリー／アルヴァロ・シザ／ケーシー・ブラウン・アーキテクチャー／冨永祥子／山下保博／遠藤政樹／イアン・ムーア／アイレス・マティウス／坂本昭／高砂正弘／有馬裕之
Works: Ryue Nishizawa; Peter Stutchbury; Álvaro Siza; Casey Brown Architecture; Hiroko Tominaga; Yasuhiro Yamashita; Masaki Endoh; Ian Moore; Aires Mateus; Akira Sakamoto; Masahiro Takasago; Hiroyuki Arima
160 pages, 88 in color　　¥2,848

98
特集号：プロジェクト2007
国内外の建築家68組による現在進行中の住宅プロジェクト68点を収録
Special Issue: Project 2007
68 Architects' 68 Works in Progress
192 pages, 104 in color

99
ミラノサローネ・レポート2007　連載：〈家具デザイナー〉⑧深澤直人　作品：隈研吾／駒田剛司＋駒田由香／キエランティンバーレイク／原田真宏＋麻魚／BGPアルキテクトゥーラ／藤森照信／川上恵一／A・L・シザ・ヴィエイラ／布施茂／長田直之／ニーソン・マーカット・アーキテクツ／D・オスティンガ
Milano Salone Report 2007　Furniture Designers: ⑧ Naoto Fukasawa
Works: K. Kuma; T. Komada + Y. Komada; KieranTimberlake; M. Harada + Mao; BGP Arquitectura; T. Fujimori + K. Kawakami; A. L. Siza Vieira; S. Fuse; N. Nagata; Neeson Murcutt Architects; D. Ostinga
160 pages, 96 in color　　¥2,848

100　新刊
日本特集
特集1：戦前後から現代に至るまで、日本の住宅を検証する
特集2：現在活躍する建築家17人「今、住宅に考えること」
JAPAN VI
Feature 1: Analysis on Residental Architecture in Japan, from WWII to Present
Feature 2: Interview with 17 Architects at the Forefront of Residental Design
288 pages, 124 in color　　¥2,848